BEATRIX POTTER

CHILDREN'S LITERATURE AND CULTURE
Jack Zipes, *Series Editor*

Beatrix Potter
Writing in Code

BY

M. Daphne Kutzer

ROUTLEDGE
New York & London

Published in 2003 by
Routledge
29 West 35th Street
New York, NY 10001
www.routledge-ny.com

Published in Great Britain by
Routledge
11 New Fetter Lane
London EC4P 4EE
www.routledge.co.uk

Copyright © 2003 by Taylor & Francis Books, Inc.
Children's Literature and Culture 27

Routledge is an imprint of the Taylor & Francis Group.
Printed in the United States of America on acid-free paper.

10 9 8 7 6 5 4 3 2 1

Library of Congress Cataloging-in-Publication Data

Kutzer, M. Daphne.
   Beatrix Potter : writing in code / by M. Daphne Kutzer.
      p. cm. — (Children's literature and culture; 27)
Includes bibliographical references and index.
ISBN 0-415-94352-3 (acid-free paper)
1. Potter, Beatrix, 1866–1943—Criticism and interpretation. 2. Women and literature—England—History—20th century. 3. Children's stories, English—History and criticism. 4. Animals in literature. I. Title. II. Children's literature and culture (Routledge (Firm)); 27.

PR6031.O72 Z5895 2003
823'.912—dc21
                                                              2002073913

For Jean: heartlove, hearthome

Contents

Acknowledgments

There are several people I would like to thank for their help in writing this book. First and foremost, the librarians, particularly those at Feinberg Library at Plattsburgh State (who have kindly not demanded the return of several books on Potter for a greater period of time than I wish to admit to); Bailey/Howe Library at the University of Vermont; and most especially the staff at the Free Library of Philadelphia, particularly William Lang, head of the Rare Book Department, and Joël Sartorius, reference librarian in the Rare Book Department. Both of these men were enormously knowledgeable and helpful to me as I made the most of a too-short sojourn in the Beatrix Potter collection.

I would also like to extend thanks to the Royal Oak Foundation of New York City, who invited me once upon a time to give a talk on Potter in conjunction with an exhibition of her original works at the Morgan Library. It was this talk that led me to reconsider her work and eventually to write this book. The gestation has been long, but I hope worthwhile.

Several individuals also deserve thanks. First, to Vincent Carey, whose questions and comments after a lecture I gave on Potter sent me down a path I had not considered. To Thomas Morrissey, without whose friendship and support my career would have had a different trajectory. A belated thanks to Ann Tracy for past and present help with cover art. To my father and to Mary Frances, who provided me with some out-of-print works on Potter they discovered in England. To all the friends and colleagues who have sent me clippings and articles about Potter over the years. And finally, to my own three "pickles," who resisted all temptation to walk across the keyboard and write their own version of Potter's tales.

Series Editor's Foreword

Dedicated to furthering original research in children's literature and culture, the Children's Literature and Culture series includes monographs on individual authors and illustrators, historical examinations of different periods, literary analyses of genres, and comparative studies on literature and the mass media. The series is international in scope and is intended to encourage innovative research in children's literature with a focus on interdisciplinary methodology.

Children's literature and culture are understood in the broadest sense of the term children to encompass the period of childhood up through adolescence. Owing to the fact that the notion of childhood has changed so much since the origination of children's literature, this Routledge series is particularly concerned with transformations in children's culture and how they have affected the representation and socialization of children. While the emphasis of the series is on children's literature, all types of studies that deal with children's radio, film, television, and art are included in an endeavor to grasp the aesthetics and values of children's culture. Not only have there been momentous changes in children's culture in the last fifty years, but there have been radical shifts in the scholarship that deals with these changes. In this regard, the goal of the Children's Literature and Culture series is to enhance research in this field and, at the same time, point to new directions that bring together the best scholarly work throughout the world.

Jack Zipes

Introduction

Beatrix Potter is a central figure in the development of the modern picture book. Illustrated books for children certainly existed before Potter, and in fact existed at least since Newbery's publication of *A Little Pretty Pocket Book* in 1744. Closer to Potter were the illustrated works of the other two central figures in the development of the picture book, Randolph Caldecott and Kate Greenaway, but none of these wrote stories that were integrated with original illustrations. Newbery's book, and many of the other books for children between 1744 and the later nineteenth century, were either illustrated alphabets, illustrated collections of rhymes and songs, or illustrated moral tracts. By the time Lewis Carroll and Edward Lear were writing, we find long original narratives for children illustrated either by the authors or a hired illustrator (Tenniel for the *Alice* books, for example). Not until Potter do we find seamlessly integrated text and illustrations; small books whose pictures comment upon and add information to the text, where indeed text cannot stand without illustrations, nor illustrations without text.

Potter's books vary in length and complexity, from the fairly straightforward texts for very small children (*Peter Rabbit, Miss Moppet,* and so forth), to lengthy and complex narratives like *The Roly-Poly Pudding* and *The Tale of Mr. Tod.* Her last works were complex narratives with minimal illustration (*The Fairy Caravan* and *Sister Anne*). Potter was always as much, if not more, interested in the words rather than the pictures in her books. She cared deeply about language and often made changes to the wording of her stories so as to make her stories more precise and effective. By the end of her career she was working hard at publishing stories without pictures, stories intended for an adult audience. She never attempted to write a novel, but it is fair to say that a number of her small children's books are in fact novels: their characters and their plots are as complex and open to interpretation as any novel published at the time. Throughout this book I will use several terms to describe her work, most often "tale" or "story" (the terms Potter herself used most frequently), but sometimes "novel" for the books deserving of that nomenclature.

Potter's books were written for children but they often had an adult sensibility and adult themes. Even if one has only read *Peter Rabbit* among her works, the seriousness of the novels is evident: Peter's adventures are life-threatening (similar adventures killed his father), and his venture into the garden is not a venture into innocence, but a venture into experience. Other Potter characters have equally dangerous excursions into experience: the Flopsy Bunnies are nearly slaughtered by the farmer and his wife; Tom Kitten nearly ends as pudding for the rats; Pigling Bland might be turned into bacon. Potter's novels take children seriously as human beings who can handle complex and sometimes frightening issues. Her respect for children is one reason her tales continue to be popular one hundred years after their original publication. Her lack of condescension toward children also helps account for her continued popularity with adult readers. There is little if any sentimentality or false emotion in Potter: her ironic tone and sharp wit speak to the adult as well as to the child.

Many adult readers of Potter experience the books through a veil of nostalgia for their own childhoods and do not always see the complexities and ironies the tales present. The books may be miniature and populated by anthropomorphic animals, but the words are as full of irony and wit as a Jane Austen novel, and the plots are often small masterpieces of social comedy. Some stories are simpler than others. *The Tale of Peter Rabbit*, for example, has a straightforward and uncomplicated plot, whereas *The Tale of the Pie and the Patty-Pan* has a complex double narrative. All of Potter's works, however, from the simplest to the most complex, are informed by the context of Potter's life and her place in Victorian and Edwardian England. Examined in this biographical and cultural context the books take on subtleties and complexities that have often been missed by critics.

Potter has had some very good critics in the hundred years since the publication of *Peter Rabbit*: Humphrey Carpenter has taken note of some of Potter's subversive qualities; Carole Scott has examined the complexities of point of view in the tales; Maurice Sendak has considered the ways in which Potter's youthful journal was a kind of artist's verbal sketchbook. Yet to date there has been no single critical study examining all twenty-six of Potter's tales in the context of her coded journal, her letters, and the social and political events of her time. *Writing in Code* attempts this task.

Potter's career can be seen as falling into three distinct periods. First was her youth, which for Potter ran from her birth in 1866 to the end of her coded journal in 1897. This is a long "youth," lasting until Potter was thirty-one, but her family was unusually constrictive and controlling and it was not until Potter was in her thirties that she was able to gain any sort of independence, and not until her late forties was she able to marry and move permanently from the family home in Bolton Gardens in London. Potter's major writing during this period was the journal she kept in code, a journal containing little about Potter's own art and hence paid little attention by the critics, although Maurice Sendak has noted that despite its complete lack of illustrations the journal is a kind of artist's sketchbook in which, "We are watching the artist learn her craft. Her purpose is to observe and record with the greatest possible accuracy the life around her."[1] In her journal, Potter observes everything from art exhibitions to odd little notices in the newspapers to political analysis to remembrances of her grandmother's house and some of the holiday spots she visited with her parents. Her social—and political—observations in the journal inform the small illustrated tales she wrote between 1902 and 1930.

The journal concludes soon after the presentation of Potter's scientific paper on fungi to The Linnaean Society. Potter's first attempt at making a living for herself centered on using her scientific skills to illustrate works of natural history. She had a theory about spore propagation of a certain fungus—a theory that later proved correct—but had difficulty convincing the scientists at Kew Gardens of her idea. Although apparently the now-lost paper was read at a scientific meeting, it was a meeting closed to women and Potter ended by feeling that this particular door to work and a life of her own had closed to her permanently.

The second phase of Potter's career spans the years of her greatest productivity, between the Warne publication of *Peter Rabbit* in 1902 to the publication of *Pigling Bland* in 1913, the year she married William Heelis. Potter's publishing career had begun before *Peter Rabbit* with the publication of some cards and illustrations for other people's words, but it is *Peter* and, to some extent more importantly, *The Tailor of Gloucester* that started Potter's career as a children's writer. The stories often begin as illustrated letters to specific children, but many of them contain sharp social commentary about the lives and situations of adult characters. Much of the social observation Potter made in the coded journal ends up coded in her children's tales as well. Not all the books reflect Potter's political and social concerns, but most of them have at least faint echoes of issues that arise in the journal: concerns about manners, social unrest, and the subtleties of social hierarchy. The journal, despite being written in code and in miniscule handwriting, held little that could dismay the elder Potters. The unhappiness the young Potter felt can be found not in overt complaints but in her joyous tone when she earns her first money by her art. When she begins to publish her children's books (to the dismay of her parents) her restlessness and rebelliousness about social propriety and domesticity is coded within the miniature children's books, which no one, least of all her parents, suspected of having subversive content.

The third phase of Potter's career occurred between 1913 and about 1930, when she published her last book for children. These years saw a decline in Potter's literary output but an increase in her involvement in farming and in local politics; she purchased land in the Lake District, which eventually enabled her to leave thousands of acres of land in the care of the National Trust. She began to refer to herself as Mrs. Heelis or as H. B. Heelis, farmer, burying Beatrix Potter the children's writer almost for good. She never lost her interest in social behavior or in politics, but instead "coded" those interests not in children's books but in letters to the press and pamphlets on free trade that she signed with her married name. Her political interests became more overt than they were in the novels, but Potter disassociated her famous public persona from these opinions by publishing under her married name. She codes herself rather than her ideas.

Writing in Code is an exploration of the three phases of Potter's career, with close attention paid to the novels themselves. My reading depends upon the context of both Potter's personal life and the cultural and political changes that occurred during her lifetime. While much of this context is given in the course of discussion of individual novels, a brief overview of the important private and public events of Potter's lifetime is in order before we look closely at the tales that arose from this context.

Potter's coded journal reveals that she was not as solitary and isolated a creature as Margaret Lane's 1946 biography would have us believe. Not only were there numerous visits to relatives, annual Easter and summer holidays spent in rented houses in Scotland, Wales, or the Lakes, but there were numerous visits to art galleries and museums and much reading of the newspaper and consideration of the wider events happening outside the confines of Bolton Gardens. True, Potter was probably more isolated than most Victorian girls of a similar social class, but she was hardly entirely isolated. Reading and family political discussions made her aware of major changes in the world beyond the walls of Bolton Gardens and the ways that world was changing.

Potter's youth coincided with events of enormous import to British political and social life in the twentieth century. She was born in the middle of the Victorian era, but by her late teens saw passage of the Third Reform Act of 1884, which expanded the voting franchise to all men over the age of twenty-one, regardless of status as property owner or salaried worker. The passage of this act had profound effects upon British politics, making it necessary for Parliament to take into consideration the interests of working men because they had been given a say in whether or not Members of Parliament could be elected. The historian Neville Kirk noted that in the 1890s "and in the immediate pre-and-post-war periods, [the claims of workers] intensify popular grievances, class consciousness, and feelings of outsider status, and promote, in part, radical and even revolutionary challenges to the *status quo*."[2] Some of these challenges took the form of strikes and other labor unrest, some of which is noted in Potter's journal. Her comments on the Third Reform Act are fairly dismissive, but they are based not so much on her opinions about the rights of workers as on her anti-Gladstone feelings. She notes that Gladstone faces difficulties over Britain's entanglement in Egypt, and that "He is going to get the Franchise Bill through as best he can, retire to the House of Lords, and leave the Tories to make the most of 20 millions deficit."[3] The franchise bill was not nearly as important to her as Britain's trade deficit. Early on she was concerned about Britain's economic policies, as she continued to be throughout her career; her concerns about free trade appear in at least one of her children's tales.

Potter came by her interest in politics legitimately, having a paternal grandfather who was a Liberal Member of Parliament for Carlisle and other relatives who had been involved in politics as far back as the days of the Jacobite Rebellions. Political discussion was apparently common in the Potter household as the journal is peppered with remarks about Mr. Potter's feelings and attitudes toward political issues and political figures, although as Potter grows older we find more and more of her own opinions, unfiltered by those of her father. The Potter family interest in politics stemmed not only from family history but also from the enormous changes occurring in the political landscape of the time. The modern party system as we know it today was being constructed; between 1867 and 1884 "the structure of parliamentary government was dismantled and the sufficiency of parliament challenged. By 1886 the contrasting assumptions and values of a modern party system were supplanting the axioms of Whig parliamentary government."[4] There are frequent comments in the journal about battles in the Cabinet and election outcomes. In 1885 Potter notes that "Some odd things happened in the House, which Radicals who are still touched by the ancient Tory failing, superstition, will treasure up" (*Journal*, 123). Later that same year she comments on the defeat of Gladstone's second cabinet, noting that "The best of the joke is they say the new electors [the newly enfranchised working men] will vote for the Tories which I quite believe. There is one thing to be said about this defeat, it is against this absurd so-called Free Trade principle which taxes British instead of foreign produce" (146). Potter was right about the new voters' penchant for Tory politics, and she was also, at the age of eighteen, incensed by the issue of free trade, an issue with which she became actively involved later in her life. Of the election of 1885 she notes, "I believe the Tories will get in. I hope so, though I am a Whig, anything is better than the Radicals" (154–55).

These are only brief examples of what amounts to a running political commentary in Potter's journal, a commentary that gives insight into her own political and social views. As Potter herself notes, she is a Whig and not a Tory, and she has little patience with Irish Home Rule and with labor unrest—but at the same time she has great respect and sympathy for the working classes and their lives. As early as 1884 she writes in her journal:

> I don't know what will come to this country soon, it is going at a tremendous speed. I think and hope that this extension of the Franchise may not be as bad as the Conservatives fear. No doubt if the labourers get power they will be greedy at first, but I think the sentiments of the lower-classes in the country are rather conservative on the whole, very loyal and tenacious of England's honours. Still, landed property is

not a secure possession at present. It is the middle-men who have pushed up, that are such mischievous radicals, like Chamberlain. (87)

Potter's politics were as idiosyncratic as she was. On the one hand she had fairly conservative political views and always would, while on the other she is sympathetic to the plight of laborers. Her politics at heart were pragmatic, as were many of the decisions she made in the course of her life.

Her pragmatism and her ability to see all sides of an issue, to be able to cross party lines in her opinions, is linked in part to her background as a Unitarian. The same year that she comments on the basic conservatism of the working man in Britain, she writes in her journal:

All outward forms of religion are almost useless, and are the cause of endless strife. What do Creeds matter, what possible difference does it make to anyone today whether the doctrine of resurrection is correct or incorrect, or the miracles, they don't happen nowadays, but very queery [*sic*] things do that concern us much more. Believe there is a great power silently working all things for good, behave yourself, and never mind the rest. (104)

This may not seem radical by today's standards, and perhaps not even by the standards of the late nineteenth century, reeling as it was with the writings of Darwin and Huxley, with Newman's defection to the Catholic Church, and with various Church of England scandals. But its radicalism is of a particular sort, marked by the philosophy of Unitarianism.

Unitarians are one of the oldest and most controversial of the dissenting sects, refusing to believe in the Trinity and in fact refusing to believe that Jesus was a part of the godhead, believing him instead to be a human messenger of a divine being. Unitarians were persecuted for many years in England, although by Potter's time they had been accepted as Dissenters. Potter was not overtly religious, and her journal records worship at Unitarian churches, Quaker meetings, and Church of England services, where she enjoyed the music. The *culture* of Unitarianism, however, had a profound impact on her. Unitarians were historically a socially conscious group that worked to better the lives of the poor and needy, not from a sense of noblesse oblige, but from a desire to raise the material circumstances of the poor and the working classes. Charles Dickens, the Gaskells, and Harriet Martineau among others were Unitarian, and the Potters had at least a glancing acquaintance with the Gaskells. What is important in understanding the impact of Unitarianism on Potter's writing is her attraction to the rebellious nature of Unitarians and Unitarian history, and to the pragmatism of Unitarian thought. The relative she loved above all others was her grandmother Jessy Crompton, who always claimed to have fought schoolyard battles "for the faith."[5] It was the fighting of the battle that attracted Potter, not the nature of the battle.

Potter was a rebel in many ways, although always a quiet one. Stories of Unitarian struggles against the majority, her closeness to her rebellious yet respectable grandmother, and Unitarian pragmatism all helped give Potter the strength to stand up for herself and her beliefs, despite parental disapproval.

Her parents were certainly problematic, as her letters show more clearly than her journal. Any Victorian household would seem constrictive by today's standards, but the Potters were constrictive even by Victorian standards. Rupert Potter was a barrister but apparently never practiced, preferring to spend his time at his club or working at the very modern hobby of photography, at which he was a talented amateur, providing working photographs for the painter Millais and taking one of the best and best-known portraits of Gladstone, despite his political dislike of the man. Mrs. Potter had a regimented life of carriage drives, visits, and trips to the servant quarters to organize semiannual house cleanings and other matters. Neither parent seemed concerned with providing the young Beatrix with friends of her own age, nor, as she grew older, did they seem concerned with giving her social opportunities by which she might meet young men. Most of their socializing appears to have been done within the extended Potter family circle, and both parents seem to have felt that their daughter's sole duty in life was to take care of them. They famously objected to Potter's 1905 engagement and objected again in 1913, despite the fact that Potter was now forty-seven years old.

The Potters claimed to object to their daughter's 1905 engagement because Norman Warne was "in trade," although they obviously objected to anyone who wanted to marry their daughter; the second engagement also met with disapproval because Heelis was a mere country solicitor, close in class background to the Potters themselves, though not a barrister like Rupert. The Potters seem to have suffered from an extreme case of what might be termed class dis-ease. Although they were more than comfortable, their family money had come from the calico business in the north of England, and they apparently had a horror of their humble class origins that, combined with a sense of not belonging to the upper classes, resulted in their failure to socialize much and their unhappiness at any connection with "trade." Their Unitarianism was also a probable cause of this dis-ease, setting them apart from more established Church of England members.

This background of relative isolation, political and social observation, and dissenting Unitarianism contributed to making Potter the woman who would create the miniature tales. Other major contributions were the literature Potter read and the holidays spent in the countryside. Potter read fairly widely, but as a child and a young woman she was particularly attracted by fairy tales, nursery rhymes, and riddles—an attraction reflected in many of her novels. She also admired Shakespeare (she memorized a number of his plays) and the novels of Jane Austen, and like most people of her time was well acquainted with the Bible—

literary influences that had an effect on her prose style. Her other attraction was to nature and to animals. Some of her happiest times were spent on holiday in the countryside, where she would sketch not only animals but plant life and fungi. She smuggled animals into her third-floor nursery to sketch them, and when she became a farmer she still found time to sketch the sheep and cows and pigs that were destined for market. She had little formal art training and complained that some of her instructors did not suit her style; she was a natural artist who could draw scientifically (as in her botanical drawings), photorealistically (as in some of the drawings of fossils and other museum artifacts), impressionistically (as in many of the landscapes she painted)—and of course she created wonderful fantasy drawings of animals.

All of these elements of Potter's background contributed to the illustrated animal tales that made her famous. Her attraction to animals and to make believe had a specific origin—her need to escape Bolton Gardens both physically and emotionally. Nature led her to her early attempts at financial independence through a failed career in science and scientific publication. Her desire to escape Bolton Gardens was thwarted by family and gender: she was rarely treated as an adult and had the lowest status of anyone in the family, including her younger brother Bertram. Her attempts to break into the world of science were blocked by family indifference and by the inhospitable scientists at Kew Gardens and in the scientific community as a whole, suspicious of women as scientists.

Yet at the time Potter began her career as a writer of children's books, other constricted members of her society were successfully rebelling: the Irish were agitating for Home Rule, the working classes were gaining political franchise, labor unions were gaining strength, and women were becoming more independent. These issues of domestic constraint and social upheaval surfaced in Potter's books, in whose miniature pages are coded references to her domestic and political unhappiness. Nearly all of them are preoccupied with hierarchy and power, many of them uneasily address the issue of domesticity, and some of them directly address political issues of the day.

Writing in Code, as a discussion of Potter's fantasy works, is thematic rather than chronological, although there is a rough chronological order to the presentation of the novels. I have chosen not to begin with her most famous work, *The Tale of Peter Rabbit*, but with Potter's personal favorite, *The Tailor of Gloucester*, and with *Squirrel Nutkin*, two early novels that together provide an overview of most of the issues Potter "coded" in her novels. The three major rabbit books are discussed as a group, as are the transitional novels before Potter moves permanently to Sawrey. The Sawrey books themselves are discussed over the course of two chapters, and two further chapters are devoted to the balance of her work. Throughout I have placed the tales in the context of the creator's journal, her letters, and the society in which she lived.

Notes

1. Maurice Sendak, *Caldecott & Co.* (New York: Noonday, 1988), 64.
2. Neville Kirk, *Continuity and Class: Labour in British Society 1850–1920* (Manchester: Manchester University Press, 1998), 155.
3. Leslie Linder, ed., *The Journal of Beatrix Potter from 1881 to 1897* (London: Warne, 1966), 116.
4. Angus Hawkins, *British Party Politics: 1852–1886* (London: Macmillan, 1998), 2.
5. Margaret Lane, *The Tale of Beatrix Potter: A Biography* (London: Warne, 1946), 9.

1

Rhymes and Riddles:
The Tailor of Gloucester and
The Tale of Squirrel Nutkin

The Tailor of Gloucester (1903) was both Potter's favorite book and her most unusual. She commented more than once in her letters that she preferred it to all her other books, noting in 1919 that *The Tailor* "has always been my own favourite" of her books, and again in 1923 that it was not only her favorite, but "it is a story that I received one of the few compliments for that I value one halfpenny," a reference to a review in a tailoring journal.[1] She preferred *The Tailor of Gloucester* to *Peter Rabbit* (*Letters*, 283). This book has several characteristics placing it apart from the rest of her work. While a few of Potter's books include human figures (most famously Mr. McGregor in *Peter Rabbit*), in none of them is the human a sympathetic protagonist. Lucie in *Mrs. Tiggy Winkle* is a sympathetic human, but she is far more passive, stiffer in both characterization and illustration than is the tailor—the hedgehog is the protagonist in that tale. *The Tailor of Gloucester* is also the only urban novel Potter ever wrote. She portrays village life in some of the novels set in Sawrey, and *Pig Robinson* has scenes in a busy seaport, but *Tailor* is the only novel to make a specific named city an important element of the tale and to illustrate it lovingly and in color. Here the novel is set in a recognizable Regency England, whereas the historical moment is less clear in her other novels.

Humphrey Carpenter, in his important essay on Potter, notes that Potter is a "subversive" writer who is "definitely on the side of the transgressor" in her books,[2] and also notes that *The Tailor of Gloucester* "was a crucially important book for Potter, a linguistic exercise, a study in establishing what she believed to be her grandmother's voice" (286). But Carpenter has to some degree failed to connect the dots in his argument; Potter's entire oeuvre is an extended complaint of repression and argument for expression of self, and her linguistic style is only a part of that rebellion. *The Tailor of Gloucester* is important not only because it helped Potter develop a distinctive prose style separating her from her own histor-ical moment, but because it allowed her to banish both Victorian prose and parental authority: in fact to excise her father, mother, and even her brother Bertram and to go back to a period her beloved and rebellious grandmother Jessy Crompton would have known well. Only by so doing can she free herself enough to write her revolutionary stories, although the stories hardly appear revolutionary at first glance: small in size and pastel in coloration, they seem unlikely candi-dates for subversive texts. But in many ways these texts, and particularly *The Tai-lor of Gloucester*, are coded texts or palimpsests—narratives that read one way on the surface and another way beneath. What they encode are complaints against hierarchy, authority, and power.

Potter kept a coded journal from age fifteen to thirty-one, and although one might expect she used code as a way to write privately about family or personal discontents, there are few complaints in the journal. Instead the emphasis is on art, travel, and politics: not unusual topics for a Victorian journal keeper, but sur-prising in Potter, whose childhood and youth have generally been considered to be extremely circumscribed. Her letters to Norman Warne, much later in life, show the same reticence as the journal, always addressed to "Mr. Warne" and hardly ever alluding to personal matters. Shortly after her engagement to Norman Warne she writes to his brother Harold to say "You will not think me very cross if I say I would rather *not* talk much *yet* about that business? though I am *very glad* you have been told" (*Letters*, 124). This is her only comment upon her engage-ment. The reticence is due largely to Potter's Victorian upbringing in an environ-ment that valued understatement or nonstatement and frowned upon emotional excess of all sorts. Yet as feminist scholarship (starting with the influential *Mad-woman in the Attic* by Sandra Gilbert and Susan Gubar) has shown, many Victo-rian women writers did manage to encode rebellion or at the least discontent in seemingly straightforward domestic fiction. Dorothea Brooke's more conven-tional marriage is a poor one, and the radical Will ends up a better choice for her; Jane Eyre rebels from childhood against authority and ends up as Rochester's savior, rather than he hers; Margaret Hale in *North and South* has a domestic life far from the Victorian middle-class ideal.

Jane Austen, a writer much admired by Potter, provides some clues to Pot-ter's own techniques. On the surface, Austen's novels (like Potter's) seem con-cerned with the superficialities of village gossip and domestic concerns—but underneath there are more serious issues at stake. As Gilbert and Gubar pointed out, Austen's heroines use "silence as a means of manipulation, passivity as a tac-tic to gain power, submission as a means of attaining the only control available to them" and finally "*seem* [*sic*] to submit as they get what they both want and need."[3] This description of Austen's heroines could apply to Potter herself, who remained silent and passive in her parents' presence yet kept a secret diary and wrote a scientific paper without her parents' knowledge; who seemed passive and ladylike when approaching scientists at Kew Gardens but who took them on acerbically in her journal; and who only seemed to submit, being willing to stand up to her parents when her own desire to marry Norman Warne and, after his death, William Heelis caused much domestic drama. To the end of her life, Potter seemed to submit to her mother's will, helping her close up Bolton Gardens and move to the Lake District after Rupert's death—but Potter was careful to keep her on the other side of Lake Windermere from Sawrey and visited infrequently.

In her novels, Potter's rebellion takes the form of rejecting almost out-of-hand the Victorian world, of banishing or criticizing family, of portraying troubled domestic spaces, and of harkening back to the time of her outspoken grandmother Jessy Crompton for inspiration. Furthermore, although her stories are often set in the Regency period or in a kind of timeless period, what McDonald describes as "no particular time, . . . yet every time,"[4] the social and political undercurrents of the tales belong firmly to the late nineteenth century. It is as if Potter had to pull herself away from her own domestic and political world in order to critique it. The "code" of *The Tailor of Gloucester* is complex, depending partly upon family circumstances, partly upon larger historical events, and partly upon Potter's' Unitarian view of the world. To unravel the code, one must start with Potter's grandmother.

Potter found much to admire in her grandmother Jessy Crompton and other Lancashire ancestors. Her grandmother claimed to have been mobbed for her beauty in Lancashire when she was young, and also claimed to have had a lover kill himself for love of her. She was a Unitarian and told Potter's mother that "Great were the battles . . . which as a girl she had waged against her non-Unitarian schoolfellows, 'for the faith'." Potter's biographer also tells us that "the Cromptons, despite their summary methods with social inferiors, were themselves great Radicals and individualists, and prided themselves on the amount of trouble they had managed to get into . . . in the eighteenth and early nineteenth centuries."[5] Late in life Potter wrote to an American friend that she was descended from generations of "obstinate, hard-headed, matter-of-fact folk" (quoted in Lane, 11). One of her ancestors (Abraham Crompton) befriended the traitor Thistlewood, who in 1820 had plotted to assassinate the British cabinet, set London on fire, and seize the Tower. Thistlewood was hung for treason and Crompton was removed from the bench of magistrates for his championship of Thistlewood (Lane, 11–12). These were exciting ancestors indeed, and grandmother Jessy Crompton was one of them, despite her gray curls and modest bonnet and shawl. Jessy was herself a kind of palimpsest, a kindly grandmother on the surface and a radical romantic underneath.

Compared to Beatrix Potter's parents, these long-gone relatives and especially her elderly grandmother Crompton must have seemed enviably free—free-spoken and free-minded. Potter's parents, on the other hand (despite Rupert Potter's flirtation with photography and his friendship with the painter Millais and other members of the Pre-Raphaelite group), were locked into a life of pro-priety and routine.[6] Whether or not Potter was as isolated in her third-floor nurs-ery as Lane's biography has it, the house must have been stultifyingly Victorian. Potter's grandparents' generation lived in a lively time of rapidly changing indus-trial culture, of a shifting and volatile class structure, of wit and sharpness, whereas Potter grew up when most of the volatility had settled (at least in her house, if not in society at large) into Victorian stolidity. Lane recounts for us the yearly rituals of Easter and summer holidays, the seasonal rituals of houseclean-ing, the daily rituals of calls and drives—a life that seems, even in the 1860s and 1870s, to have been unusually regimented and constrained. We can imagine this regimentation when we remember that at the time Potter was growing up in this household, George Gissing was prowling New Grub Street, Hardy was beginning to reshape the English novel into modern form, and the Pre-Raphaelites were shaking up art, poetry, and morals. (Rupert Potter may have been an acquaintance of some of these revolutionaries, but he hardly seems to have been affected by their outlook on life, remaining a political and social conservative.) At the same time Potter began to publish her children's novels, we find E. Nesbit publishing her very modern-sounding Bastable books, Walter Crane illustrating children's tales with Pre-Raphaelite and aesthetic flourishes, and Winsor McKay inventing the modern comic strip with *Little Nemo in Slumberland*. In this context Potter's books certainly seem old-fashioned even for her own time, although as we shall see they often refer to Edwardian issues.

The Tailor of Gloucester is specifically set in a pre-Victorian period, "In the time of swords and periwigs and full-skirted coats with flowered lappets,"[7] and in a particular city, Gloucester. Details of clothing, crockery, and language specify (for the adult if not the child reader) that the story takes place somewhere during the Regency period and probably somewhere between 1785 and 1800, a hundred years before Potter sat down to write the story. The tricornered hat and cutaway coat the gentleman mouse wears, the crockery under which he is trapped by Simpkin, and above all the gorgeous waistcoat the tailor is making for the mayor's wedding are all visual clues that we are in the Regency. For the child reader these details simply place the story "once upon a time" (for the child reader of a hundred years ago as well as the child reader of today), but if Potter had simply wanted to suggest "once upon a time" she could have mixed all sorts of historical periods together in her illustrations instead of so carefully recon-structing the Georgian world. The language of the story has the same effect: words like "lappet" and "paduasoy" and "pipkin" have a magical sound but were old-fashioned even in Potter's day, and in the illustrated letter that formed the manuscript of the novel, Potter provides definitions for some of these outdated words at the conclusion of the story.

The details of clothing and crockery are quite specific in the novel, as is the setting of Gloucester, a city whose origins go back to Roman times and a city favored by the Plantagenet kings. In 1643 the city held out for a month against the Royalists and paid for its insurrection by having the city fortifications demolished after the Restoration. It is, in other words, not only a beautiful city but one with a history of insurrection, something that no doubt appealed to Potter, who herself first visited Gloucesteshire in 1894 to stay with her cousin Caroline Hutton in Stroud, close to the city. In her journal Potter wrote of the visit that "I used to go to my grandmother's, and once I went for a week to Manchester, but I had not been away independently for five years. It was an event."[8] Potter was twenty-eight at the time. "It was so much of an event in the eyes of my relations that they made it appear an undertaking to me, and I began to think I would rather not go. I had a sick headache most inopportunely, though whether cause or effect I could not say" (*Journal*, 312). She went, and referred to her first visit to Gloucester as being "like a most pleasant dream" (312).

The trip to Gloucester was a turning point in Potter's development as a writer, coming directly after the 1893 *Peter Rabbit* letter to Noël Moore and only a few years before her paper on fungi was presented to the Linnaean Society. It marked nearly the first time she had traveled on her own, and if not in direct defiance of her parents, certainly against their wishes. She had gone to visit her cousin, with whom the young Potter seems fascinated. She writes in her journal of Caroline that "It is well in this world to discover there can exist a young woman, clever, brilliantly attractive and perfectly well principled, although knowing her own mind" (313). She compares Caroline to Austen's Emma, and says that "She is so completely self-possessed as to be a little unobservant of feeling in others, and may do mischief unwittingly like a kitten" (314). Caroline does not always observe social propriety and mildly shocks Potter by having "flopped" down in her chair before grace was said at dinner (314). Potter considers Caroline to be "a pickle," a word she uses in her novels to describe characters who are mischievous but also somehow admirable (315). "I was once or twice shocked with that young person; at other times I thought her perfect. The prevailing impression was of freshness and extreme amusement. The keynote of her character is decision and complete absence of imagination" (315), and "she is absolutely fearless, strong in innocence as in triple-mail. . . . [S]he has in many respects a strong self-reliant disposition and plenty of commonsense" (316).

Caroline's common sense extended far outside the family. Potter notes in the 1894 journal entry that "Caroline talked of labourers, their miserable wages of eleven shillings a week, their unsanitary cottages, their appalling families and improvidence. All with feeling and sense, and a refreshing unconsciousness of the world's obstinacy and difficulties, always with common sense and courage" (316). Potter clearly admires Caroline and her impassioned interest in the laboring classes—an interest Potter to some extent shared and which is reflected in some of the books she was to write, including *The Tailor* with its sympathetic portrayal of a working man.

Potter's characterization of Caroline Hutton and of her visit to Gloucester is the single longest entry in the journal, and further stands out because of the liveliness of the prose and the attention Potter pays to detail. The Caroline entries are full of life and energy—Potter's life and energy, not only Caroline's—for Caroline seems to have brought it out in Potter. Potter is both attracted to and taken aback by the very qualities in Caroline that she herself had but often repressed: forthrightness, honesty, fearlessness, humor. It was Caroline who had "carried off" Potter when her family had doubts about the wisdom of the visit, Caroline who pursued exciting discussions about Darwin, Huxley, Unitarianism, and other modern topics. Caroline, in many ways, brought to life the Potter who would write not only *The Tailor of Gloucester* but nearly two dozen other books for children that often had a streak of independence and subversion beneath their attractive surfaces—much like Caroline herself, and like Potter.

Not only Caroline but the city of Gloucester itself provided Potter with tropes of rebellion and subversion. Potter had ancestors who supported seditious activists, and here she was in a city that had stood against the Royalists and had paid a price for it after the Restoration. Furthermore, she was in a city that had strong links with the beginnings of the Unitarian Church in England. Gloucester had stood for Cromwell, one of whose first official acts in 1653 was to set forth an Instrument of Government in forty-two articles. Three of these articles spoke to religious freedom and guaranteed freedom of worship to all Christians who professed the fundamentals of Christianity. Although these fundamentals were not specified and led to later difficulties for Cromwell and the country, this Instrument of Government provided the first real protection dissenting Christians had experienced in England, and in fact provided some protection for the early practitioners of what was to become Unitarianism.[9]

Gloucester was also home to John Biddle, born in 1615 in Gloucestshire to a tailor and his wife and an important figure in the history of the Unitarian Church in England.[10] An Oxford-educated independent thinker, he became convinced that the doctrine of the Trinity had no basis in either Scripture or reason and made his beliefs publicly known, leading promptly to the first of his many arrests for heresy and in fact for occasional calls for his death. Biddle published well-constructed arguments against the Trinity, was followed by other preachers (John Knowles, also a Gloucesterman, among them) and is considered by many to be one of the founding fathers of Unitarianism.

Potter's family was Unitarian, and while she was visiting Caroline Hutton the subject of Unitarianism was sometimes the focal point of lively discussion. Potter notes that Mr. Hutton

> says grace only at dinner, and prayers only on Sunday night. Goes to church once on Sunday, reads the lessons and sleeps regularly during the sermon, and afterwards discusses the historical aspects of the Athanasian Creed with an open mind. . . . He

considers the Creed of St. Athanasius was an admirable fighting invention and is now a document of historical interest. (*Journal*, 315)

Athanasius was the fourth-century defender of the concept of the Trinity, then under attack by the heresy of Arianism, which held that Christ was human, not divine, and a messenger of God rather than an aspect or part of the godhead. Arianism is at the root of Unitarianism, a religion that denies the Trinity and the divinity of Christ. Early forms of British Unitarianism were among the most radical of the Dissenting sects. Practicing Unitarians were often persecuted, and if they did not subscribe to the Thirty-Nine Articles were effectively closed out of civic life.

That Mr. Hutton considers Athanasianism of merely historical interest and that he can discuss it with an "open mind" certainly marks him as a Unitarian, someone whose beliefs are founded as much in rationality and logic as they are in faith and belief. The discussion apparently veered off into talk of Huxley and Darwin, and Potter suggested to Caroline that although "Huxley was sufficient for an educated person like Caroline, it would be a poor exchange and indeed an impossible creed for the lower classes" (315). This sort of discussion over and after dinner in the Hutton household must have been both refreshing and liberating for Potter. None of her brief remarks in her journal concerning family discussions at Bolton Gardens hint at subjects more contentious than Gladstone's shortcomings or the concerns of various relatives. Although the Potter family members were practicing Unitarians, they do not seem to have participated in the kind of freewheeling Unitarian discussions that were ordinary fare in the Hutton household.

Potter's Unitarianism has not been much explored by scholars, but I think that combined with the family stories of radical free-thinking ancestors it had a profound effect upon her. Unitarianism as a whole was "in principle, an open, ever-developing religion, with no subscription to articles of faith"[11] and was notoriously difficult to define accurately. It was not unusual for Unitarians to move from preacher to preacher (as the Potters did), nor was it unusual for them to engage in a wide variety of theological viewpoints. Unitarians, if nothing else, were famously open-minded and often concerned for the welfare of others and for the reformation of societal ills. Potter's own maternal Grandmother Leech started a school for the children of mill hands in the 1870s (*Letters*, 196). Many of the important Unitarian families in the north of England must have been close acquaintances of the Cromptons and Potters because the Gaskells and others were also involved in the cotton and textile trades. In fact, the name "Crompton" shows up repeatedly in Unitarian histories, and although it is unclear how closely related Jessy Crompton's family was to the Manchester Cromptons, important in Unitarianism, it seems likely that at the least they were distant cousins.

For Potter, Unitarianism equaled rebelliousness. Unitarianism was not only a dissenting religion, which like Presbyterianism, Quakerism, and others, rejected the Thirty-Nine Articles of the Church of England, but was so radical it refuted the idea of the Trinity. The term "Unitarian" was itself both illegal and blasphemous before 1813 (Watt, 4). It was not the theology of Unitarianism that affected Potter, but rather the culture of Unitarianism and the elements of rebellion and stubbornness that attracted her. Although there is no evidence that she knew the specifics of the story of John Biddle, it is likely that she would have heard at least some of it within Unitarian circles or at the home of the Huttons, and she could not have helped admiring the man who stood up for his beliefs, was arrested numerous times, and suffered mightily without ever giving in to higher authority. Even if she did not know of John Biddle, she did know of her grandmother Jessy, who also "suffered for the faith."

All of this is part of Potter's background when she visited Gloucester for the first time in 1894 and heard the story of the tailor, which was the inspiration for the little story she wrote for Freda Moore for Christmas 1901. Potter had failed in her efforts to be taken seriously as a scientist and still thought of herself as a private not a public writer, but that was beginning to change. She began to think she could earn money not through scientific illustrations but through fantasy books for children.

Both *Tailor* and *Peter Rabbit* began as private illustrated letters to children of her acquaintance (the *Peter* letter in September 1893 and the *Tailor* letter in 1901). Potter finished the first draft of *The Tailor of Gloucester* during the same year she published *Peter Rabbit* privately, and in which Warne agreed to publish a colored edition the following year. Thus *The Tailor of Gloucester* and *Peter Rabbit* together are the seminal works in Potter's development as a novelist of illustrated texts. Both are suffused with rebellion and subversion, but of these two important early works it is the *Tailor* that spoke most deeply of Potter's own dreams and desires.

The plot of *The Tailor of Gloucester* seems more a fairy tale than a call to revolution. It is the story of a tailor who is aided in the project of his life by some grateful little mice. The mice who help the tailor (who is ill) are omnipresent though largely unseen in Gloucester, as Potter tells us: "For behind the wooden wainscots of all the old houses in Gloucester, there are little mouse staircases and secret trap-doors; and the mice run from house to house through those long narrow passages; they can run all over the town without going into the streets" (17). Like Potter herself, these mice are secreted in houses, unseen by larger humans, and able to escape and move from house to house with no one being the wiser—much as Potter herself could leave Bolton Gardens in her imagination, if not very often in fact, and much as Potter as a child hid beneath her grandmother's table to listen to stories of the past and as she hid herself in the coded pages of her journal.

The mice suggest a kind of secret life within the larger life of the city, and as the story progresses they turn out to be persecuted by Simpkin the cat and to sympathize with the poor tailor, whose entire livelihood depends upon the whim of the mayor. Although in their dress and demeanor the mice are not working class at all, their small stature and status as prey to cats puts them in a position to sympathize with the difficulties of the working life of the tailor, whom they thank for his kindness by finishing the wedding waistcoat for him. Humphrey Carpenter has pointed out that this story has a "nice sharp social edge" and "reverses the usual order of power" (285), and we can see this in the hierarchy of creatures and power that the story presents. Within the world of the animal characters the most powerful creatures are the ones most often thought of as useless vermin (the mice), who both taunt and outwit their traditionally stronger enemy, the cat. Moreover, these "weak" mice are the creatures enabling the equally weak tailor to raise his social status by pleasing the powerful mayor. The mayor himself, though clearly important, never appears in the book. He is represented by the wedding waistcoat, effectively suggesting the presumably powerful mayor is only an "empty coat," albeit a beautiful and rich one.

The "empty coat" of the mayor is a sly comment on the emptiness of ritualized power in the city. The mayor is all ceremony and surface, separate from the lives of the people he supposedly governs. His splendor, symbolized by the coat, is entirely dependent not only upon the poor tailor but upon the largely unseen and usually despised mice of the city. The mayor's inability to provide properly for the citizens of Gloucester is suggested by the imagery of food and kitchens that runs throughout the manuscript and the privately printed edition of the book, although the Warne edition of 1903 excises much of this. The manuscript tells us that "the Mayor was a grocer, at the sign of the Golden Candle" and that the tailor himself lives in a "kitchen cellar." The tailor has only a bit of bread and some milk to eat. The manuscript reads, "And when the bread should be finished, and the milk in the pipkin—what would become of Simpkin and the tailor?"[12] When the fire goes out, the manuscript reads "there was very little left to eat—except the mugs and pewter plates." The mice and their rat cousins—again missing from the Warne edition—are present in an energetic illustration of dancing and carousing rodents plundering the mayor's cellar. Apparently the rich grocer of a mayor is unable to ensure that his citizens have enough to eat, so that they must either steal or work extremely hard to afford the bare necessities.

Potter's emphasis on the imbalance of power is much clearer in the manuscript than in the edition published by Warne and familiar to readers today. One of the most telling changes from manuscript to printed text occurs when the tailor releases the mice from beneath the tea cups. The text of the printed edition reads, "Was it right to let loose those mice, undoubtedly the property of Simpkin?" (29). The manuscript version reads, "Was I wise to *unfranchise* [my emphasis] those mice, undoubtedly the property of Simpkin?" The use of "unfranchise" specifically links the tailor's action to governmental, civic action because "franchise" is only granted by governments. The tailor is worried that he has overstepped his authority by intruding upon the rights of the cat, showing more concern for his "citizens" than does the mayor. The word "unfranchise" here is especially interesting because Parliament had only recently (in 1884) passed the Third Reform Act, which essentially extended the voting franchise to all men over the age of twenty-one, regardless of their status as property owners, and Potter herself refers more than once to the extension of the franchise in her journal. Potter may set her story in Regency England, but late Victorian concerns filter in nonetheless.

The disenfranchised working-class tailor is the pivot upon which all three elements of the story turn: the story of Simpkin, the story of the mice, and the story of the waistcoat. Potter suggests the common fairy-tale motif of the weakest turning out to be the strongest, but beneath the resemblances to such fairy tales as "The Shoemaker and the Elves" there is a strong social commentary about the lives of the artisan and working classes. Potter gives the reader this commentary in a triple narrative, each narrative mirroring the others. First is the story of the imprisoned mice who, with the help of the tailor, outwit the predatory Simpkin. Then the tables are turned and the tailor, imprisoned by poverty and ill-health, is aided by the mice, who free him from his "prison" by working through the night to finish the waistcoat that has been promised to the mayor. The mayor is not imprisoned at all, but he is predatory in that he is certainly living well—feeding himself, if you will—at the expense of the working people he serves at his grocery store and whom he governs. His power will not be overturned at the end of the story, but will instead be turned to the tailor's use.

Simpkin stands between the narrative lines of the mice and mayor and is tied to the other two narratives through the imagery of hunger and food. The mayor is "hungry" for his coat and is feeding himself on the labor of others, some of whom (like the tailor) are nearly starving. The mice, nearly dinner for Simpkin, taunt him with his hunger after the tailor has helped them escape, and they do so through rhyme and riddle. Their taunting and Simpkin's search for a mouse dinner occupy seven pages of text in the Warne edition, which includes only six of Potter's original twelve rhymes and riddles. All of these rhymes refer, in one way or another, to food. The first rhyme in the manuscript version is a Christmas wassailing song, ending with a reference to "pockets full of money, the cellars full of beer." The second is a much longer version of what appears in the Warne edition as "Dame get up and bake your pies" (41) and includes references to ducks with clipped wings who are destined for the Christmas dinner table. The third is a quotation from the well-known Old Mother Hubbard rhyme about the empty larder, to which Simpkin compares his own larder. Simpkin then moves on to a stable-yard that houses "fat horses" and we hear a rhyme about riding a horse to Banbury cross—a reference not only to the horses but perhaps also to hot cross buns. Then we hear a bit of Old King Cole and his blackbird pie followed by another rhyme featuring cooking. Simpkin sees rats frolicking in the mayor's cellar singing "And he ate up all the good roast beef / And he ate up all the good fat tripe." There are several other rhymes concerning "cuttery corn," a "cup of sack," and a "race of ginger," and a song about a nut tree. Simpkin goes on to hear the mice taunt him with a rhyme about Jack Sprat, and they end by singing

Hark! Hark!
The dogs do bark,
The beggars are come to town,
Some in tags
And some in rags
And one in a velvet gown!

The velvet gown here is an ironic reference to Simpkin's natural fur coat.

Simpkin's extended journey in the manuscript version of *The Tailor of Gloucester* puts more emphasis on his hunger and on his punishment for having trapped the mice than exists in the published version. While Warne managed to tighten the story by dropping so many of the rhymes (to Potter's dismay), the publisher also diluted Simpkin's purpose in the tale. Simpkin is the tailor's servant and ought to be on the side of the poor and the working classes. Instead, he looks out only for himself and selfishly keeps his potential mouse dinner under the china, then punishes the tailor for releasing them by hiding the necessary twist (thread) in a tea pot. Simpkin acts as a kind of independent entrepreneur who cares little for the welfare of others. The price he pays is to remain a servant at the end of the tale, where his purpose is to care for others. The mice and the tailor, on the other hand, help one another escape the prisons of crockery and poverty to become more substantial citizens of Gloucester—and they do so at the expense of the mayor, who has paid handsomely for his embroidered waistcoat. There is, in this tale, a subtext of class hierarchy thwarted by hard work rather than outright rebellion.

Simpkin's narrative echoes that of another famous literary cat, Perrault's Puss-in-Boots, who shares much with Simpkin. Both cats are successful hunters and are sly and clever; both have impoverished masters; both cats use clothing in their schemes; both cats are illustrated as having large boots and heroic stances. But whereas Puss-in-Boots aids in raising his master to a higher status by providing him the clothing to pass as a Marquis, Simpkin denies the tailor the essential piece of "twist" to finish the clothing that can make the tailor's future and by extension Simpkin's future as well. In Potter's tale the cat is subverted by the mice, whereas in Perrault's tale the cat triumphs when the ogre transforms himself into a mouse—who is then eaten by Puss.

The changes Potter made to Perrault's tale give us clues as to some of her philosophy. Whereas Perrault gives us a poor miller's son who is passive and dim-witted, Potter's tailor is talented and passive only because of illness and hunger. He clearly is a hard-working and talented artisan, having designed, cut, and pieced the waistcoat himself. The miller's son in Perrault's tale can achieve nothing without the help of the cat; in Potter's tale the cat is not a help but a hindrance.

A combination of generosity and hard work leads to the tailor's success, whereas all the miller's son must do is listen to Puss and obey his instructions. Whereas Puss becomes as wealthy as his master in Perrault's tale, Simpkin reverts to servant status at the end of *The Tailor of Gloucester.*

One of the messages encoded in *The Tailor of Gloucester* is that it is hard work, cooperation, and generosity that will improve the lot of the working classes, not deceit and not selfishness. Those who exist unseen in the nooks and crannies of society, as the mice exist in the nooks and crannies of Gloucester, have substantial power to improve their lot in life if they work hard and cooperate, rather than compete with one another. In both Perrault's tale and in Potter's, clothes quite literally make the man: the miller's son is mistaken for a marquis because of the way he is dressed, and the mayor's waistcoat not only shows his status but raises the status of the tailor. But the tailor is made through his own hard work on that waistcoat, while the miller's son is made through deceit and through the cleverness of his cat. Furthermore, the mice are also made through their hard work. They can dress as ladies and gentlemen because they have taken the tailor's scraps of fabric and put them to good use. The tailor helped the mice raise their status, and they in turn help him. Potter is validating hard work and cooperation as a way to improve oneself. Simpkin, who fails at both, cannot rise above his feline servant status. By the end of the tale he, of all the characters, is without clothing, without a symbol of social status.

This subtext of class, status, and hierarchy is consistent with Potter's general political viewpoint as we can piece it together from her journal and her letters. She was always a political conservative, anti-Gladstone and anti-Irish Home Rule, for example, yet she had a profound respect for the working classes and a desire to treat them fairly and give them opportunities to improve their lives. She made clear her feelings about the working classes and their relationship to those above them in a letter in 1929, in which she said that "A man's attitude towards his subordinates, and their opinion of him, is an acid test of character" (*Letters,* 317), a test the tailor passes and Potter passed as well in her lifetime. Potter's relationships with the Cannon family (her tenants at Sawrey) and with other farmers in the area were respectful and cooperative. As her letters and comments to others make clear, she worked in tandem with these farmers, who were not gentleman farmers but working farmers on small holdings. She knew she could learn much from these men and women and consulted with them rather than ordering them to do various chores and tasks on the property. She not only consulted but actively worked in the fields and with the sheep and pigs; she well deserved the title "farmer," which in later life she signed after her name in letters to the press. Unlike her parents, who preferred to forget that their own family fortune had its origins in "trade" and in hard work in textile mills in the north of England, Potter remembered her roots and knew what riches hard and honest work could bring. She was never a social radical, but she did believe in fairness and equity, a theme that runs throughout all her novels, not only in *The Tailor of Gloucester.*

Potter may also, in *The Tailor of Gloucester*, have been influenced by her own status in Bolton Gardens as an absolutely necessary but undervalued member of the household, someone who lived out of the way and largely unseen on the third floor but who was increasingly relied upon to deal with the hiring and handling of the household staff. Even after she married and moved permanently to the Lakes, leaving her parents behind in London, Potter had to travel down from Sawrey to deal with her mother's servant crises. Potter lived "between the cracks" much as the mice in *Tailor* do, and like the mice depended upon artistry to build an independent life for herself. The mice are artists both in words and in action. Although they do not create their own rhymes and songs, they know how to string together the right quotations to tease and taunt the cat who wants to consume them. They do exquisite embroidery, with stitches so tiny they can hardly be seen. In some ways the mice can be seen as stand-ins for Potter, herself both a visual and a verbal artist who lived largely unnoticed until someone needed her help.

Potter wrote the letter forming the basis of *Peter Rabbit* in 1893, seven years before she wrote and sent the Christmas letter about the tailor. Between these two events, in 1894, Potter made that crucial visit to Gloucester, a visit that freed her from parental authority, gave her an example of a modern and free woman in Caroline Hutton, and stirred in her subconscious ideas and feelings about rebelliousness and revolution. It is not until after the visit to Gloucester that Potter decides she might try to publish *Peter Rabbit*, a story she had already written. *Peter Rabbit* may have been the first book she published, but I do not think she would have had the independence of mind and spirit to pursue publication had she not visited the Hutton household near Gloucester in 1894. By December 16, 1901, the first private edition of *Peter Rabbit* had been published and Potter was in negotiation with Warne over the possible commercial publication of the book, the contract for which had been more or less settled by December 18, 1901. Potter sent the first manuscript of *The Tailor* to Freda Moore as a letter dated Christmas 1901.

The timing of the manuscript of *The Tailor of Gloucester* was not coincidental. The story had clearly been in Potter's mind in some form or other since her initial visit to Stroud and had clarified in subsequent visits. The acceptance of the *Peter Rabbit* book by Warne gave Potter the confidence to give full voice to herself, and even if coded and embedded deep within the illustrations and the text, her rebelliousness and longing for a more independent life shine through in *The Tailor of Gloucester*. It is not coincidental that Potter always claimed this was her favorite of her books, nor is it coincidental that the illustrations are by far the most detailed and gorgeous of any to appear in her novels. There is much about *The Tailor of Gloucester* that is unique in the Potter oeuvre: the urban setting, the importance of the human character, the specific historical period, the detail of the illustrations. There is also much that will be echoed in later books, all of which are, as Humphrey Carpenter pointed out, not "moral" tales so much as "immoral" tales, tales that demonstrate "the rewards of nonconformity" and that encourage readers "to question the social system into which they found themselves born" (279).

The tale published directly after *Peter Rabbit* (a novel that will be discussed at length in Chapter Two) is thematically closer to *The Tailor of Gloucester* than to *Peter*, and like *Peter* sheds light on some of Potter's embedded social and political themes. This book is *The Tale of Squirrel Nutkin* (1903), which also had its genesis in a 1901 letter to one of the Moore children, this time Norah instead of Freda. Both *Tailor* and *Nutkin* reflect Potter's interest in fairy tales and in riddles and rhymes, and both are set in recognizable and beloved settings for Potter: Gloucester for one and the shores around Derwentwater for the other. Although both *Tailor* and *Nutkin* appear in print after *Peter Rabbit*, their genesis in letter form predated both the private and commercial publications of *Peter*. Like *Tailor*, *Squirrel Nutkin* is influenced by fairy-tale motifs, rhymes, and old songs. Like *Peter*, the book is an overt exploration of rebellion and its consequence.

The strongest link between *The Tailor of Gloucester* and *The Tale of Squirrel Nutkin* is the reliance of both on fairy tales and old rhymes, songs, and riddles. Potter had a long-standing fascination with rhymes and riddles. She was familiar with the rhyme and fairy-tale collections of both Robert Chambers and James Halliwell and had illustrated fairy tales herself from a young age. She was an admirer of Randolph Caldecott, perhaps the most famous illustrator of nursery rhymes, and her father had collected some original Caldecott drawings. The fairy-tale connection in *Squirrel Nutkin* is less obvious than in *The Tailor of Gloucester*, and lies not so much in an echo of a Grimm fairy tale as it does in the loose employment of several fairy-tale motifs and narrative techniques, as well as an echo of Aesop's *Fables*, which she was to use again later in her career. *Squirrel Nutkin*, like many fairy tales, has a rural rather than an urban setting, contains a threatening figure (Old Brown) who lives at the center of the woods, and uses a great deal of repetition: the squirrels arrive at Old Brown's island on six consecutive days. Each time they arrive with a present for Old Brown, and each time Nutkin taunts the owl and tempts fate, refusing to behave like the good squirrels who are collecting nuts for winter consumption. The riddles Nutkin recites to torment the owl are similar to the repetitive rhymes or incantations that one sees, for example, in the Grimms' "Ashiepattle," in the song or chant to the helpful tree; in "The Juniper Tree" with the dead son's song; or in the chant to the mirror in "Snow White." However, Potter ends her tale in a nontraditional way. Instead of our young hero completing a series of tasks or outwitting an antagonist, he is caught by the antagonist and punished. Potter in fact does an interesting reversal of a fairy-tale motif, in that she asks the *reader* rather than the protagonist to solve the riddles.

Squirrel Nutkin, like *The Tailor of Gloucester*, is a tale where food is at the center of things. The plot hinges on the squirrels' need to obtain food from lands belonging to Old Mr. Brown. Mr. Brown is an owl, most likely a tawny owl,[13] a species that preys primarily on rodents, including moles and mice (both of which are provided him by the squirrels), as well as larger rodents such as rabbits—and squirrels—when available. They nest in tree cavities (as does Old Brown), and have been known to appropriate squirrel nests for their own.[14] There is a wonderful irony in this story: the squirrels need the food in Old Mr. Brown's dominion, but they are in danger of being eaten by him. The solution is to ask politely for permission to gather nuts and to provide the old owl with a combination bribe/present of other foodstuff to distract him from the temptation of squirrels on his island.

Because Old Mr. Brown is the owner of the island and because he is dangerous to the squirrels, they approach with caution and obeisance. As we saw in *The Tailor of Gloucester*, issues of class structure and hierarchy often play out in Potter's work, and they do in *Squirrel Nutkin* as well. The squirrels make "an offering" to the owl, they bow to him, and they ask "politely," "Old Mr. Brown, will you favour us with permission to gather nuts upon your island?"[15] The language here is formal. The narrator has referred to the owl simply as "Old Brown," but the squirrels add the honorific of "Mr." when they address him. They also make an "offering" and lay their presents down at the owl's feet rather than deliver them into his claws. While the squirrels are certainly realistically cautious here—no need to get closer to an owl's claws than you must—the placing of the dead mice at his feet, in both text and illustration, makes the squirrels appear something like obedient, obsequious servants of a ruler. The same formality is repeated when the squirrels show up a second day with an offering of a dead mole, which they carry to Old Brown in a kind of solemn funeral procession, and ask him again, "Mr. Brown, will you favour us with your gracious permission to gather some more nuts?" (22). Now they are even more polite than they were during their first visit, dropping the "Old" but keeping "Mr." when they address the owl and qualifying his permission as "gracious." In all of their subsequent visits to the island they are equally formal in their presentation of gifts.

In *The Tailor of Gloucester* we had a human hierarchy of mayor and tailor, and an animal hierarchy (reversed in the end) of cat and mouse. There are no humans in *Squirrel Nutkin* but there is still a sense of hierarchy, class, and power and a desire to overturn it. Old Brown and the squirrels, in fact, behave something like a landowner and his underlings. Old Brown owns the island and all that is upon it, much as a landowner owned not only his land but the game and everything else that lay upon it. In the human world anyone who tried to take something from this land without permission would be poaching, for which there were severe penalties in the nineteenth century. (Indeed, the infamous "man traps" of spiked pits meant to catch poachers had only been made illegal in mid-century.) Potter may have been born in London but she spent many formative summers and holidays in the country and would have been well aware of poachers and the laws against them: *Squirrel Nutkin* reflects her knowledge of country law. The squirrels know there is a penalty for taking nuts without permission. Likewise, humans in Potter's time knew there was a penalty for poaching rabbits, even if the land-lord had no earthly use or desire for rabbits, or even if he considered the rabbits vermin. Poaching is a violation of sovereignty, not merely a violation of land and property.

One of the squirrels visiting the island, Nutkin, is not interested in helping with the harvest, and certainly not interested in appeasing Old Brown. His behav-ior can be seen as mirroring that of both a disobedient child and of a rebellious underling. Nutkin refuses to give respect to Old Brown and instead taunts and teases him, oblivious to the consequences. At the end of the story, when Old Brown finally runs out of patience with Nutkin, he snaps him up, "carried Nutkin into his house, and held him up by the tail, intending to skin him" (56) and no doubt eat him. Nutkin defies social conventions and uses rude language in doing so. Here he imitates not only the behavior of a rude child but also the behavior of many rebellious working-class people of Potter's own time. His exceedingly rude behavior and language stand in stark contrast to the behavior and language of the other squirrels, the squirrels willing to play by Old Brown's rules.

Nutkin is the voice of rebellion here. Just as the mice in *The Tailor of Gloucester* taunt Simpkin with a number of rhymes about food, Nutkin taunts Old Brown with old English riddles. Owls have long been personified as "wise" crea-tures and Nutkin torments Old Brown by presenting intellectual puzzles in riddles he thinks the owl will be unable to decipher. Nutkin is challenging the very nature of the "wise owl" by riddling him.

Nutkin quite literally needles the owl when on the second day he sings a rid-dle whose answer is "nettle," all the while "tickling old Mr. Brown with a *nettle*" (25; Potter's emphasis). The accompanying illustration shows a daring Nutkin standing close enough to touch the owl, "tickling" him under the chin with a thorny nettle. Here Potter is using "tickle" in its British ironic sense of "to chas-tise," as in schoolboys being "tickled" with birch rods when they disobey: Nutkin does not want to give the owl pleasure, but wants to irritate or punish him. The owl ignores Nutkin and carries his latest present (a dead mole) into the house, shutting the door in Nutkin's face. Nutkin, not to be dissuaded, peeps through the keyhole and taunts the owl with another riddle. He further needles the owl by refusing to take the nut-gathering seriously, instead choosing to play games on the owl's land. We are told he gathers "oak-apples" and uses them to play marbles while he keeps an eye on the door to the owl's house rather than collecting the useful nuts. He also gathers "robin's pin-cushions off a briar bush" and sticks them full of "pine-needle pins" (37) and plays ninepins "with a crab apple and green fir-cones" (42). He is more interested in play and in leisure than he is in work.

Nutkin's interests remind the reader of children's desires to avoid work in favor of play, but the kind of play Nutkin engages in suggests he also has links to the working classes. The games he plays—marbles and ninepins—are games associated with working-class children and adults, not with the upper classes. Ninepins was a game played in alleys behind pubs and grew out of the older game of bowls, which had actually been made illegal for the working classes to play until the mid-nineteenth century (although this law was largely ignored by both the populace and officials).[16] The owl treats Nutkin the way the upper classes often treated the working classes: he ignores the annoying underling, but when pushed too far he resorts to violence to contain the threat of uprising. What Potter does in *Squirrel Nutkin* is to combine her own understanding of the natural world and her interest in rebellion against authority with echoes of the working-class dissent and dissatisfaction of the period.[17]

Potter was not only the quiet and cloistered girl of Bolton Gardens, but also a keen observer of the political world, and the political world she grew up in was one of rebellion and change. Some of her earliest journal entries concern the agitation for Irish Home Rule, which led to terrorist activities such as an attempted bombing of government offices in 1883. Potter, sixteen at the time, writes, "What will be blown up next? . . . Papa says it is Mr Gladstone's fault. He takes the side of these rogues and then, if they think he is slackening, they frighten him a bit— really we shall be as bad as France soon" (*Journal*, 32–33). The eighties and nineties were also a period of agitation for increased trade unionism in Britain, and Potter was in London for the Dock Strike of 1889, a highly volatile strike that marked an important point in both the rise of "new trade unionism" and the eventual rise of a labour party. Potter's journal for 1889 is very brief and sketchy and contains no mention of this important event in British labor history, but Potter was a voracious reader of the press and observer of political and social doings and would have been well aware of the Dock Strike and its implications. G. D. H. Cole notes of 1889 that the year is one "in which the gathering storm of industrial unrest suddenly burst, and the New Unionism became a recognized power in Great Britain."[18] Hobsbaum argues that the British working class as we know it today "did not emerge much before the 1880s and took shape in the next couple of decades."[19] Angus Hawkins, in his study of British party politics, points out

By the 1870s and 1880s traditional communities were finding themselves under growing economic and social pressure. Old ties of affiliation and obligation were being eroded. The historic vocabulary of estates, degrees, orders and ranks was becoming out-dated. Notions of social status, as much as being dependent upon region or religion, were becoming increasingly defined in terms of class. . . . By the 1890s religion was giving way to class as a major impetus to popular activism.[20]

This is the social and political climate at the time Potter begins to write her tales. Class and class issues were at the forefront of political discourse and widely discussed and debated in the popular press. While not all writers, and certainly not all children's writers, reflect the contemporary social climate in their works,

Potter does. The reader can ignore this layer of meaning in texts like *Squirrel Nutkin* and still enjoy the tale, but a recognition of the context of the story adds to its meaning. In *Squirrel Nutkin* Potter is writing of disobedience, as she often does, but she does so in the context of working-class agitation.

Nutkin's celebration of disobedience is given to the reader through the trope of play, a trope that also has links to changes in culture. Leisure was a relatively new concept for the Victorians and a problematic one for the middle classes as well as for the working classes. The mid-Victorian years saw public debate on the morality and usefulness of leisure for the increasing middle class, with debates over the morality of billiards, dancing, cards, and so forth. The middle classes also increasingly became concerned with working-class leisure, as the increase in labor legislation and unionization and the decrease in working men's hours allowed the working classes a certain amount of leisure time as well. As Peter Bailey notes

> the anxieties that beset the middle class during their initiation into the new leisure world of industrial society were never completely extirpated, but rather displaced onto the working class. . . . If the proper exercise of this responsibility had tested the moral resources of the middle class, how then could it be safely entrusted to untutored working people?[21]

Leisure posed particular problems for the Potter family itself. The Potters were not aristocrats, whose lives in the nineteenth century were largely defined by leisure and by recreational activities on landed estates (hunting, riding, and so forth), but they were not typical suburban middle-class Victorians either. Rupert Potter was a barrister but rarely if ever practiced law, spending his time instead at his club and in pursuit of the modern leisure activities of photography and attendance at art exhibitions. More significantly, although the Potters were not landed gentry, they masqueraded as such during their long holidays in rented country houses such as Dalguise in Scotland. Even in London, Mrs. Potter's fastidiousness concerning the social pattern of her day mimicked the pattern of the class above her, not below her. The Potter family fear of association with "trade" had to do with their own insecurities about their class situation and the origin of their wealth in the cotton and calico manufacturing business. The entire second half of the nineteenth century was a period of shifting class consciousness, of which the Potters seemed acutely aware. Both Beatrix and Bertram Potter rebelled against this class consciousness, Beatrix by going into "trade" herself with her novels, and Bertram by secretly marrying the daughter of a wine merchant—a tradesman's daughter—in Scotland. The Potter children, perhaps feeling more secure in their class situation than their parents, were comfortable transgressing the class boundaries upheld by their parents.

Nutkin's games, then, emphasize both the challenges and the dangers inherent in breaking class boundaries. While the good squirrels collect nuts that will feed them in the winter, Nutkin challenges the wisdom and authority of the owner of the island with his riddles and also eschews the world of work for the world of leisure. Leisure has its dangers, however, and the botanical imagery of Nutkin's games foreshadows the potentially fatal consequences of ignoring work in favor of play. The oak-apples Nutkin gathers are a kind of gall that grows on oak trees, are useless as food, and disfigure the tree: Nutkin won't collect the useful and edible acorns, but he will collect useless gall as game pieces. The briar bush is not good for much of anything except an overabundance of thorns. Nutkin plays ninepins with inedible crab apples and fir cones that are too green to go to seed and lead to new growth. Nutkin's game playing—both in terms of the riddles and in terms of his physical games—challenges the owl and is aimed at getting a rise out of him and engaging him in some sort of relationship. The owl, living apart in his own world, is untroubled by these antics until the very end, when Nutkin leaps on his head in a genuine attack. At this point the owl does wake up, and threatens Nutkin with the death that his games have foreshadowed.

If we think of Old Brown as an emblem of political or social power, what Potter seems to suggest is that such powers will pay little, if any, attention to the agitation of workers until the workers actually attack—in which case the claws come out and death (or at least disempowerment) is the probable outcome. If we think of Old Brown as an emblem of adult authority over a disobedient child, the same logic holds: there is tolerance for misbehavior up to a point, but then the child is put in her place. The illustration accompanying the text where Nutkin "takes a running jump right onto the head of Old Brown" (50) shows that the owl is no easy victim. He is tensed for a spring into the air, his very sharp beak is wide open, and one of his large claws is raised for the attack. It is a fearsome little drawing, and the good squirrels know enough to run away from the action. The page turn tells us that when the good squirrels come back "very cautiously" to see what has happened, Old Brown is sitting still, "with his eyes closed, as if nothing had happened" (53). Potter then sets off the drama of what has happened with a series of asterisks and italic print, to tell the reader, "*But Nutkin was in his waistcoat pocket!*" (53; Potter's emphasis). The next page turn gives us the single line of text, "This looks like the end of the story; but it isn't" (54), accompanied by an illustration in which the very large and predatory owl has Nutkin pinned, lying on his back, looking as vulnerable as Tom Kitten will a few books later when he is tied up by the rats.

Of course Nutkin escapes, but the nature of his escape and the denouement of the story tell us something of Potter's often ambivalent views of power and powerlessness, rebellion and disobedience. Old Brown holds Nutkin by the tail, intending to skin him, "but Nutkin pulled so very hard that his tail broke in two" and he manages to escape. The final words of the story are, "And to this day, if you meet Nutkin up a tree and ask him a riddle, he will throw sticks at you, and stamp his feet and scold, and shout—"Cuck-cuck-cuck-cur-r-r-cuk-k-k!" (59). The accompanying illustration shows Nutkin without his tail, high up in a tree, chattering away at four other squirrels. Nutkin still looks fairly defiant but at the same time he looks as if he is ready to turn and flee from the good squirrels, all of which Potter manages to capture in fluidity of line and attention to squirrel posture.

The story began with the narrator telling the reader "This is a Tale about a tail," and at the end of the story, Nutkin loses both his tail and his tale, his verbal ability to taunt Old Brown and other authority figures. Throughout the story he has riddled Old Brown with English riddles, has been anthropomorphized by Potter into a squirrel/boy who has difficulty dealing with authority and echoes working-class discontents. She conflates the working classes with childhood, a common tendency of journalists of the period. In the end Nutkin is not completely vanquished by authority, but he does lose his tail and his voice. His tail is the very essence of who he is. Squirrels in nature express much of themselves and their mood through their tails, which twitch and switch and express (to the human eye) their emotions. Nutkin has lost the essence of squirrelhood in losing his tail. But more significantly he has also lost his voice, lost his "tale" or the ability to tell it, through his disobedience. He is no longer verbally quick and clever but is reduced to squirrel chatter, rendered admirably by Potter in her onomatopoeic last line. He has challenged authority and escaped with his life, but he is somehow diminished.

The disobedience and its outcome here are not uncommon for Potter. On one hand she celebrates rebellion and is clearly on the side of the mice and not Simpkin, of Nutkin and not the owl, of Peter and not Mr. McGregor, and so forth. On the other hand there is a price to pay for rebellion. In *Squirrel Nutkin*, that price is loss of voice. Potter was a Victorian woman challenging her family's expectations for her as a daughter and a woman. Women novelists by Potter's time had become at least somewhat respectable and sometimes admired figures in the literary world. It was still difficult for a woman novelist to make a living and to gain respect through her writing, but it was not impossible and there were numerous role models to follow. In Potter's family, however, anything that connected the family with trade and with a public voice was to be frowned upon. The Potters wanted their daughter to be silent and under their control; she wanted to express herself in her own voice and to make a living for herself outside the confines of her family. The ending of *Squirrel Nutkin* suggests that one of Potter's fears was that if she actually attacked the authority figures in her life, if she actively fought against them rather than trying to "riddle" them with secretive forays into card publishing and picturebook writing, that she might lose her voice entirely. She was equally ambivalent about the demands of the working class and changes in the larger social and political world, remaining conservative in her politics but often sympathetic to such problems as poverty and disenfranchisement of the poor and the Irish. This uneasy balance of a desire for change and rebellion, and a fear and dislike of it, is the base upon which most of her novels rest.

Notes

1. Judy Taylor, ed., *Beatrix Potter's Letters* (London: Warne, 1989), 261, 283.
2. Humphrey Carpenter, "Excessively Impertinent Bunnies: The Subversive Element in Beatrix Potter," in *Children and Their Books: A Celebration of the Works of Iona and Peter Opie*, ed. Gillian Avery and Julia Briggs (Oxford: Clarendon, 1989), 287.
3. Sandra Gilbert and Susan Gubar, *The Madwoman in the Attic: The Woman Writer and the Nineteenth-Century Literary Imagination* (New Haven: Yale University Press, 1979), 163.
4. Ruth McDonald, "Why This is Still 1893: *The Tale of Peter Rabbit* and Beatrix Potter's Manipulations of Time into Timelessness," *Children's Literature Association Quarterly* 10, no. 4 (1986): 185.
5. Margaret Lane, *The Tale of Beatrix Potter: A Biography* (London: Warne, 1946), 9, 10.
6. Lissa Paul, "Beatrix Potter and John Everett Millais," in Margaret Mackey, ed., *Beatrix Potter's Peter Rabbit: A Children's Classic at 100* (Latham, Mary. and London: Children's Literature Association and Scarecrow Press, 2002). See pp. 43–54 for an interesting discussion of Millais's influence on Potter's art.
7. Beatrix Potter, *The Tailor of Gloucester* (London: Warne, 1903; 1995), 9. All references will be to this edition unless otherwise noted in the text.
8. Leslie Linder, ed. *The Journal of Beatrix Potter* (London: Warne, 1966), 312.
9. Earl Morse Wilbur's *A History of Unitarianism in Transylvania, England, and America* (Cambridge: Harvard University Press, 1952) provides a good short history of these events. See especially pp. 202–206.
10. Although it is unlikely that Potter had Biddle's history in mind when writing *The Tailor of Gloucester*, the link to tailoring is a pleasing coincidence.
11. Ruth Watt, *Gender, Power and the Unitarians in England, 1760–1860* (New York: Longman, 1998), 3.
12. Beatrix Potter, Manuscript of *The Tailor of Gloucester* (RBD BP MSS 97-528, Philadelphia Free Public Library), n.p.
13. There are five owl species in Great Britain, the most common being the tawny owl (*strix aluco*). Potter's illustration is a beautiful rendition of this species, and other details of his life mark him as a tawny owl as well. I am indebted to Deane Lewis of Maryborough, Queensland, Australia, for help in identifying this species.
14. Potter's brother Bertram had had a pet tawny owl and Potter was well acquainted with their behavior.
15. Beatrix Potter, *The Tale of Squirrel Nutkin* (London: Warne, 1903; 1987), 17. Unless otherwise noted, all text references are to the 1987 edition.
16. See *Encyclopedia Britannica: Macropedia* (1973), entry on "Bowls," for a brief and informative history of this game.
17. Later in life, Potter herself was approached by locals in Sawrey who wanted to use one of her fields for a bowling green. She was not adverse to the idea, but

specified that if one were built, it should be available to all the citizens of Sawrey, and not just the landed ones.

18.   G. D. H. Cole, *A Short History of the British Working Class Movement: 1789–1947* (London: Allen and Unwin, 1948), 243.

19.   Ernest Hobsbaum, *Uncommon People: Resistance, Rebellion, and Jazz* (New York: New Press, 1998), 62.

20.   Angus Hawkins, *British Party Politics, 1852–1886* (London: Macmillan, 1998), 5.

21.   Peter Bailey, " 'A Mingled Mass of Perfectly Legitimate Pleasures': The Victorian Middle Class and the Problem of Leisure," *Victorian Studies* 2, no. 1 (1977), 28.

2

Into the Garden:
The Story of Peter and His Family

The Tailor of Gloucester was Potter's favorite book and the book giving us critical clues about how to read the rest of her novels, but it is the first of her published works, *Peter Rabbit*, that made the publication of *Tailor* possible and that set Potter on the path to becoming probably the single best-known writer for children in English (with the possible exception of J. K. Rowling). *Peter Rabbit* is the text that has received the most extensive treatment by Potter scholars, and many contemporary readers know only this of all of Potter's works for children. Yet for all that has been written about the book, little attention has been paid to how the novel fits into the entire Potter oeuvre, nor to its importance in Potter's growth as businesswoman and entrepreneur. *Peter Rabbit* and its companion volumes (*The Tale of Benjamin Bunny* and *The Tale of the Flopsy Bunnies*) gave Potter crucial business experience and made possible her own transformation into a profit-making working farmer.

The story of the genesis of *Peter Rabbit* has been told often and well by scholars such as Leslie Linder, Ruth McDonald, and Judy Taylor. The illustrated letter to Noël Moore dated September 4, 1893, that was the beginning of the story has been reprinted in facsimile form in several places, including Judy Taylor's *Letters to Children from Beatrix Potter*.[1] Potter retrieved this letter some seven years after she wrote it as the basis for a privately printed edition of *Peter Rabbit*, illustrated in black and white with a color frontispiece, which she sold to friends and acquaintances and used to try to find a commercial publisher (with the help of Canon Rawnsley, Vicar of Crosthwaite, a pioneer in the formation of the National Trust and a verse-writer for children). Potter published a second private edition, and Warne agreed to publish the book if the illustrations were redrawn in color and if the number of illustrations were cut from forty-one to thirty-two. Warne did four printings of the novel; the fifth printing of 1903 is the edition that has been canonized and that is familiar to readers today (and which will be the text referred to here, unless otherwise noted). But there is far more to the story of how Peter came to life than is generally discussed by commentators on Potter's work.

Potter had long been interested in rabbits and had at least two pet rabbits that she sketched obsessively: Benjamin Bouncer and, later, Peter Piper. Rabbits gave Potter her first ideas for using her artistic talents to make money for herself. Whalley and Hobbs point out that the date at which Potter first moved away from realistic paintings of flowers, fungi, and animals and into the fantasy drawings that would eventually lead to the illustrated novels is difficult to determine, "but many of her best imaginative paintings date from the 1890's" when Potter was in her early twenties. "The main reason for this sudden burst of energy," they note, "was the need for money."[2] Bertram was finishing up at Charterhouse and heading to Oxford, but Potter was still at home, still unmarried (and apparently uncourted), and anxious for some independence of her own. The constraints of Victorian gender expectations and of her conservative and not very social family contributed to Potter's isolation as she grew into her twenties.

Bertram, on the verge of leaving home, had been her ally in a number of schemes that involved commercial rather than fine art. By May 1890, Potter titles an entry in her journal "A Visit to Hildesheimer and Faulkner," the printers, and notes that "The root of this happy business was pique and a desire for coin to the amount of £6."[3] She and Bertram "work[ed] a mutual admiration society" and Potter had created a series of fantasy-animal Christmas cards to put under the plates of her relatives on Christmas morning. They provide "a five minute wonder," and her uncle says "any publisher would snap at them. All the same I might have waited till doomsday before he would have moved a finger. He is a provoking person" (*Journal*, 204). Undeterred, Potter worked on a series of six designs, "taking for my Model that charming rascal Benjamin Bouncer" (204). It was not until May that she heard from Hildesheimer and Faulkner, the second publisher she and Bertram approached, who gave her the desired £6 as well as a request for more sketches.

The journal entry that follows this exciting news shows Potter more animated and happier than she has been or will be elsewhere in the journal, with the possible exception of the entries about Caroline Hutton dating from 1894. She gives Benjamin a "cupful of hemp seeds, the consequence being that when I wanted to draw him next morning he was partially intoxicated and wholly unmanageable" (205). Potter herself seems to have had a sympathetic reaction to those hemp seeds because she lay awake until two in the morning, "and afterwards had an impression that Bunny came to my bedside in a white cotton night cap and tickled me with his whiskers" (205). Tellingly, she says nothing to her aunt and uncle (and fails to mention her parents at all) until after she gets the check back from Bertram, to whom she had to send it for endorsement. Her success is a private one, not to be shared with the "provoking" uncle and not to be shared with disapproving parents. Although painting was a respectable Victorian occupation for young ladies, getting paid for it and going off to publisher's offices to discuss contracts was not, and Potter must have known that she would struggle with her parents over her desire to move into the commercial world of art.

Potter was motivated by "pique" at her relatives and also by a desire for money of her own, and she reacted by working in secret with her brother. She could not completely escape the constraints of family and gender, but by allying herself with her equally rebellious brother managed her first successful rebellion from her parents. She managed this coup in secrecy and kept the pleasure of her success largely to herself. She chose not to pursue escape from Bolton Gardens through the traditional means of marriage, but instead quietly began what was to be a successful career as artist and businesswoman.

The journal entries about her first business success are followed directly by another entry headed "Reminiscences of Grandmother Potter," probably written at about the time of Jessy Crompton's death in 1891. In this brief entry Potter tries to capture the rhythm of her grandmother's speech, giving us a re-creation of some conversation with the grandmother in the grandmother's own words, complete with phonetic spellings and dashes to indicate pauses in the older woman's thought and speech. At the close of the entry, Potter writes in her own voice:

> I put an unfortunate fishing question about the politics of the family in the rebellion of '45—she thought of 1640 (the one who had his head cut off?), but having got her right, "Oh that one, Bonny Prince Charlie, he did not make much disturbance. She referred to him much as she might to Charley Crompton—nothing could I make of that lead." (207)

There are several interesting things about this particular entry. First, Potter's thoughts after having her first success with commercial publishing were of her grandmother, not her parents. Her grandmother's fortune had come from trade and specifically from the calico-printing trade; her grandmother had been a forthright and independently minded woman; and her grandmother was the woman Potter admired above all others in her family. Later in life Potter would write to a child friend that "I was very much attached to my grandmother Jessy Crompton and said to be very like her."[4] Second, Potter wants to find out something about the family "politics." The Potter family had a passion for genealogy and for family stories, and one that had been handed down over the years was that Abraham Crompton had connections with the second Jacobite Rebellion of 1745. Abraham owned Chorley Hall, which he had been able to purchase in 1715 because its owner, Richard Chorley, had been beheaded for his support of James II during the first Jacobite Rebellion. In 1745, when Bonnie Prince Charlie was making his way south to Lancaster in an attempt to gain the British throne, he showed up at the Chorley estate and was, with or without enthusiasm, hosted by Abraham Crompton. The prince used his own silverware and table linen, and the Crompton family was still in possession of some linen napkins with the royal arms of Scotland woven into them.[5] Although the Cromptons were no friends of Catholicism, they did apparently have an attraction for the lost causes of rebels, something Beatrix herself seems to have shared. Directly after making her own first rebellion, Potter again is thinking about revolution and insurrection, as she would four years later in Gloucester. She had just engaged in what was her own first revolt against the family "antitrade" ethos, had taken it upon herself to move toward financial independence, and seems to have recognized that financial independence would give her at least some emotional independence from her parents.

All of this fledgling revolt and independence came right before Potter sent her illustrated letter to Noël Moore in 1893 and the 1894 visit to Gloucester, and coincides with another aspect of her rebellion, her involvement in science and natural history. The years between about 1890 and 1900 are crucial ones for Potter's development as an artist and storyteller. She was restless and eager for some emotional and financial independence. She attempted not only the cards for publishers but was also seriously collecting and sketching fungi during this period. A scientific interest in fungi and spores was hardly a usual occupation for a Victorian young lady. Potter had been interested in fungi since at least 1888, did the majority of her collecting between 1887 and 1901, and studied and photographed them intensively between 1893 and 1898. Although her botanical illustrations are both beautiful and accurate, her interest in fungi was more scientific than artistic. She learned a great deal and obtained a number of specimens from Charlie McIntosh, a postman she had known at Dalguise and a self-taught expert on fungi. Her rebellious streak ran not only to an interest in science but also to collaboration with a postman, something of which her parents remained unaware. She also had help from her scientific uncle Sir Henry Roscoe, the same "provoking" uncle who had initially been of little help over the illustrated cards. Sir Henry was a scientist (with specialties in chemistry and river pollution), a fellow of the Royal Society, and Vice-Chancellor of London University. It was he who provided Potter with the works of Pasteur and the German mycologist Brefeld, and who provided her with introductions to and help working with the scientists of Kew Gardens.

Potter's journal entries concerning her work with spore germination, her meetings (and occasional heated discussions) with scientists at Kew, and her attempts to have her paper on spore germination read and accepted by leading scientists of the day are the last she wrote, the journal ending at the disappointment of not being able to go forward with her scientific work and before the excitement of having her first children's book accepted by a commercial publisher. All of the work with fungi involved subterfuge with her family: they had little if any knowledge of her friendship with Charlie McIntosh, and were unaware that she slipped out after dark to collect specimens of dry rot and bury them in the garden for fear of parental discovery; when they did discover Potter's work they did not take it seriously. Her father did read the paper Potter was working on for the Linnaen Society, but only made corrections in the grammar, thus implicitly criticizing his daughter rather than supporting her.

Potter's science was sound: she was the first to contrive a way to germinate the spores of *agaricineae*, the subject of her paper, and was among the few English scientists who were aware of the symbiotic nature of lichens. She was in the grand Victorian tradition of the amateur scientist, but because she was female she had much difficulty both gaining access to scientific institutions and to major scientists, none of whom took her seriously. Although she had to steel herself to meet the intimidating (and rather abrupt and rude) director of Kew (she often was "so seized with shyness" that she "bolted" [*Journal*, 425]), she also confronted him. Thiselton-Dyer had treated her patronizingly, called her opinions "mares' nests," and neglected to look at her drawings. Potter "informed him that it would all be in the books in ten years, whether or no," and noted in her journal that "it is extraordinary how botanists have niggled at a few isolated species and not in the least seen the broad bearings of it. He would never have found out the bearings of the lichen" (*Journal*, 426). Potter was clearly thinking of writing an illustrated book on fungi; in a letter in 1897 she writes, "I have been drawing funguses very hard, I think someday they will be put in a book but it will be a dull one to read" (Quoted in *Artist and Storyteller*, 88).[6] Potter's paper was presented on April 1, 1897, apparently read by George Massee, the Assistant Director of Kew Gardens, without Potter herself being present. There are no journal entries regarding this event, although Potter did write to Charlie McIntosh about it. Her journal ends January 31, 1897. Her interest in fungi seems to have diminished after this point, perhaps finally done in by the lack of support from the scientific community. She continued sketching fungi and they show up in amusing ways in many of the illustrations in her children's tales, but she seems to have realized that science was not going to provide an easy route to financial or emotional independence from her family. After 1897 she focused her attention on fantasy sketches and the work that would lead to the novels that did provide her a means to free herself from the entanglements of Bolton Gardens.

These restless years of scientific work and card production coincided with Bertram's departure into the larger world, the end of Beatrix's nursery years with no adult future in sight, the visit to Gloucester and the exciting Caroline Hutton, and the death of the beloved Jessy Crompton, which perhaps prompted Potter to emulate that woman's independence of spirit. Despite the scientific disappointments, Potter had her first commercial success and earned her own money for the very first time. All of these events culminated in *The Tale of Peter Rabbit*, the most famous of Potter's artistic treatments of rabbits, but not her first.

Whalley and Hobbs mention more than a half-dozen Potter publications in the 1890s, many featuring rabbits. There are the rabbit illustrations in *The Happy Pair* with verses by Frederic Weatherly (1890); Christmas card designs with rabbits pulling sleds and walking in the snow; card designs of well-dressed rabbits walking down village streets, and more. There are also unpublished illustrations for "Cinderella" in which rabbits pull the pumpkin coach (c. 1895), more rabbit illustrations in her pictures for *Uncle Remus* (1893), and some illustrations of the White Rabbit for *Alice in Wonderland* in 1895 (*Artist and Her World*, 51–70). Here, Potter's rebellious nature takes two forms. First, in the commercial card designs published most frequently by either Hildesheimer and Faulkner or Ernest Nister, Potter was rebelling against the family horrors of both being in trade and of being publicly known. Potter herself was notoriously shy but seems to have been able to steel herself to approach publishers and, increasingly, negotiate with them over terms. Her rebellion may seem a mild one by contemporary standards, but it led to enormous changes in her perception of herself and in the increasingly independent way she led her life.

Second, the tales she chose to illustrate as private exercises, rather than as commercial properties, are generally tales that concern rebellion or transformation or both. The *Uncle Remus* tales, for example, provide the reader with the trickster Br'er Rabbit, who gives hope to the oppressed that cleverness may lead to freedom, and as we shall see had an impact on both *Peter Rabbit* and some other of Potter's stories.[7] *Alice in Wonderland* is, among other things, a complaint against stuffy Victorian conventions and arbitrary authority figures. "Cinderella" is the quintessential transformation tale, whereby the hard-working and persecuted girl is rescued and restored to her rightful place with the help of a good fairy. Potter almost seems to have anticipated how her own transformation was to be accomplished, replacing the mice of Perrault's version of the tale with rabbits to pull the coach that takes Cinderella to the ball. Rabbits would, metaphorically speaking, take Potter to her own ball and prince, in the form of Sawrey and William Heelis, by way of *Peter Rabbit* and Norman Warne.

By the time *Peter Rabbit* was actually written—from the initial letter to Noël Moore in 1893 to Potter's recall of the letter in 1900, to the initial private printing of 1901 and the first Warne printing of 1902—Potter had spent many years thinking about, living with, and sketching rabbits. Rabbits, in fact, may be seen as her alter-ego during the first phase of her career. Like rabbits, Potter was shy and not easily seen by others. Also like rabbits, Potter was surprisingly strong and feisty: anyone who has ever held an unhappy rabbit can attest to the strength of legs and sharpness of claws. In a journal entry commenting on the nature of her pet Benjamin Bouncer and of rabbits in general, Potter writes that the rabbit is

> one moment amiably sentimental to the verge of silliness, at the next, the upsetting of a jug or tea-cup which he immediately takes upon himself, will convert him into a demon, throwing himself on his back, scratching and spluttering. . . . He is an abject coward, but believes in bluster, could stare our old dog out of countenance, chase a cat that has turned tail. Benjamin once fell into an Aquarium head first, and sat in the water which he could not get out of, pretending to eat a piece of string. Nothing like putting a face upon circumstances. (*Journal*, 300)

Much of this description could apply to Potter herself. Although no one would ever accuse her of sentimentality, she certainly did have a sense of humor as well as a great deal of suppressed anger, some of which surfaces in the novels. Potter was also "cowardly," or at least shy, but she certainly knew how to bluster and to "put a face upon circumstances," as she had in her experiences with the scientists at Kew.

Peter Rabbit is, in some ways, Potter's way of working out some of her own difficulties with families, independence, rebellion, fear, and danger. She writes, as she nearly always does, of a male protagonist, not a female one. As we will see, when there are female protagonists (as in *Jemima Puddleduck, Mrs. Tiggy-Winkle,* and *The Pie and the Patty-Pan,* for example) she often criticizes aspects of traditional womanhood, while at the same time her rebellious female characters, like Jemima, tend to be failed rebels. The successful rebels are the males, with whom Potter seems to have closely identified.

The first sketch in the letter version of *Peter Rabbit* is of the four rabbit children, unclothed, labeled by name, with Peter to one side, staring directly at the reader. The second shows the mother rabbit in the foreground, still unclothed, with the four rabbit children behind her, partially obscured by the root of the fir tree. By the time of the final Warne edition, these two illustrations have been combined into a single one, with the unclothed mother rabbit making eye contact with the reader, while behind her, beneath the fir tree, one can see three rabbit heads and one rabbit hindquarter, and none of the rabbit children is identified by name. One suspects, however—particularly given the nature of the second illustration—that the rabbit child to one side of the others, separated visually by both the trunk of the tree and his mother's body from his siblings, and looking off into the distance rather than at his mother or the reader, is indeed Peter, already contemplating escape and adventure. The text also, very early on, suggests Peter's different and in fact more human nature. His sisters have the pet animal names of Flopsy, Mopsy, and Cotton-Tail—but Peter is ennobled with a human name, and will have adventures that resonate with human children.

The second illustration in the Warne edition, that of Mrs. Rabbit instructing her children before she heads off to market, makes clearer what is only hinted at in the first illustration. The three girl rabbits have their attention focused completely on their mother, are neatly dressed, and carry baskets in imitation of their mother, who will be seen two pages later making her way through the woods. The girls, it is perfectly clear, are happy to model their behavior after that of their mother. Peter, on the other hand, is standing to one side, his back to his mother and sisters, jacket unbuttoned and shoes off, an annoyed expression on his face. Indeed, the other child character in an illustrated book that shares a nearly identical facial expression is Max in Sendak's *Where the Wild Things Are,* when he is tapping his foot in annoyance at being sent to his room for a "time out." Like Peter, Max is a figure with both animal and human nature, someone in rebellion against maternal authority and interested in exploring the wider and more enticing world outside domestic borders.[8] Peter is next seen with his shoes, looking very uncomfortable as he is buttoned into his blue jacket and his mother says, "Now run along, and don't get into mischief. I am going out."[9]

Potter then leaves the reader to guess what Peter is up to while she explains Mrs. Rabbit's errand to the baker and provides us with a full-length portrait of Mrs. Rabbit going through the woods. This illustration, although not much commented upon by Potter scholars, is an early example of the sly kinds of visual irony in which Potter excelled, and of the ways in which subversive messages were often encoded in her illustrations. As McDonald has pointed out, Mrs. Rabbit "looks suspiciously like Little Red Riding-Hood."[10] Potter had done some illustrations for this fairy tale as early as 1894, in a style not at all like the mature style we are familiar with today. The 1894 illustrations are in grisaille and pencil, finely detailed, so much so that they have the quality of an etching rather than a drawing. The reference to Little Red Riding Hood in the finished *Peter Rabbit*, though it seems slight at first, is not so. Little Red, after all, is traditionally a child character who disobeys her mother's instructions and (in the Perrault version with which Potter was familiar) is eaten by the wolf and not resurrected to live another day. Given the plot of *Peter Rabbit*, the reader might expect the boy rabbit to somehow be linked to Little Red Riding Hood, but Potter unexpectedly links the mother rabbit to the fairy tale figure. Mother Rabbit is clearly dressed as Little Red Riding Hood: she wears a red cloak with a distinctive hood, she carries a basket (albeit an empty one, rather than Red's full one) and is walking through a rather dark and dismal wood, a wood without leaves on the trees or wildflowers on the path. Furthermore, she carries an umbrella, which McDonald suggests "underscores the sense of motherly anxiety" and shows that Mrs. Rabbit is "cautious about the unexpected" (32). McDonald feels that the Red Riding Hood reference helps Potter make a point about the generally anxious nature of Mrs. Rabbit. However, the Little Red Riding Hood of the tale is not a generally anxious character—far from it—although her own mother is. Potter is conflating the mother/daughter figures of the fairy tale to her own subversive ends.

The traditional story of Little Red Riding Hood is, no matter which version one reads, a fairly moralistic tale about obedience to one's parent. Here, Potter visually suggests the parent is as vulnerable to disaster in the woods as any child, may not have a happy ending in store for her, and at the very least has a lesson to learn. We know that Mr. Rabbit was put into a pie by Mrs. McGregor for transgressing the boundaries of the garden, but Mrs. Rabbit as Red Riding Hood suggests that danger exists even for proper bunnies who dress up to go to market rather than steal from gardens.

The Riding Hood reference is an oblique reference to food and its dangers, which is one of the themes of *Peter Rabbit* (as it is in *The Tailor of Gloucester* and *Squirrel Nutkin*). The entire tale of Little Red Riding Hood is about appetite and the trouble it can land one in: Red's appetite for adventure off the path leads to her death, and the wolf's appetite for human flesh leads to his in some versions of the tale. *Peter Rabbit* is also about the attractions and dangers of both food and adventures off the path. The father rabbit has gone in search of food and been turned into food instead; the mother rabbit is headed to market to get food, but is ominously dressed as Red Riding Hood; Peter seems destined to repeat his father's fate by entering the forbidden garden for food. Mrs. Rabbit does return home safely without meeting a wolf on the path, but she nearly loses a son while she is gone. The reader understands that Mrs. Rabbit's rules have very little effect upon the young. If "Little Red Riding Hood" is a moral tale about the fatal dangers of appetite, *Peter Rabbit* is about the pleasures of appetite and the rewards of risking danger. There are consequences for Peter, as we shall see, but the adventure seems to have been worth it for him by the end of the tale.

Peter's tale is further delayed by a two-page spread devoted to the sisters, who have taken off their jackets in order to better collect blackberries. Peter, of course, will later lose his jacket as well, but the detail of the clothing is dealt with very differently where the sisters are concerned. They are, after all, picking blackberries, whose juice stains easily and deeply and whose thorns are sharp. Putting their jackets to one side does not reveal their innate rabbit nature so much as it shows how careful they are of their belongings, unlike their brother Peter. They are aware of the consequences of their actions. Furthermore, the success of the blackberrying expedition is in some doubt. Later in the story Peter will have some helpful sparrows on his side, but here Potter pictures some blackbirds who are busy eating the berries nearly as soon as the rabbits put them in a basket. We know by the end of the tale that they do collect enough for dinner, but surely the birds have taken much of what the girl rabbits have harvested. Like their brother, the girls have enemies in their search for food, in both the birds and in the protective thorns of the blackberries (which Potter is careful to include in her illustration). When they return home they get a nursery tea of bread and blackberries, and although Peter may seem to be punished by not sharing in the meal, his adventures in the garden have provided him ample reward.

Finally, on pages eighteen and nineteen, we get to Peter's story. The narrative line concerning mother and sister rabbits not only delays Peter's appearance, thus making the reader eager to know what that particular rabbit has been up to, but by its slowness also suggests the caution and carefulness of the female rabbits. Peter, however, appears explosively at the beginning of his adventure. Whereas we hear about the sisters going "down the lane" and see Mrs. Rabbit venturing down the wooded path, Potter telescopes Peter's journey to Mr. McGregor's garden. We hear only that "he ran straight away to Mr. McGregor's garden, and squeezed under the gate!" (18). Peter's expression is alert and watchful—he knows about Mr. McGregor, after all, and is keeping a sharp lookout, but is in no way deterred from entering this forbidden garden. The illustration further foreshadows some of the dangers that Peter is about to face by framing the gate with a holly bush and by showing the ground beneath Peter scattered with dead leaves.

Potter chooses to illustrate holly not only for the chance to add some color to the illustration, but also to suggest the sharpness and danger of what is to come. Although we often think of holly as cheerful winter and Christmas greenery, in fact its leaves have points as sharp as thorns. The holly bush provides a visual counterpoint to the thorns protecting the sisters' blackberry bushes, but it also suggests that the entire garden is protected and dangerous.

The action again moves quite swiftly to the next illustration, the famous one with Peter blissfully eating one radish while holding the next in his other hand, eyes half-closed in pleasure, while a third radish is already half-pulled from the ground. He is oblivious to evidence of the human gardener (the hoe), and his enjoyment is amplified by the cheerful robin sitting on top of the hoe, whose beak is raised in song and whose entire posture—down to the one raised foot—echoes Peter's. The animal figures are set off by a screen of beautifully drawn French beans and some lettuces. There is extravagant abundance in this garden. Given the scale of Peter himself, who we know is small but who fills the vignetted illustration, the beans and radishes look enormous. Indeed, the radishes are so long and luscious that they have been mistaken by readers for carrots (a more traditional rabbit food), but they are not. The tastes that Peter indulges in are not tastes that children are likely to enjoy, but they are tastes rabbits enjoy. More importantly, they are sharp and vivid tastes, with a hint of bitterness to them. Radishes are sharp and hot in taste; undressed lettuce often has a sharp bite to it; the beans are French beans and not butter beans or sweet peas. Potter is suggesting not only the richness of the garden's delight but is also foreshadowing the bitter edge Peter is about to discover in this garden, the beginnings of which we find at the next page turn when Peter feels rather ill and goes in search of parsley, then and now an herbal remedy for indigestion.

At this point in the story, of course, Peter meets up with Mr. McGregor and the chase begins. If we pause here and consider what Potter has thus far told us about rebellion and about family dynamics, we can see that she has set up some interesting themes. *The Tailor of Gloucester* banishes families entirely—there are simply masters and servants and groups of helpful mice. *Squirrel Nutkin* tells us Nutkin has "cousins," but again family is marginalized and workers and owners take the foreground. The early scenes of *Peter Rabbit* do provide us with a family but it is not a traditional one, at least in the human sense. Mrs. Rabbit is a single mother, whose husband has "met with an accident" and been turned into a pie by Mrs. McGregor. Mrs. Rabbit's euphemism for rabbit-murder is consistent with her concerns about propriety and proper dress and behavior in her youngsters. It is, in fact, the kind of euphemism that would have been common in Potter's own Victorian household, not in the more frank period of Grandmother Crompton. Peter clearly understands that there is mortal danger in the garden—hence his watchful gaze when he squeezes under the gate. But he chooses to ignore the safety of home and mother's rules in favor of the potential richness of the world outside of home, despite its dangers. And in the end, of course, Peter manages to escape where his father did not. He taunts both mother and father and ends up, I will argue, triumphant at the end, despite the chamomile tea. Family is physically present in *Peter Rabbit*, but psychically Potter manages to banish family authority and specifically maternal authority.

Up to the point where Peter is taken ill, Potter pictures him as either a small rabbit in comparison to his mother, but still a rabbit who takes up a fair share of the illustration; or as a rabbit who nearly completely fills the vignette as in the first three illustrations of Peter alone in the garden. However, by the time Peter is pictured as ill from too many vegetables, Potter is already beginning to show his increasing vulnerability. When Peter is eating radishes, Potter gives the illusion that he is larger than he really is by posing him next to only the handle of the hoe, not the entire tool. Peter, it seems, is as tall as the hoe, when in reality he is only as tall as its handle. When he is holding his swollen stomach, looking rather ill, the potted plants behind him tell us that he is really quite small. (And the robin again comments upon Peter's state, its own crop looking as overstuffed as Peter's belly.) When we finally see Peter next to Mr. McGregor for the first time, on page twenty-four, he is quite small in relation to the farmer. While Peter does appear larger than Mr. McGregor on page twenty-seven, when the chase begins in earnest, this is a trick of perspective, and the content of the illustration makes clear Peter's great danger and vulnerability.

The illustration of Mr. McGregor chasing Peter with a rake gives the reader a sense of real menace and emphasizes Peter's human qualities. Peter not only is still dressed in his blue coat, but he is running on two legs, not on four. Mr. McGregor yells, "Stop, thief!" as he would at a human, not a rabbit, invader. The large tined rake Mr. McGregor brandishes gives a visual representation of dangers we have only been told of earlier. Furthermore, the earlier illustrations are all vignetted, but here Potter gives up the vignettes in favor of two small figures on a very white page, neither enclosed by a vignette, but connected through a thin shadow of wash. Peter literally has room to run off the page, through the white space, unrestricted by a vignette. At the same time, however, he remains connected to and in danger from Mr. McGregor.

The page turn gives the preliterate reader cause for the jitters, for Peter is nowhere to be found. We see instead only a row of cabbage plants and a puzzled robin examining a lost shoe. Peter has vanished from the page. Has he also vanished from the story, captured by Mr. McGregor and carried off to the kitchen and Mrs. McGregor's culinary skills? The text does not tell us that he has been captured, but neither does it tell us that he is safely out of the garden. We learn only that "he had forgotten the way back to the gate" and that, frightened, he "rushed all over the garden" (29). The next we see of him, he has been stopped in his headlong rush by the gooseberry net. Peter again takes up most of the vignetted visual space, but he is now stationary, vulnerable, and literally as well as metaphorically upside down and inside out.

Peter gets caught in the net not because he is a rabbit, but because he is a rabbit in human clothing. Potter explicitly tells the reader that he "got caught by the large buttons on his jacket" and then goes on to draw further attention to the jacket by writing, "It was a blue jacket with brass buttons, quite new" (30). Peter is vulnerable because he is doing what his mother told him to do—wear clothing—and not because he is behaving the way all rabbits behave in gardens. Earlier in the novel, the illustration for the words "Now run along, and don't get into mischief. I am going out" (13) is of Mrs. Rabbit buttoning Peter into his jacket so tightly he looks nearly strangled. The irony is that later he is very nearly strangled courtesy of the jacket, which catches him in the net. It is the very domestic jacket, insisted upon by a well-meaning but constrictive mother, that is nearly the end of Peter Rabbit. The danger to his life lies in his domesticated nature, not in his wild nature.

Carole Scott has suggested that for Potter "clothes, and the social self they represent, are imprisoning; they mar and hide the real, natural self, rather than provide a means to express it."[11] She is certainly correct about this, and supports her contention with examples from *Jemima Puddleduck*, *Tom Kitten*, and *Samuel Whiskers*, as well as from *Peter Rabbit*. But in *Peter Rabbit*—despite the fact that the illustration of Peter after he sheds the jacket gives us an absolutely natural sketch of a fleeing rabbit, with no human personality to it at all—Peter's jacket represents not only his social self but also his maternally dominated, domesticated self, which is suffocating him and threatens to "kill" him as much as Mr. McGregor threatens him. If his mother were not so insistent upon domesticating and taming her wild son, he would not be in so much danger in the garden. When he "wriggle[s] out" of the jacket "just in time," he is wriggling out of domesticated family life as much as he is out of the jacket.

Peter is now unprotected by clothing, by home, by family, and is hunted relentlessly by Mr. McGregor, whose large hands and hobnailed boots take on a nightmarish scale in the illustrations. He attempts to hide in a watering can full of water and finally manages to escape when Mr. McGregor tires of the hunt and cannot follow Peter as he flees out of a small window. Peter is nearly caught, not in the out-of-doors but in a tool shed filled with gardening tools. While not a house, the shed does represent an enclosed and relatively domesticated space, one used to store implements used in bringing young plants to life. But this enclosure does not provide nurturance and safety from harm, the way Peter's own house might. Instead it is a potential trap, and not even the enclosure-within-an-enclosure of the watering can protect Peter for long. He can only be safe once he is, again, outside and in the garden.

Once rested, Peter goes "lippity—lippity" as he looks for egress from the garden. Potter apparently lifted the word "lippity" from Joel Chandler Harris's Uncle Remus tales, for in the "Tar-Baby" story, Br'er Rabbit goes "lippity-clippity, clippity-lippity—dez ez sassy ez a jay-bird."[12] Whalley and Hobbs note that

Peter is more "subdued" than Br'er Rabbit as Potter drops the "clippity," but the reference to the Harris tale is, again, a bit more complicated than it first appears, as was the earlier reference to Little Red Riding Hood. Peter may not be feeling as "sassy" as Br'er Rabbit after his close brush with death, but he shares with his American cousin a certain cleverness and speed (of foot if not of thought and word) that save him from death at the hands of a larger and stronger opponent. Peter is not as consciously a trickster figure as is Br'er Rabbit, but as his story progresses he is pulling tricks on the unsuspecting reader, as well as on Mr. McGregor, who will have other tricks pulled on him in the later rabbit books.

Peter must still navigate the dangers of locked doors, predatory cats, and Mr. McGregor in person before he can find the gate out of the garden. The cat is unaware of Peter behind her, distracted by the goldfish in the pond, who appear to be looking up at her rather than swimming away. They appear to be either taunting her or expecting her to provide them with food, as perhaps the humans on the farm do. Either way, the theme of eat-and-be-eaten is sounded again here and in the following illustration, where Peter spies the gate just beyond Mr. McGregor, who is hoeing onions. Potter may be making a subtle reference to one of the usual accompaniments to cooked rabbit: onions or onion sauce.[13] If Peter cannot find a way past Mr. McGregor, he and the onions might become one in a pie, repeating his father's fate.

Peter does manage to slip by Mr. McGregor, who is again running after him with the rake, and he is "safe at last in the wood outside the garden" (50). This reverses the usual fairy-tale motif of danger lurking in forests, but is perfectly suited for the story of a wild rabbit, for whom the wild woods are a safer haven than a tidy and domesticated garden ruled by humans. In fact, it is domestication in general that provides the greatest danger to Peter, not the potential predators in the woods (owls, foxes, and so forth). We have already seen this in his struggles in the garden. It is nature tamed, not nature wild, that tempts Peter to risk his life for radishes and lettuces, and it is domesticity embodied in his jacket that traps him in the gooseberry net. And when Peter returns home to the burrow under the fir tree, seemingly safe at last, he is still threatened by domesticity.

When Peter returns home, "His mother was busy cooking; she wondered what he had done with his clothes. It was the second little jacket and pair of shoes that Peter had lost in a fortnight!" (54). The illustration shows Peter, unclothed, sound asleep on his side, his wondering mother looking on while stirring a pot full of dinner. The other rabbit children are peering in from outside the door. Only the last three illustrations in the text (and the frontispiece, showing Peter in bed about to be dosed with chamomile tea) are interior views of the rabbit home. They are, on the one hand, cozy drawings, the rounded vignette shape echoing the soft roundness of the mother rabbit as she prepares food and tea for her children. The predominant colors are brown and blue: there is a warm golden brown for the burrow itself and the rabbits, and the only patch of blue is on the mother rabbit's dress. There is, on the surface, something very comforting about the enclosed domestic space of the burrow and the nurturing mother preparing food. On the other hand, given the story and the illustrations that have preceded these final pictures, there is a certain undercurrent of claustrophobia at work here.

Peter originally abandoned his mother, her rules, and the burrow to go off into the forbidden garden to satisfy his own tastes and desires. Yes, the garden is dangerous, but it is also delightful, and in fact is less dangerous to Peter the more of his domesticated nature he abandons. The blue coat he abandons is closely connected with his mother: she has provided the jacket, she has buttoned him into it tightly, and the jacket matches the color of the dress she wears while indoors. Only by abandoning this object so closely associated with his mother can Peter save his life in the garden. Mr. McGregor uses the abandoned coat and shoes to form a scarecrow in the garden, but the scarecrow is of little use: we see it pictured surrounded by birds who are not the least bit intimidated by it. The domestication by which Mrs. Rabbit swears has little power out in the world.

Another interesting aspect of these final illustrations is that Peter, in relation to the other figures, is quite small. In fact, he is nearly invisible in the illustration on page fifty-seven, where the foreground shows us the mother rabbit pouring out tea as the three sisters watch and the background shows a very tiny Peter poking his head out from beneath the bedcovers. In the final Warne version of the book, the last illustration excludes Peter altogether in favor of a close-up of his sisters enjoying their meal of blackberries and milk. Peter is as small in these final pictures as he is in the illustrations including both him and Mr. McGregor earlier in the text, and the scale once again indicates Peter's vulnerability, this time at the hands of his mother rather than Mr. McGregor. Peter has, in fact, been captured after all, but captured by the forces of domesticity, the very forces he was trying to escape by running to Mr. McGregor's garden. He cannot escape his mother's ministrations, cannot escape being fed chamomile tea against his will. He has managed to escape becoming rabbit pie, but he does have to pay a price for having eaten ill-gotten greens: by the end he has become invisible. The price is both small and large, and speaks to Potter's ambivalent feelings about obedience and disobedience, domesticity and rebellion.

The illustration that now serves as the frontispiece to the Warne edition of *Peter Rabbit* shows Mrs. Rabbit leaning over a cowering Peter, preparing to dose him with the chamomile tea. We can see nothing of Peter but his ears and paws sticking up from beneath the covers as he attempts to avoid his medicine. He is reluctant to take the tea, something with which any child who has been forced to take bad-tasting medicine can empathize. But for the adult reader, something more subtle is suggested by the illustration and by the ending of the story. Chamomile tea is not bad-tasting at all, but it is a mild purgative. Mrs. Rabbit wants to purge Peter of the forbidden greens he has indulged in, but also wants to purge him of his adventuresome spirit. He has, after all, lost not one but two jackets. Her posture whenever she is near Peter is mildly threatening, despite her plump figure and softly-drawn clothes. She quite literally seems to want to suffocate Peter into domesticity. We can see this when she buttons his jacket up so closely to his chin that he appears to be choking, and we can also see this in the frontispiece where she looms claustrophobically over her reluctant son, who is trapped in the bed and cannot escape.

Potter, at the end of this novel, suggests both the attractions and dangers of home, just as she has earlier presented both the attractions and dangers of the garden. Yes, home is comfortable and safe from gardeners and other dangers, but home is also suffocating, closed, and airless. Yes, home provides the caring figure of the mother, but that same mother stifles all the energy, activity, and passion of her son. There is tension at the end of this story, a tension between the attractions of home and the attractions of the wider world. Both, Potter suggests, contain dangers to the self. The danger in the garden is to Peter's physical self: he is in mortal danger as he trespasses. But the danger at home is to his spiritual self, to his rabbit nature and the self he truly is. He is as trapped in that bed, with mother looming over him, as he was in the gooseberry net with Mr. McGregor about to descend. Had he been turned into a pie, at least he would have fulfilled his desires before his demise. At home, he is at the mercy of his mother and her rules, all of his own desires stifled and suffocated. Potter does not seem overly enthusiastic about Peter's return to the safety of home. She does not tell us that he is relieved or happy to be home, simply that "He was so tired that he flopped down upon the nice soft sand on the floor of the rabbit-hole and shut his eyes" (54).

It is possible to look at Potter's last words in the novel—"But Flopsy, Mopsy, and Cotton-tail had bread and milk and blackberries for supper"—as implying that Peter has been punished by being excluded from this feast. But has he? Two of his good sister bunnies are pictured with napkins tied tightly around their necks, again suggesting suffocation, and the food they eat is the equivalent of a nursery supper, whereas Peter has indulged in a veritable feast of adult tastes, and more to the point adult rabbit tastes. He has risked all in order to satisfy his rabbit nature; his sisters stay closer to home and eat food that is delicious but not suited to the tastes of real rabbits. Potter clearly wanted the reader to be on Peter's side throughout the tale, and she is still on his side at the end. The sisters, although adorable, are not meant to be models of behavior for the reader; it is Peter who has a human name, Peter who has exciting adventures, and Peter who outwits Mr. McGregor. The price Peter pays is to be returned to the forces of domesticity, but the reader suspects he will escape yet again. And he will, in the two sequels to *Peter Rabbit*, but those books complicate and shift the presentation of the problems of domesticity.

That Potter's first published book for children explored these tensions regarding domesticity is not surprising. The book represents, in many ways, her own first escape from the constraints of home. She would not be able to leave home entirely for many more years, but *Peter Rabbit* was her first substantial opportunity to rebel against the strictures of Victorian domesticity that reigned in

Bolton Gardens. Mrs. Potter herself was at least as concerned with propriety as is Mrs. Rabbit, and Potter often felt constricted by her and by the household, as evidenced both in journal entries and in letters. In 1902, in the course of negotiations with Warne concerning royalties and copyrights, she writes

> If my father happens to insist on going with me to see the agreement, would you please not mind him very much, if he is very fidgety about things—I am afraid it is not a very respectful way of talking and I don't wish to refer to it again, but I think it is better to mention beforehand he is sometimes a little difficult; I can of course do what I like about the book being 36. I suppose it is a habit of old gentlemen, but sometimes rather trying.[14]

As early as age seventeen, in her journal, she complains about having a new governess and writes, "If they said I must, I'd do it willingly enough only my temper'd be very nasty—but father wouldn't force me . . . I thought to have settled down quietly—but it seems it *can not* be. Only a year, but if it is like the last it will be a lifetime" (*Journal*, 38). In the course of writing *Benjamin Bunny* she writes to Norman Warne, "I hardly ever go out, and my mother is so 'exacting' I had not enough spirit to say anything about it. I have felt vexed with myself since, but I did not know what to do. It does wear a person out." After a paragraph where she returns to discussing the illustrations for *The Tale of Two Bad Mice*, underway at the same time, she adds, "As far as the book is concerned I think I can do it from the photograph & my box; but it is very hard to have seemed uncivil" (*Letters*, 85). In 1903, after the success of *Peter Rabbit* and during the process of publishing both *The Tailor of Gloucester* and *Squirrel Nutkin*, Potter apologizes to Harold Warne for not visiting the office before she leaves town with her parents, for "If I had not supposed that the matter would be dealt with through the post, I should not have mentioned the subject of another book at present. I have had such painful unpleasantness at home this winter about the work that I should like a rest, while I am away" (78).

These circumspect complaints about her parents and the restrictions they placed upon her life surface in the small children's books. *Peter* can be read as a critique of domesticity, and *The Tailor of Gloucester* and *Squirrel Nutkin* both excise family and domesticity and explore rebellion and subversion. The two other major rabbit books, *The Tale of Benjamin Bunny* and *The Tale of the Flopsy Bunnies*, are sequels to the original *Peter Rabbit*, but unlike *Peter* they do not complain of the strictures of domesticity as much as they acquiesce to them to some degree—the question is why? The question is particularly interesting because *Benjamin Bunny* was underway at the same time Potter was working on *The Tale of Two Bad Mice*, which in some ways is an allegory of her warming relationship with Norman Warne and potential flight from her family; and *The Tale of the Flopsy Bunnies* comes in the middle of a series of books set in Sawrey,

Potter's refuge from Bolton Gardens. Potter bought Hill Top in 1905, and although Norman's unexpected death meant that she was still tied to Bolton Gardens, she had a garden of her own to escape to at Hill Top, and the stories set there are, like *Peter* and *The Tale of Two Bad Mice*, critiques of domesticity. Yet the two sequels to Peter seem oddly moralistic and not up to Potter's usual standards of narrative (although the illustrations, particularly in *Benjamin Bunny*, are as exquisite as anything she did at this period in her career). This view of Potter's work is reflected in at least one of the reviews of *Benjamin Bunny* that appeared in *The Times Literary Supplement* of October 28, 1904, which read in part, "Among the little books which have become as much a manifestation of autumn as falling leaves, one looks first for whatever Miss Beatrix Potter gives. . . . In her new book . . . although there is no diminution in the charm and drollery of the drawings, Miss Potter's fancy is not what it was. The story is inconclusive. Next year we think she must call in a literary assistant. We have no hesitation in calling her pencil perfect" (106).

There are several factors accounting for the greater morality present in the second two rabbit books and their lesser complexity and ambiguity. *Peter* had grown out of Potter's letter to Noël Moore and out of Potter's increasing loneliness in Bolton Gardens. *Benjamin Bunny* and *The Flopsy Bunnies*, respectively, grew out of leftover illustrations from Peter and the public's desire for more "bunny books," rather than from any deep-seated desire on Potter's part to continue Peter's saga. Furthermore, Potter was consciously trying to write simpler texts for her younger readers, shorter and less complex texts than *The Tailor of Gloucester* and *The Tale of Squirrel Nutkin*.[15] Potter may have felt that more "moral" tales were better suited for her younger readers.

Another factor in the creation of the second two rabbit books was public demand. Not only had Potter turned into a money-making author for Warne & Co., but the public had especially fallen in love with *The Tale of Peter Rabbit* and wanted more of the same. Successful sequels to original works of genius are rare, then and now, and in the rabbit books Potter was working under some commercial pressure, as well as under the demands she made of herself in her art. *Peter Rabbit* and *The Tailor of Gloucester* had been written with no public other than herself and the Moore children in mind; in her subsequent books she had to consider both the demands of her publisher and of her public. As Ruth McDonald points out, "When Potter first turned to write *Benjamin Bunny*, she frankly admitted to her publisher that she had run out of ideas for drawings and that she would have to spend some time collecting more sketches of bunnies and gardens" (38). Although she did have in mind, in vague form, several possible stories for Warne, it is clear that neither of the sequels to *Peter Rabbit* spoke to her emotionally the way the original had.

It is also possible that for Potter, rabbits were connected with her earlier years in Bolton Gardens. As she began to act more independently of her parents, the rabbits may have been more connected in her mind to the constrictions of her home, and she no longer felt the need to critique home in the ways she had in *Peter Rabbit*. She effectively devised her own escape from home, both by way of royalties and by way of Norman Warne's increasing attentions. Potter wrote to Norman Warne while in the process of writing *Benjamin Bunny*, surprised at the amount of money *Squirrel Nutkin* had brought in, noting that "It is pleasant to feel I could earn my own living" (92). The initial printing of *Peter Rabbit* ran to only eight thousand copies, but then a few books later her initial print runs were closer to twenty thousand, so she was indeed beginning to earn her own living (103). At the same time she was beginning to gain some financial independence she was also seemingly on the verge of gaining emotional independence from her parents. Norman Warne's attentions were becoming more than strictly professional, and while she was working on *Benjamin Bunny* she was also collaborating closely with Norman on *The Tale of Two Bad Mice*, which in some ways can be seen as an allegory of Potter's feelings about leaving one domestic space for another. (See Chapter Three for a fuller discussion of this point.) The tensions about rebellion and domesticity in *Peter Rabbit* are, in some ways, divided between the texts of *Benjamin Bunny* and *Two Bad Mice*: *Benjamin Bunny* demonstrates the attractions of safe domesticity, and *Two Bad Mice* demonstrates the delight in destroying domesticity, or at least a certain kind of domesticity.

The Tale of Benjamin Bunny was published by Warne in 1904, and in many respects can be seen as a kind of anti-*Peter Rabbit*, reversing much of what Potter explicated in the first book. The two novels cover much the same ground—illegal trespass and theft in Mr. McGregor's garden, danger to life and limb, and eventual escape—but Peter is quite a different rabbit here, and the two bunnies are physically punished by Old Mr. Benjamin Bunny at the end, whereas Peter was not explicitly punished at the end of *Peter Rabbit*. Benjamin, Peter's cousin, is the more active rabbit in this tale, a rabbit who observes Mr. and Mrs. McGregor riding off in their gig, with Mrs. McGregor in her best bonnet, suggesting that the two of them will be gone for the entire day. No sooner does Benjamin observe this than he is off "with a hop, skip and a jump"[16] to "call upon" his relations. This is typical understated irony from Potter, who knows full well that Benjamin is not polite nor mature enough to be making a formal call. In fact, we are told that he "did not very much want to see his Aunt" (14). Peter's mother is here pictured (in an illustration that was originally intended for *Peter Rabbit*) as a shopkeeper, industrious and domestic, and of course Benjamin wants nothing to do with someone who might draft him into either work or good behavior. Instead, in time-honored bad-boy fashion, he comes around the back of the fir tree and tumbles upon his cousin Peter, who "looked poorly, and was dressed in a red cotton pocket-handkerchief" (17).

Peter, in the first illustration we have of him after his adventures in Mr. McGregor's garden, looks chastened. He is not suffering the physical effects of his orgy in the garden so much as he is the moral effects. He is bundled up in the handkerchief, nearly swaddled in it, so that his arms do not show and we can only see the tips of his feet. He is also sitting in an enclosed space between the roots of the fir tree, sitting below the level of Benjamin, whose clogged feet we see above Peter. He is, in fact, pictured as a fairly timid looking rabbit, one sticking close to home and wrapped up in a "security blanket": he bears little resemblance to the energetic and disobedient Peter of the first novel. Now he seems to welcome the suffocating closeness of his "clothes" rather than suffer their imposition. Instead of the implicit criticism of Mrs. Rabbit's attempts to bring Peter back into the folds of domesticity, we have here a presentation of Mrs. Rabbit's near-complete victory over Peter, a victory that will be even clearer by the end of *The Tale of the Flopsy Bunnies*. Lack of clothes and lack of domesticity saved Peter's life in his first adventure, but now it seems not only his mother but he himself feels the need for clothing of some sort. The red handkerchief links him to the cloaks his sisters wore in the first adventure, and he seems to have taken on much of their timidity with the adoption of their favorite color. Benjamin reassures him that the McGregors have gone for the day, and Peter does not immediately leap up to continue his adventures but only hopes it will rain, thus ruining the McGregors' "adventures" as they ruined his. Peter then hears his mother call to his sisters to collect some more chamomile and decides he would feel better if he went for a walk.

Peter is in an ambivalent state here. He feels vulnerable and sickly after his close call in Mr. McGregor's garden. Yet he is not feeling so vulnerable that he wants to stay home to be dosed with more chamomile tea. The initial illustration in the novel, one developed for but not used in *Peter Rabbit*, shows Mrs. Rabbit at work in her shop, accompanied by the three sisters, who appear to be either helping out or keeping close company with their mother. As in the first novel, Peter stays apart from his sisters and is not pictured in this illustration. This is partly because he is not feeling well, but both pictures and text suggest that Peter is not entirely happy being in the presence of his mother and sisters. He still finds Benjamin Bunny's call to adventure more appealing than staying at home, although Peter has grave misgivings and doubts about the wisdom of this decision. He may not want to ally himself entirely with the forces of femininity and domesticity represented by his mother and his sisters, but he is unwilling to go into the garden again to retrieve his clothes unless Benjamin leads the way, which Benjamin is more than happy to do.

Ruth McDonald has suggested that the interplay between these two rabbits is reminiscent of that between Huck Finn and Tom Sawyer, with Benjamin as Huck and Peter as the reluctant Tom. Like Huck and Tom, these two rabbits are struggling with both the attractions and dangers of the domestic life. Huck feels nearly suicidal at the beginning of *Huckleberry Finn*, trapped in the house of the Widow Douglas and by the conventions of the domestic life. Tom, on the other hand, has reconciled himself to life at Aunt Polly's and has argued for the benefits of the domestic life with Huck. Like Huck, Benjamin counts himself a man (or bunny) of the world, one who knows that "it spoils people's clothes to squeeze under a gate; the proper way to get in, is to climb down a pear tree" (25).[17] He is more proficient at this task than Peter who, hampered by the handkerchief, falls down head first into the garden, a comic sidekick to his cousin. The following illustration tells us everything we need to know about the relative moods of Benjamin and his cousin Peter. Benjamin has reached down to sample the tender little lettuce seedlings that have been set out in the garden, while Peter has his handkerchief wrapped tightly around him, standing on his hind legs with a nervous expression on his face, alert for danger, anxious about what might be waiting for them in the garden. Before his experiences with Mr. McGregor, Peter had Benjamin's confidence, and like his cousin had gone straight to the serious business of eating. Now, however, wiser through his experiences, he can do nothing but wrap himself in the domesticity represented by that handkerchief and look around for danger. He no longer needs his mother to smother him in domesticity—he does it to himself.

Together, then, *The Tale of Peter Rabbit* and *The Tale of Benjamin Bunny* show us how experience alters innocence forever, how experience makes it impossible for us to see anything in the old innocent way again. Part of what experience does for us is to change the way we look at the world. The world itself stays the same, but our perception changes radically. As Blake puts it in "The Tyger," "Did he who made the lamb make thee?" Experiencing the tiger forever changes our understanding of the lamb. Experience teaches us that the world contains both good and evil, pleasure and danger, simultaneously. One looks at the lamb and sees not only the lamb, but also the tiger who eats the lamb and the creator who made both. Peter can no longer look at the garden as a paradisiacal pantry filled with lettuces and radishes, but knows that it harbors death as well as life. He does not have the wisdom or the confidence to refuse to follow his cousin Benjamin into the garden and so becomes, however unwillingly, Benjamin's companion in Benjamin's own discovery of experience.

The rabbits reenter the garden not only to enjoy lettuces, but to collect Peter's clothing from the scarecrow. However, "There had been rain during the night; there was water in the shoes, and the coat was somewhat shrunk" (29). Peter's clothing here suggests that he no longer fits into his old role, that he has outgrown the clothes he wore in his first experience in the garden. Those clothes are now linked not only to Peter's domestic life, but also to the loss of his innocence. As he has gained experience he has lost clothes, and now those clothes no longer fit. When Peter attempts to wear his discarded clothing, Potter is suggesting that he would like to go back to the innocence he had before his first adventure in the garden, before he lost his clothes through experience. He wants to be the boy he was before Mr. McGregor chased him all over the garden, but of course this cannot be. Peter cannot enjoy himself, cannot return to the state of innocence even after he puts on his ill-fitting jacket: "Peter did not seem to be enjoying himself; he kept hearing noises" (30). Peter, alas, is all too aware of the potential consequences of the action of entering the forbidden garden, while Benjamin remains oblivious and concentrates on the vegetables. Benjamin "was perfectly at home, and ate a lettuce leaf. He said that he was in the habit of coming to the garden with his father to get lettuces for their Sunday dinner" (33).

In the company of the experienced elder rabbit, expeditions to the garden are apparently permitted. Like many youngsters, Benjamin (mistakenly) assumes that if an activity is acceptable when performed with a parent it is also acceptable when performed solo. Benjamin is full of bravado, the same sort of bravado Peter himself had in the past, but Peter knows that bravado will only get you so far when you are in forbidden territory ruled by an angry human who wields rakes and sieves. Benjamin is more concerned about placating the aunt and the other adult rabbits when they return home. He sees only family consequences, not consequences in the wider world containing both rabbits and humans. In hopes of disarming his relatives he decides to collect some onions for Mrs. Rabbit. Here we have the same botanical irony that we saw in *Peter Rabbit* itself, with a rabbit collecting a vegetable that humans like to serve with cooked rabbit, botanical irony that will be even more complex in later texts like *The Tale of Jemima Puddleduck*. The onions also foreshadow the danger that lies in wait for the rabbits just beyond the next page turn, when they come face to face with a cat and must hide themselves (and the onions) beneath the basket. If the cat turns over the basket the cat will eat them; if Mr. McGregor finds them beneath the basket he will be saved the trouble of collecting his own onions for his rabbit stew or rabbit pie. Collecting the onions not only puts the rabbits in mortal danger but also foreshadows their potential fate if they are captured by the farmer.

The young rabbits, however, are saved by old Mr. Benjamin Bunny, who appears "prancing along the top of the wall of the upper terrace" (49). The fact that he is above both the cat and the young rabbits suggests his greater age and his superior wisdom, as does the fact that he is confident enough to "prance" upon the wall. Furthermore, he carries a switch and his purpose is to look for and punish his son. Mr. Benjamin Bunny has clearly benefited from some experience himself: he knows his son is missing, knows he has probably headed for the forbidden garden, and he comes armed with a switch to punish his son and, potentially, to use as a weapon against whatever enemy might be awaiting him in the garden. Unlike the young rabbits, old Mr. Benjamin Bunny takes a proactive stance with the cat, attacking before he is attacked and locking the cat safely within the greenhouse. Only then does he rescue his son and nephew, to soundly whip them with his switch. Mr. Bunny is no fool, however: he leaves the garden but takes the onions with him. Thievery is an acceptable but dangerous occupation, and one not to be attempted by inexperienced boy rabbits.

The last illustration in the book returns us to domesticity. Despite the title of the book, the last illustration is not devoted to Benjamin's homecoming but to

Peter's. Potter gives us a domestic scene within the rabbit burrow, with Mrs. Rabbit holding two of her little girl bunnies upon her lap while "Cotton-tail and Peter folded up the pocket-handkerchief" (59). The family is safely intact in their cozy burrow. Of the four rabbit children, Peter is the only one who is dressed, in his old blue jacket. Whereas *The Tale of Peter Rabbit* ended with Peter still in a rebellious mood, naked, his jacket abandoned in favor of his life, unwilling to take his medicine, *The Tale of Benjamin Bunny* gives us a completely domesticated Peter. Here we see him wearing his jacket—physical proof of his experiences in the wider world and at the same time is a reminder of the domestic life in the burrow. He has, it seems, brought his experience home with him, and the result is that he helps his sister with the traditionally feminine chore of folding laundry. At the same time he makes eye contact with his mother, as if asking for her approval. The end of *The Tale of Peter Rabbit* is hardly moral and it is certainly not a tale about the punishment that awaits children who disobey. The end of *The Tale of Benjamin Bunny* is decidedly moral, making clear that physical punishment is the cost of disobeying parental authority, and that one may end up entirely tamed and happy to stay at home rather than venture into the wider world. This second novel does indeed seem to have been written with a younger audience in mind, one not yet ready to leave home, one not entirely certain that experience is worth the price.

In this tale, the rabbits outwit Mr. McGregor not so much by stealing his onions as by leaving him puzzling over the missing scarecrow clothes, the tiny clog footprints, and the cat locked in the potting shed. As in *Peter Rabbit* the trickster qualities of the rabbits are muted but they are present nonetheless and will be even more evident in *The Tale of the Flopsy Bunnies*. It is in the nature of all tricksters to outwit the seemingly more powerful, and even though the actions of Peter and Benjamin in these first two rabbit books are mitigated by the punishments dealt by the adult rabbits, they still manage to trick Mr. McGregor. Within the hierarchy of the rabbit world, neither Benjamin nor Peter is ascendant, but both rabbits (and old Mr. Bunny himself) become ascendant over the human world.

The illustrations for *Benjamin Bunny* are lovely; there is greater detail and greater facial expression than Potter managed in *Peter Rabbit* and more attention paid to the garden backgrounds, but the story is less satisfying. Potter has opted for a more traditional Victorian moral tale rather than for a subversive and rebellious plot—although even here she does not condemn thievery in the garden, simply thievery by inexperienced rabbits who lack the skill and confidence to thieve successfully without being caught. The next installment in the series of stories about Peter and his friends is *The Tale of the Flopsy Bunnies*, published in 1909; in it the dangers to small rabbits are quite clear and they must be rescued by the adult rabbits. In this book it is not the young rabbits who take center stage, but the adult Peter and Benjamin, thus making the story less appealing to child readers.

There will be a final return to the rabbit family in *The Tale of Mr. Tod*, but that novel more properly belongs to the badger and the fox, not to the rabbits. It is a coda, in more ways than one, as we shall see.

The young rabbits in *The Flopsy Bunnies* are known by their collective name, not by individual names, because as the narrator tells us, "I do not remember the separate names of their children."[18] They are clearly a handful, as we see on the facing page where the six young rabbits race around the burrow, demanding attention from parents and chasing each other and generally causing the sort of mayhem not uncommon in large families. There are also hints that Benjamin (now married to Peter's sister, Flopsy) has learned from his experiences in Mr. McGregor's garden. While his own father allowed his son to accompany him on garden raids, this adult Benjamin Bunny depends upon "borrowing" cabbages from Peter to make ends meet, or when Peter is unable (or unwilling) to spare some cabbages, "the Flopsy Bunnies went across the field to a rubbish heap, in the ditch *outside* Mr. McGregor's garden" (17; my emphasis). The illustration on the page facing this text shows the young bunnies in the rubbish heap, barred from the garden by a high (to them) brick wall, and watched over by their father. These bunnies, adult and child alike, are not on a thieving expedition. Benjamin apparently learned his lesson in his own youth and is not encouraging his offspring to violate Mr. McGregor's garden, but instead to depend upon rubbishy leavings. Pickings are slim in the rubbish heap: "There were jam pots and paper bags, and mountains of chopped grass from the mowing machine (which always tasted oily), and some rotten vegetable marrows and an old boot or two" (18). We are a long way away from the radishes and French beans and lettuces of *The Tale of Peter Rabbit*. The only lettuces these rabbits get—and they are delighted to get them—are overgrown lettuces that have shot into flower. All of the rabbits stuff themselves, to the extent that they fall asleep, with Benjamin "sufficiently wide awake to put a paper bag over his head to keep off the flies" before he too sleeps (21). The irony, of course, is that he is not sufficiently awake to protect his children or to move them to a less vulnerable spot.

As in *Peter Rabbit*, but not in *Benjamin Bunny*, Mr. McGregor is the antagonist here, who finds the sleeping rabbit children and pops them into a sack to be killed and eaten later. Mrs. Flopsy comes along to find what has happened to her family and Benjamin (now awake) tells her the "doleful tale" (37). The helpful Mrs. Tittlemouse (later to be the heroine of her own tale) nibbles a hole in the sack so that the little rabbits can escape. Flopsy and Benjamin together, turning into trickster figures, fill the sack with vegetable marrows and other garden rubbish to fool Mr. McGregor into thinking the sack is still full of rabbits, and consequently the entire rabbit family lies in wait to see how their trick will turn out.

While in this story Mr. McGregor is not quite as fearsome as he was in *Peter Rabbit*, he is fearsome enough, positively gleeful over his unexpected windfall of baby rabbits. The situation may seem even more frightening to child readers because the rabbits are vulnerable not only because they are sleeping, but because their parent has neglected to protect them. Despite his fearsomeness Mr. McGregor becomes a comic foil, more so than in the previous two rabbit books. In *Peter Rabbit* he is merely a grumpy farmer who gets revenge by using Peter's clothing for a scarecrow; in *Benjamin Bunny* he is puzzled by the disappearance of his scarecrow, the tiny footprints in the garden, and the cat who has managed to lock herself inside the shed. In this last tale Mr. McGregor has a larger role and a fair amount of dialogue. The rabbit family follows him as he goes back to gloat with Mrs. McGregor over his fine catch of baby rabbits. The McGregors apparently have a cantankerous marriage because Mr. McGregor wants to sell the rabbits and buy tobacco with his earnings (thus reminding us of Mrs. Rabbit who, in the first illustration, is a seller of tobacco), but Mrs. McGregor wants to line her old cloak with their skins. Mrs. McGregor here sounds even more bloodthirsty than her husband, declaring that "I shall skin them and cut off their heads" (50). All of this would be terrifying to small readers if it were not for the fact that we know the rabbits are safe and are watching the kitchen argument from the window. The only damage done is to the youngest rabbit, who is hit with a vegetable Mr. McGregor throws from the window when he discovers the truth of what is now in the sack. The adults then "thought it was time to go home" (56), and leave the garden while carrying the youngest, injured rabbit. In the end, the last we hear is that the helpful Mrs. Tittlemouse gets a Christmas present of warm rabbit-wool clothing in thanks for her role in rescuing the rabbit children.

No one is punished in this story, unless we count the injured young Flopsy, who is "rather hurt" but seems to survive the adventure in the sack and at the kitchen window. Like *The Tale of Benjamin Bunny*, domesticity is implicitly approved of in this novel, but the treatment of domesticity indicates an important shift in both Potter's life and in her career. The tale begins with some news of Peter, who is now in business with his mother as a florist, and whose business sign reads, "Peter Rabbit and Mother, Florists. Gardens Neatly Razed. Borders Devastated by Night or Year" (12). Unlike Benjamin, Peter has not married, but has stayed on with his mother (still wearing his blue jacket) to run a business. He has, in effect, become Mr. McGregor; he has his own "nursery garden" now (13). He no longer wants to raid the farmer's garden but has his own plot to tend which, moreover, he must save from being raided by Benjamin Bunny. There is a very amusing illustration accompanying the text: "Sometimes Peter Rabbit had no cabbages to spare," showing Benjamin and his family looking longingly over the fence at Peter's garden, where the few cabbages that have not been harvested are being hidden from sight by Mrs. Rabbit, who is spreading her skirt to obscure their presence. Moreover, Mrs. Rabbit is holding a rake and Peter is holding a hoe, and there is a sieve or basket in the background, all implements that remind the reader of how Mr. McGregor chased Peter in the first book. Additionally, the fence surrounding Peter's garden is not only a picket fence, but a fence faced with chicken wire to keep small predators (like rabbits) away.

Peter has both grown up and not grown up, just as Potter had both grown up and not grown up by 1909. He lives at home with his mother, but he has adult responsibilities as a businessman and is not only reluctant to raid gardens (as he was in Benjamin Bunny), but has obviated the need to raid by growing his own food. He has become a worker, an adult, and not an improvident and impudent child. Peter is still Potter's alter ego, but the alter ego of an older and more experienced woman. Like Potter, Peter cannot entirely escape his mother, but also like Potter he can support himself and can guard against those who would exploit his hard work. The rabbits in *The Tale of the Flopsy Bunnies* are rather dull compared to those of the earlier two rabbit books, reflecting both the relative dullness of adulthood and Potter's own increasing boredom with drawing rabbits. In fact, the humor in *The Tale of the Flopsy Bunnies* comes from the joke played on Mr. McGregor by the adult rabbits, not on much that has to do with the personalities of the younger rabbits. The rabbits in this book are not as important as the garden and house backgrounds in which they exist and upon which Potter lavished most of her artistic attention.

By this point, of course, Potter had been spending quite a lot of time in Sawrey and had been sketching many of the farm and village buildings and their gardens. Eight of the illustrations (of twenty-six total) include Mr. McGregor or his wife; seventeen contain garden walls, farm houses, or outbuildings; and there are almost no close-ups of the rabbits themselves, and certainly none with the detail of the rabbit portraits in *The Tale of Benjamin Bunny*. Nearly all the rabbit-pictures contain many rabbits, and thus are painted from the middle distance in order to include all of them as well as the farm background. Of the three fairly close-up views of the (unnamed) rabbit children, only one shows us the complete face of the rabbit, whereas the other two, respectively, give us first a rabbit face partly obscured by a geranium leaf and then the back view of a rabbit, so we can see no facial expression at all. It is almost as if Potter is on the side of the farmer here, seeing the rabbits as an undifferentiated nuisance, not as individual characters. This of course makes perfect sense for Potter the farmer, who was battling infestations of rats and other vermin at Hill Top and Castle Farm, bought the same year *The Tale of the Flopsy Bunnies* appeared.

From the point of *The Flopsy Bunnies* on, Potter concentrated her books on farmyard and household animals, not on farmyard pests. Her interests moved to cats, dogs, ducks, and pigs among the domesticated animals she writes about, and to frogs, wild mice, hedgehogs, and badgers among the wild animals—wild animals that pose little difficulty for the farmwoman. When potential wild predators appear, as in the fox figures of *Jemima Puddleduck* and *Mr. Tod*, they are dealt with summarily. The virtual end of the rabbits in her work signals the end of her own rabbitlike existence in Bolton Gardens and her own need to steal time and energy (instead of lettuce and beans) from the household in order to nurture herself. *The Tale of Peter Rabbit*, and rabbit drawings in general, begin Potter's emancipation from the confines of Bolton Gardens and her parents' wishes and desires for her. By the publication of *Benjamin Bunny* she is beginning to see that she can make her own living—not just "pin money," but a living—from her little books, and by *The Flopsy Bunnies* she is a substantial landowner in the Lake District, has fought and won a battle with her parents over her engagement, and has met her future husband, William Heelis.

Her growing confidence shows not only in the demise of her interest in rabbits as subjects but also in her growing interest in business affairs, as evidenced in letters of the period, and in some of her activities. Her business acumen shows up quite early. While it is impossible to know if the impetus for her discussion of terms with publishers came from herself or from her father or uncle, the likelihood is that Potter herself was the driving force in her dealings with publishers. She certainly was from the point of *Peter Rabbit* on, but we can see her bargaining with publishers and clarifying contracts quite early in her career. For example, in 1894 the publisher Nister had offered to buy some of Potter's illustrations of frogs for an annual publication known as *Comical Customers*.[19] They offered her a guinea, and she wrote back, "I have received your letter of 2nd inst with reference to the pen & ink drawings, but regret to inform you that I am not satisfied with your terms." She suggests other terms, and says, "unless you care to pay that price I am afraid I must trouble you to return the remaining 9 drawings which you still have" (*Letters*, 28). Potter got her terms.

When she and Warne were discussing the possibility of publishing *Peter Rabbit*, a letter of December 18, 1901, shows us a Potter willing to proceed on her own and to defy male authority figures. Canon Rawnsley, who had been trying to help Potter publish her book, had translated Potter's prose into fairly insipid rhyme, thinking this might improve her chances of publication. Warne was interested but made clear that they preferred Potter's text to Rawnsley's. Potter writes

> I do not know if it is necessary to consult Canon Rawnsley; I should think *not*. Speaking for myself, I consider your terms very liberal as regards royalty; but I do not quite understand about the copyright. . . . For instance who would the copyright belong to in the event of *your* not wishing to print a second edition? . . . I should like to know what I am agreeing to. (56; Potter's emphasis)

One might think that Potter, daughter of a barrister, might have consulted with her father and, prompted by him, asked intelligent questions regarding copyright, but an addendum to the same letter reads, "I have not spoken to Mr Potter, but I think Sir, it would be well to explain the agreement clearly, because he is a little formal having been a barrister—" (57). This letter suggests first that although Potter was grateful for Canon Rawnsley's help, she did not feel beholden to him in any way, and firmly took control of her own text and the terms by which she was willing to subject it to commercial publication. Second, the addendum quite clearly indicates that Potter had not spoken to her father about her plans and that she was acting on her own—but that she would consult him. There is almost a veiled warning in that addendum, an indication to the Warnes that not only was she no fool, but she had access to free legal advice in her own home.

Her letters to Warne become rapidly more self-confident and self-assured, both on the subject of copyright and contracts and on the subject of printing methods and printers. In May of 1902 she writes, "I should wish, before signing an agreement, to understand clearly what arrangement it would imply about the copyright; and what stipulations would be made about subsequent editions, if required" (61), returning to the subject of her letter of December 18, which apparently Warne had not addressed to her satisfaction. Later in May, on the verge of signing an agreement, she writes to the Warnes that "If my father happens to insist on going with me to see the agreement, would you please not mind him very much. . . . I think it is better to mention beforehand he is sometimes a little difficult; I can of course do what I like about the book being 36" (62). Potter clearly neither wants her father's company at the Warne offices, nor feels she can ban him. Her reminder to Warne that she is thirty-six is also a reminder to herself: she is an adult and can do as she pleases, despite her parents' wishes. She is philosophical about Warne's failure to register the copyright to *Peter Rabbit* in America, where the book was promptly pirated, writing, "I was very sorry to hear about the American edition, I trust they have not got hold of a copy of the mouse book [*The Tailor of Gloucester*] also; but perhaps the private edition is not worth stealing" (74). She was still a polite Victorian lady, anxious to please and offering to redo illustrations to Warne's specifications, but her spine does show through in comments such as this one, in a letter to the Warnes in 1903, when she writes, "I am afraid I generally say what I think, but I assure you I will draw it any way you like!" (73).

Potter was as active in the discussion of printing methods and production as she was in discussion of copyright and royalty. On January 7, 1902, she told the Warnes "I think Hentschel would make the best job of [printing the illustrations for *Peter Rabbit*]; if the money part of the business can be arranged, which I do not doubt it can be somehow" (57). When discussing the illustrations for *The Tailor of Gloucester*, she suggested adding "a line-work frame in pink or blue" to the plates, elaborating that "I was not thinking of a plain straight line; the enclosed may look rather heavy on the present bits of paper, but if you put them down on a page of the right size beside the sample page of type, it seems to me that they prevent the plates looking too dumpy" (77). Again concerning *The Tailor of Gloucester*, she writes in 1903

> I think these are very good blocks; but I am much afraid they have cut away my black line round the plates? I am very much vexed if it is so; I think that one of the gateway is intirely [*sic*] spoiled by it. . . . It is different when a thing is vignetted, but if there is an edge there ought to be a line, otherwise they look rotten; I asked particularly last winter if the line would be left. (79)

She is just as testy on July 25, 1905, in a letter to Norman Warne concerning *Mrs. Tiggy-Winkle* (interestingly, the same day she received a letter from Norman proposing marriage). She writes, "I am rather staggered with the blocks I confess. Please ask Hentschell's [*sic*]—civilly but *firmly*—to take the trouble to rub down the spottyness as much as they can" (123; Potter's emphasis) and then goes on to suggest a scientific reason for the spottyness. She is equally firm about *The Roly-Poly Pudding*, of which she writes to Harold Warne in 1908

> I am sorry to say I don't like the cover at all. You & Fruing are fond of that subject—but look at it across the room; it would never show in a shop window, or sell the book. I think it would be very much safer to follow the Peter Rabbit style of cover, which has been a success. This is after the style of Patty pan which was a relative failure. (157)

In a mere five years Potter has taken her publishers firmly in hand and shown that she not only has artistic concerns, but also commercial concerns regarding the publication of her books.

In many ways Potter is an unrecognized entrepreneurial pioneer. True, Newbery had offered his first children's books in 1744 with an accompanying toy, but Potter was shrewd enough to see the commercial possibilities of her books, and she saw them quite early on. She registered a patent on a Peter Rabbit doll on December 28, 1903, and wrote to Norman Warne, "I am cutting out calico patterns of Peter, I have not got it right yet, but the expression is going to be lovely. . . . I think I could make him stand on his legs if he had some lead bullets in his feet!" (83). In April of 1904 she was still working on these dolls, again writing to Norman that "I had intended to colour the white *woolly* rabbit, but it will not take watercolour at all; I think that explains why the Peter dolls were coloured so coarsely. . . . Do you think it would be worth while to let them make a sample one? Telling them carefully that the doll is copyright" (93–94; Potter's emphasis). Her next idea, in 1904, is for a board game based on Peter Rabbit, for which she provided a sketch of a gameboard and a detailed set of rules. She writes to Norman in December of 1904

> I think this is rather a good game. . . . I have another copy of the map, in case you wanted to register this. It might be well to register it, & then put it aside till some less busy time; it is too late to do anything with it this season; but I think it is a game that children might find exciting, if they were fond of the book." (110–11)

By 1908 Beatrix Potter merchandising was in full swing, with licensing of characters for use on wallpaper and china, and for construction of dolls. Apparently the impetus for licensing came from Potter and not from the Warnes, and certainly Potter was in close collaboration with the publishers about every detail concerning the licensing of her characters. She writes to Harold Warne in January of 1908

> I have been thinking about that china agreement, it is rather an awkwardly worded document. I think the words 'all earthenware' would prevent me from offering the statuettes to other firms. . . . But if you decide to let them go on making *tea-sets*—with a promise of *improvement*—I should think the agreement had better be written out again? in a less wholesale style? The agreement with Hughes seems a much better model. (157; Potter's emphasis)

Later in her life Potter would allow her characters to be used to raise money for the Invalid Children's Aid Association, and she would also use the characters to fight against free trade in political battles in the Lake District.[20]

During the years that Potter was drafting the miniature world of Peter Rabbit and her other animal characters, her own world was moving from the miniature and constricted life in Bolton Gardens to a world of much greater scale and interest to her. Although she never stated so directly in the journal or in her letters, one can infer that her impetus to write the earliest of her novels was threefold. First, she had a genuinely complex interior fantasy life, one she wanted to share with children to whom she felt close. Second, she was a committed artist who could not stop drawing whatever it was she observed. Third, she wanted financial and emotional independence from her parents. There are scattered comments in the letters spanning the first two years of her commercial publication that tell the Warnes, as well as those of us reading the letters today, that her parents were alarmed by and resistant to this growing independence, even before Norman Warne's proposal. Potter was rebelling, in a quiet but very firm way, not only against the strictures of her family but also against some of the strictures of gender roles in the late nineteenth century. She would not have considered herself a rebel (nor was she much in favor of female suffrage), but she felt constrained by the restricted role both her family and society wanted her to have. She rebelled by writing in code—her first version of a private world, which blossomed into the private fantasy world of the animals she then shared with the world. She rebelled by taking up amateur science out of a genuine passion for fungi, but also from a hope that she might somehow make a living through scientific illustration. She rebelled by secretly publishing her first cards, then privately publishing *Peter Rabbit* and going on to commercial publication. She rebelled by becoming an astute businesswoman (and later an astute farmer) at a time when women had a very small role in business of any sort, unless it be working-class women in factories and pubs. Later in her life she rebelled by becoming politically active.

Potter found her rebellion against family and gender expectations echoed in the rebellious behavior of the working classes of her time. These class echoes do not resonate in the rabbit books, which as I have argued are most closely linked to Potter's struggles with herself and her place in her family. They are, however, echoed in the non-rabbit books, as early as *The Tailor of Gloucester* and *Squirrel Nutkin*.

In the widest sense, Potter's rebellion was against the strictures of Victorian domesticity, but her rebellion was an ambivalent one: she is not necessarily against all forms of domesticity, but she is certainly against forced domesticity. Her difficulties with the question of what domestic life is and what it meant in her own life are most clearly reflected in the non-rabbit books published from *The Tale of Two Bad Mice* (1904) onward, the subjects of the following chapters.

Notes

1. Judy Taylor, ed., *Letters to Children from Beatrix Potter* (London: Warne, 1992).
2. Judy Taylor, Joyce Irene Whalley, Anne Stevenson Hobbs, Elizabeth M. Battrick, eds., *Beatrix Potter 1866–1943: The Artist and Her World* (London: Warne, 1987), 49.
3. Leslie Linder, ed., *The Journal of Beatrix Potter* (London: Warne, 1966), 204.
4. Judy Taylor, ed., *Beatrix Potter's Letters* (London: Warne, 1989), 322.
5. Margaret Lane, *The Tale of Beatrix Potter* (London: Warne, 1946). 14–15.
6. Her illustrations were finally used in a book on fungi published in 1967 in W. P. K. Findlay, *Wayside and Woodland Fungi* (London: Warne).
7. Harris's Uncle Remus tale of tale "Mr. Fox and Miss Goose," in particular, seems to have had an influence on Potter's tale of Jemima.
8. Sendak is a Potter admirer and an astute commentator on the nature of her work. See his two essays in *Caldecott & Co.: Notes on Books and Pictures* (New York: Noonday, 1988), "Beatrix Potter/1" 61–70 and Beatrix Potter/2 71–76.
9. Beatrix Potter, *The Tale of Peter Rabbit* (London: Warne, 1902; 1987), 13. Unless otherwise noted, all references in text are to the 1987 edition.
10. Ruth McDonald, *Beatrix Potter* (Boston: Twayne, 1986), 32.
11. Carole Scott, "Clothed in Nature or Nature Clothed: Dress as Metaphor in the Illustrations of Beatrix Potter and C. M. Barker," *Children's Literature* 22 (1994): 79.
12. Taylor et al., *Artist and Her World*, 69.
13. Five years later Kenneth Grahame makes use of the same image when Mole taunts the rabbit at the toll-gate in *Wind in the Willows* by crying, "Onion sauce! Onion sauce!"
14. Judy Taylor, ed., *Beatrix Potter's Letters* (London: Warne, 1989), 62.
15. This is especially true of her simplest rabbit tale, *The Story of a Fierce Bad Rabbit,* and of *The Story of Miss Moppet* both published in 1906 in panoramic wallet format, rather than in the standard format of the little novels. Both of these small books have very simple narrative lines and equally simple, not very detailed, illustrations.
16. Beatrix Potter, *The Tale of Benjamin Bunny* (London: Warne, 1904; 1987), 10. Unless otherwise noted, all text references are to the 1987 edition.

17.   Here again is the characteristic Potter verbal irony: climbing down a pear tree is hardly proper by any definition of the term.

18.   Beatrix Potter, *The Tale of the Flopsy Bunnies* (London: Warne, 1909; 1995), 10. Unless otherwise noted, all text references are to the 1995 edition.

19.   Some of these were later to be redrawn for use in *The Tale of Jeremy Fisher.*

20.   See Leslie Linder, *A History of the Writings of Beatrix Potter* (London: Warne, 1971), 398ff. for a discussion of some of Potter's political writings and illustrations.

3

Bad Mice, Lost Laundry, and Disastrous Tea Parties

The Tale of Two Bad Mice (1904), *The Tale of Mrs. Tiggy-Winkle* (1905), and *The Pie and the Patty-Pan* (1905) are all transitional works for Potter, reflecting changes in both her artistry and her life—and indeed, the changes in her life precipitated the changes in the art. All three of these works had input from Norman Warne, the last of his help before his death in 1905. The year of Norman's proposal and untimely death was also the year Potter bought Hill Top Farm, which was to be her refuge even after her marriage to William Heelis, when she used Hill Top as both a working farm and as a place to retreat and write. But the transitional tales from 1904 to 1905 are each transitional for a different reason. *The Tale of Two Bad Mice* can be seen in part as an allegory of Potter's desires for a home of her own, and in it she expresses some of her frustrations and fears about domesticity. *Mrs. Tiggy-Winkle* has a clearly defined Lake District setting and is also a domestic novel of sorts. In *The Pie and the Patty-Pan*, Potter for the first time features domestic animals as her protagonists, setting them clearly in a village setting reminiscent of Sawrey itself, and the size of the book expands to 177 mm by 138 mm, from the standard of 139 mm by 104 mm for the earlier books. Despite the differences among these three texts, each shows Potter working through questions of the meaning of domesticity, the meaning of work, and the meaning of social hierarchies, all of which were enduring themes for her throughout her career. Political issues and larger social concerns continue to lie beneath the surface of the tales, but as we shall see, once she leaves London for the Lakes, more or less permanently, her political interests shift to the local level. Whereas the earlier *Tailor of Gloucester* and *Squirrel Nutkin* reflect elements of broad class issues, the interest in the later books is in the concerns of working farmers.

The Tale of Two Bad Mice is a crucial transitional work for Beatrix Potter. She was working on it and *The Tale of Benjamin Bunny* simultaneously, but clearly her heart was with the mouse book and not the rabbit book. As McDonald has pointed out, "One suspects that the publisher [Norman Warne] was as indispensable in its creation as was the author-illustrator."[1] Norman Warne certainly was instrumental in the simple mechanics of the illustrations for the tale, supplying Potter not only with photographs of the dollhouse he had built for his niece, but also with the dolls themselves, the plaster food, and a glass-fronted mouse box, so Potter could draw mice in an interior setting. Potter also corresponded regularly with Norman Warne regarding the progress of the book, items to be included in the illustrations, and other matters. As McDonald and other commentators have pointed out, Potter was unable to meet personally with Norman or to sketch the dollhouse in situ, because Mrs. Potter objected to her daughter's warming relationship with a "tradesman." Norman had acquired a nickname from Potter, "Johnny Crow," after the Leslie Brooke text Warne had published the same year they published *Peter Rabbit* (Leslie Brooke had recommended to Warne that they publish Potter). Their courtship, leading to Norman's proposal of marriage in July of 1905, was conducted through the medium of *The Tale of Two Bad Mice* and the correspondence concerning it. These letters contain some of Potter's rare complaints against her parents and grow increasingly warm and familiar in tone, although to twenty-first-century ears they sound formal from beginning to end. Her letters remain circumspect, never referring directly to the engagement once it has occurred, but the novel is quite suggestive of Potter's complex and conflicted feelings about domesticity and rebellion, feelings that must have been brought out by her "rebellious" engagement and her desire to flee the domestic space of Bolton Gardens for a domestic space she would build with Norman.

The setting of the story is "a very beautiful doll's-house"[2] and its environs, including the mouse hole. There are actually three settings to the story, a kind of Russian-nesting-doll scenario of a human house, holding a doll house, which is invaded by mice who live in an even smaller abode within the human house. We have, as we did in *The Tailor of Gloucester* and as we will again in *Roly-Poly Pudding*, a sense of hidden worlds within the conventional human world, miniature worlds that are livelier and more interesting than the human-scale world within which they exist. One of the attractions of both *The Tailor of Gloucester* and this second mouse book is the invitation to the reader to enter a hidden, interior, miniature world that is entirely real and far more interesting than our own everyday world.

The story thus suggests, from the outset, that one theme will be domesticity and the role of domiciles within domesticity. The story also presents us with tensions about both the pleasures and dangers of domesticity, the pleasures and dangers of rebellion and insurrection. Of the human world that encloses the two miniature worlds, we know very little but can infer much. The dollhouse, with its "red brick" and "white windows" and "real muslin curtains and a front door and a chimney" (9) is no ordinary doll house, but an extravagant and beautiful one. The illustration shows us a substantial dwelling, one with a fashionable bow window and dormer windows for a third-floor nursery or servants' quarters. The dollhouse sits on carpet and is set against a wallpaper background (badly faded in current reproductions), and is framed by badminton equipment, helping to give it a sense of scale, and also hinting that this is a house whose inhabitants can afford leisure. One doll sits on the roof, and the other on the floor. Later in the story we learn that although the house "belonged to two Dolls called Lucinda and Jane" (10), in actuality the house is possessed by a little girl who takes the dolls for rides in the perambulator, and the girl herself is managed by a governess: the nesting-doll technique extends to the human or humanlike figures in the tale. Obviously both the human and the dollhouse are upper-middle class, an impression borne out by other illustrations of the interior of the dollhouse and its many middle-class furnishings: gilt clocks, carpets, flowers, a separate dining room, and so forth.

The dolls, drawn with exquisite stiffness and immobility by Potter, must be enlivened by human action, by the girl who owns them. But the girl herself is also a doll or a puppet in some ways, her activities controlled by the off-stage nurse who cares for her, accompanies her on her trips out with the dolls, and arranges for mousetraps at the end of the story. The girl is a nice middle-class girl, playing with dolls and houses, being encouraged through childhood play to look forward to running an adult household of her own with cooks and servants. She is obviously a proper little girl, one concerned with order, because she buys a policeman doll to protect her property at the end of the story. But Potter is not on the side of middle-class propriety in this story: she is on the side of subversion, insurrection, and individualism.

McDonald and other commentators have noted that *The Tale of Two Bad Mice* can in some ways be seen as a "gentle mockery" (McDonald, 74) of the sterile and static lives of Potter's parents, but there is little that is gentle in the mockery. In fact, the book is a miniature declaration of Potter's increasing independence from her family and her desire to have a home of her own, rather than to be a permanent resident and kind of head-housekeeper for her parents; but at the same time the novel shows some of Potter's indecision and ambivalence about leaving home and her parents. If rabbits were her alter ego in the beginning stages of her career, here, her stand-ins—hers and Norman's—are Hunca Munca and Tom Thumb, those two bad mice. Their story is as complex and multilayered as the nest of houses providing the setting of the story and is Potter's most complex narrative since *The Tailor of Gloucester*.

The dolls who inhabit the house, even Jane the cook, have nothing to do. The food has been bought ready-made from a store and the dolls' only activity is to go for a ride with their child owner—even in this "activity" they are passive. On their own, they initiate nothing and do nothing until put into action by some outside agent. They move, in the illustrations, from the outside of the doll house to the inside and back again, but clearly cannot move on their own: they are puppets to their human owner. They also do not fit easily into the house: Lucinda, outsized, sits on the roof in the initial illustration, and the interior picture of the two dolls in the next illustration shows them stuffed uncomfortably into a cluttered interior. They are not appropriately sized for the dollhouse, and the illustrations of them are visual foreshadowing of their displacement by the smaller, livelier mice.

The dolls' primary concern is appearances. They appreciate their box of food for its bounty and its beauty, not for its nutritional value. These are dolls who will starve because they have only plaster food, but of course they don't need real food because they are dolls: they are already, in a sense dead, or figures of life-in-death. Potter, growing up in her parents' house, must have felt that there was a lack of life in the ironically named Bolton Gardens, that the lives of her parents were enervated and empty ones, that they were as overwhelmed by their house and their belongings as the two dolls are. She wrote to Norman Warne, after receiving photographs of his niece's dollhouse, that "The inside view is amusing—the kind of house where one cannot sit down without upsetting something, I know the sort!"[3] The dolls are concerned not with reality or utility but with surface attractions. Like the self-satisfied upper-middle class, show for the dolls is everything; utility is nothing. Potter herself grew up in a house where show and appearances mattered, not for the sake of ostentation, but for the sake of showing and knowing one's proper place in the social world. For Potter, the practical amateur scientist and budding farmer, show is nothing and utility everything. If we know anything at all about Potter, we know that she does not approve of the dolls' lives (or, perhaps, of her parents' lives) and is setting them up for a fall, even before the mice are introduced.

At the same time, however, there is some ambivalence at work: the dollhouse is attractive and the plaster food is beautifully realistic. The reader is meant to be attracted to the miniature wonders of the dollhouse world, just as the mice are attracted, but both the house and the food appeal because of how they *look*, not because of what they *do*. Houses should protect owners from the elements, but this house is only for show because it is protected by the larger human house and would probably be ruined by exposure to the elements. Food should help us live, but here the food is beautiful but inedible, a product of art rather than nature. We never see the dolls making any use at all of the middle-class comforts the house holds, but as we shall see, the mice (and Potter) are practical beings and manage to turn the useless into the useful.

When the mice appear, we see them first peeking out from their hole in the skirting board, looking inquisitive and ready for action. They are unclothed, natural-looking mice, except for the faintly anthropomorphic expressions on their faces. They are also cautious, as mice need to be, making certain the coast is clear before venturing into the nursery and across the rug to the dollhouse. The mice approach the house and discover that the door has been carelessly left "not fast" (*Bad Mice*, 18). Thus, Potter implies that the mice are not really bad for entering the house: their entrance is the price the dolls (and their owner) pay for carelessness. But if we pause and consider for a moment, dollhouses don't usually have locks on the doors. On the one hand the dolls are careless; on the other hand they have no choice but to leave the house unlocked. If we consider further, they would have no need to lock up their elegant house from outside marauders because the dollhouse is protected from the outside by the larger human house surrounding it. What the inhabitants (of both doll and human house) have not taken into account is that danger and disruption can come from within as well as from without. Mr. and Mrs. Potter were about to discover the same thing with their daughter. The Potters, ever alarmed by social unrest and labor strikes and protests in London, alarmed enough to leave the city at times, never expected their own daughter, the "mouse" within their house, to cause more disruption in their lives than working-class unrest ever could.

Potter's mice are given names that perfectly fit their roles. Hunca Munca and Tom Thumb are not original names on Potter's part, but names she lifted from Henry Fielding's play, *Tom Thumb, a Tragedy*, a farce first performed in 1730. The play, hugely popular in London in its time, is a mock heroic ridiculing what Fielding saw as the bombast of many of the grandiose tragedies of the period. The plot, such as it is, concerns Tom Thumb, a man who lives up (or down) to his name in his small size, who is lauded as a great hero for supposedly having conquered dozens of giants. His reward is the Princess Huncamunca, to be given over to him by her parents, King Arthur and his queen. Unfortunately the queen wants Tom Thumb for herself, and all ends quite tragicomically, with everyone dead on stage, including the ghost of Tom Thumb, who manages to be killed twice.

Potter chose to reference a parodic play in her own miniature parody of middle-class life. She dropped the courtly setting of Fielding's play and replaced it with an upper-middle-class house, and she also drops the jealous queen. In fact, in her very loose adoption of Fielding's characters she drops interfering parents and adult authority altogether. She allows her "giant killers," the mice, to win against the dolls and not only to live, but to live together as mouse and wife. Whereas Fielding's play leaves the stage littered with dead bodies at its end, Potter not only allows the mice to live, but in fact brings life to the dollhouse through the agency of the mice. It is the small, unseen, quiet mice with their secret lives that both bring down the dollhouse and bring life to it, just as Potter herself disrupted the propriety of Bolton Gardens by accepting a proposal from the "tradesman" Norman Warne.

I do not think it is stretching a point to consider that Potter is, in some ways, commenting upon her own situation in this small book. All of Potter's books predating *The Tale of Two Bad Mice*—*Peter Rabbit*, *The Tailor of Gloucester*, *Squirrel Nutkin*, and *Benjamin Bunny*—deal with disobedience and misbehavior, but none is situated so squarely in the domestic world as *The Tale of Two Bad Mice*. Two of the four stories do not deal with domesticity at all, and the two rabbit books, as we have seen, have conflicting messages about the attractions and dangers of life at home. By the time of *Two Bad Mice*, Potter is actually making a living from her books, which at least in theory would make it possible for her to have a home of her own, with or without a husband, although to do so would violate late-Victorian ideas of female propriety, not to mention parental dictates. She is on the verge of buying Hill Top Farm in the Lake District, and in the course of finishing *Two Bad Mice* gains a proposal of marriage, has strenuous arguments with her parents over whether or not she should accept, and finally wins a compromise of wearing Norman's ring but not announcing the engagement. She can see, shimmering on the horizon, the possibility of her own home, smaller perhaps than Bolton Gardens, but hers. That her initial hopes were cruelly dashed when Norman died suddenly of leukemia mere weeks after proposing marriage does not mean that she is not thinking of home and what it means to her. Her conflicting feelings about home—her parents' home, Grandmother Crompton's Camfield Place, vacation homes, the hope of a home of her own—are reflected in *Two Bad Mice*.

The mice, upon first seeing the interior of the house, are as attracted by appearances as the dolls and the reader have been. When they see the dining room table laid with plates and food, they "squeaked with joy! Such a lovely dinner was laid out upon the table! There were tin spoons, and lead knives and forks, and two dolly-chairs—all *so* convenient" (21). Potter makes very clear that the mice are attracted by the appearance of the dining room and its appointments, but also suggests that they will be disappointed in the food, which the reader already knows, having been given a lengthy description and illustration of the toy food. She writes that a lovely "dinner" was laid out, but the rest of the sentence does not talk about the food, commenting instead on the tableware and dining room furniture. The tableware itself is as insubstantial as the food, made of flimsy tin and soft lead rather than real silver. Again, it looks attractive but turns out to be useless, as we learn at the page turn when Tom Thumb attempts to carve the ham and the knife "crumpled up and hurt him" (22).

That the mice are at heart practical creatures is indicated by Tom Thumb's remark that the recalcitrant ham "is not boiled enough; it is hard" (22). Jane, the cook of the house, the cook who never cooks, would know nothing of the proper preparation of a ham, but Tom Thumb—the male mouse, at that—knows precisely how ham should be prepared and disapproves of the "beautiful shiny yellow, streaked with red" ham he has found in the dollhouse. Hunca Munca concurs with her husband, noting that the ham is "as hard as the hams at the cheesemonger's" (25), a lovely observation that, like the best of Potter's writing, includes a wealth of information in very few words. Hunca Munca's observation first sets her out as a good housewife, one who is a careful shopper and knows that the hams at a particular shop are not up to her standards. Second, because we are beginning to know these mice we suspect that Hunca Munca does not buy her hams at the cheesemonger's, but rather pilfers ham when she can get it. Third, we know that she is a good wife, waiting for her husband to carve before she tries, and concurring with his opinion. All of this is accomplished in a mere eight words.

The mice quickly become enraged with the uncooperative food that will not be sliced and that stubbornly remains stuck to its plates. They try all the silverware on all the dishes, to no avail. "Then Tom Thumb lost his temper. He put the ham in the middle of the floor, and hit it with the tongs and with the shovel— bang, bang, smash, smash!" (29). Discovering that the food is actually plaster, that it is nothing but false appearance, "there was no end to the rage and disappointment of Tom Thumb and Hunca Munca" (30) and the real destruction in the house begins. They put the fish into the "red-hot crinkly paper fire in the kitchen" (30), but of course the fish will not burn in the make-believe fire. Hunca Munca discovers that the canisters in the kitchen contain only shiny beads. The mice move on to the bedrooms and begin to pull out and destroy the dolls' clothes.

For such small creatures, the mice are quite destructive—true of real mice as well as of these fantasy mice. And what is it they are destroying? The staid, false appearances of a respectable home. Ironically, their destructive behavior is the first sign of life the house has seen. All of our other views of the house have been static ones, with the dolls sitting or standing stiffly and inactively. Once the mice invade, however, the house has life in it. In her typically ironic fashion, Potter gives us the dollhouse come to life just as it is being destroyed by the mice. If the dolls have been drawn to look stiff and dead, the mice are so alive they practically twitch off the page. They are, in fact, the first living beings to enter the house. We can see their energy in the force Tom puts into his shoulder as he tries to carve the ham; in Hunca Munca's helpful reach as she hands the plate of fish to Tom; in the joyful cooperation of the two mice as Tom hammers the ham to pieces and Hunca Munca stands on a chair ready to give him the next plate of plaster food to destroy; in the effort the mice put into muscling an unwieldy bolster down the stairs.

If we think of this novel as Potter's conscious or unconscious comment on her own life, at this point in the story we can see her absolute delight in bringing disruption, destruction, and energy into a house as stifling and life-denying to the dolls and mice as Bolton Gardens was to her. There is, in fact, more overt destruction and violence portrayed in this novel than in almost any of her other books, and certainly more than we have seen so far in her career. Although there is implied danger and violence in the earlier books, the violence comes not from the protagonists of the stories but from their enemies—Mr. McGregor, Simpkin the cat, Old Brown the owl. There is plenty of violence in the later books as well, particularly in *Jemima Puddleduck* and *The Roly-Poly Pudding*, but again, it is not the protagonist who creates the violence but rather the nemesis of the protagonist, the fox or the rats. Only in *The Tale of Two Bad Mice* (and much later in *The Tale of Mr. Tod*, a dark little story that marks the end of Potter's best work) do we see the protagonists engaged in violence, and the violence they are engaged in also wrecks a home.

The story does more than suggest that destroying a respectable but life-denying house is an understandable, if not entirely condoned, act. For the mice come to their senses halfway through their rampage. Hunca Munca, in the midst of destroying the dolls' bedroom, has second thoughts. "Hunca Munca had a frugal mind. After pulling half the feathers out of Lucinda's bolster, she remembered that she herself was in want of a feather bed" (37). She gets her husband's assistance, and they turn from destroying the house to pilfering its contents for their own use. The bolster is squeezed into the mousehole. So are two chairs, some odds and ends, and a cradle. However, "the book-case and the bird-cage refused to go into the mousehole" (41), which we can clearly see in the illustration. The birdcage contains a stuffed toy bird, and the bookcase an encyclopedia, neither as useful as the smaller iron, tea-kettle, fireplace tool, and hand-mirror that the illustration also includes and that the text suggests the mice do appropriate for their own uses.

The mice take the items that the dolls can make no use of to their mousehole where the stolen goods provide a solid beginning to their family life. The doll-house utensils go from uselessness to usefulness. Hunca Munca is going to need that cradle, for she has four baby mice on the way, whom we see in one of the last illustrations in the novel. Potter suggests that it is not the goods themselves that are at fault, but rather the uses to which they are, or are not, put. Potter was an intensely practical woman and a frugal one who knew the worth of money and of goods. When she finally gained her own homes at both Hill Top and then at Castle Farm, those homes were used—they did not merely symbolize her station in life. Both were working farms and Potter kept Hill Top as a working studio for herself after she married William Heelis. Hill Top, still filled with Potter's furnishings (representations of which can be seen in *The Roly-Poly Pudding*, set in the interior of Hill Top), gives a sense of a woman who had good taste but who did not clutter up her life with useless objects. She had little patience with appearance for appearance's sake, something that comes through clearly in *Two Bad Mice*. Hunca Munca, after all, "has some *useful* pots and pans, and several other things" (50, my emphasis) after her adventures with the useless food. Food they can get from the cheesemonger; mouse-sized cradles, kitchen utensils, and clothing are far more difficult to come by, and the mice take advantage of their opportunities.

The mice remain attached to the dollhouse and in fact to the human house, because their mousehole is contained in the nursery that contains the dollhouse, which itself is contained by the larger house. They further remain attached because their own domestic bliss is largely furnished with goods they have taken from the dollhouse. Unlike the rats in *The Roly-Poly Pudding*, they do not leave the site of their thievery but remain, although hidden from sight. They have taken what is useful to them and, although tempted by useless items, have found there is no way to make them fit, literally or metaphorically, into their household. Potter herself never left home completely, even after she married William Heelis and moved permanently to the Lake District. A mere two weeks after her marriage she writes to a friend that "I am going to London this next week, Thursday, as my mother is changing servants. It is rather soon to have to leave the disconsolate Wm. People are sure to say we have quarreled!" (*Letters*, 213). One suspects Mrs. Potter of wanting to disrupt the marriage. Neither she nor Mr. Potter were enthusiastic about William, and Potter notes in a letter of September 14, 1913, weeks before her marriage on October 15, that "I was feeling the going away [from Bolton Gardens] very much, but William has actually been invited up for a week-end soon—they never say much, but they cannot dislike him" (212). The "actually" here is telling, indicating Potter's surprise that her parents would invite her fiancé for a visit. The letter also suggests Potter's ambivalence about leaving home, where her father was not well and her parents had come to depend upon her. After her father's death in May 1914, Potter writes to Harold Warne that she has been to Bolton Gardens "eight times=sixteen journeys since New Year" (217). Potter moved her mother to a house on the other side of Lake Windermere from Sawrey, and Judy Taylor notes that "Beatrix rarely crossed the lake to see her mother and when she did make the effort she was not always welcome," Mrs. Potter being unwilling to lend her car to meet her daughter.[4] Potter never stopped being the dutiful daughter, never ended her connection with a difficult parent, but also insisted on a home of her own and a large degree of independence. In this she is not much different from the mice in her tale.

The story does not end with the return of the mice and their stolen goods to the mousehole. Potter remains both ironic and ambivalent about domesticity, order, and rebellion to the end. The dolls return to the house and in their doll-like way, "Lucinda sat upon the upset kitchen stove and stared; and Jane leant against the kitchen dresser and smiled—but neither of them made any remark" (*Bad Mice*, 46). The proper middle-class inhabitant of the house and her cook are struck speechless by this invasion of troublesome outsiders. They in fact are powerless to do anything about the assault upon their property. The human inhabitants of the nursery, however, have other plans. The girl who owns the dollhouse says "I will get a doll dressed like a policeman!" (53) and the nurse replies "I will set a mouse-trap!" (54). Here the child is still involved in the fantasy that dolls are people and have real powers, although the reader is well aware of their static quality. The illustration showing the policeman doll underlines this: the policeman is looking down at Hunca Munca, who is holding up one of her children to get a better look at the officer, while other mouse children have invaded the dollhouse once again. Not only does the doll policeman have no authority over the mice, but

Potter seems to be suggesting here that the forces of law may not be able to contain the determined forces of an "underclass" of mice determined to get more of the goods it feels it deserves.

Although *The Tale of Two Bad Mice* is largely a reflection of Potter's personal and domestic concerns; the entire novel is nested within a larger context, just as the dollhouse is nested within the human house. In this small novel Potter gives us a glimpse of her attitudes toward her own domestic situation, a glimpse of her own quiet, hidden, but disruptive rebellion against her family's constraints and their class values, but there is also a faint echo, as there was in *Squirrel Nutkin*, of some of the larger class issues of the time and specifically of labor unrest. The mice can be seen as representative not only of Potter's rebellion, but also of the various rebellions of the working classes against working conditions in England. The period between the 1890s and the beginning of the First World War was marked by "the growing number of local political and industrial conflicts revolving around issues such as the recognition of the new unionism, conditions of work, employer 'tyranny', living standards, unemployment and 'relief without pauperisation', the 'right to work, minimum wages and the eight-hour day' and the closed shop."[5] Workers made some gains with the passage in 1889 of the Technical Instruction Act, the passage of the Housing of the Working Classes Act in 1890, an important factory act in 1892, among other reforms. Most of these occurred under Salisbury's cabinet (formed after Gladstone's defeat in 1886), but Salisbury was not an enthusiastic reformer, fearing that "even desirable limited change might whet the appetite for confiscation of property."[6]

Potter's attitudes toward the working classes and class agitation for greater rights and protections under the law were as complex and ambiguous as her attitudes toward domesticity. She might be expected to approve of Salisbury's actions because he was Gladstone's foe, and Potter was anti-Gladstone from beginning to end, but her difficulties with Gladstone were mostly due to his support for Irish Home Rule and his foreign policy in Egypt and elsewhere. Her journal entries suggest that she approved, to some extent, of Gladstone's efforts to extend the franchise and democratize the British electoral process. Potter commented on working-class unrest in her journal, noting in 1885

> There was a demonstration of the unemployed on the Embankment on the 16th. Two or three thousand only, on account of the rain, most violent speakers. One young man, who was arrested for throwing stones at the police, stated he had left a situation to better himself, and as the magistrate said, if many of the *unemployed* [sic] were out of work by the same means, they deserved very little sympathy.[7]

Here she disapproves of violence as a means to social reform. However, this does not mean she disapproves of reform itself. She notes a few pages later on in the journal that "They say that, supposing cabmen were really paid at the rate of sixpence a mile, they must go forty-two miles before they begin to make any profit.

They pay sixteen shillings per day to a cab-owner for a cab and two horses, and have incidental expenses as well" (*Journal*, 144). Potter provides no editorial comment on these facts, but her observation comes after a trip to Camfield, which involved using cabmen. Her lack of negative commentary may not mean that she supports better compensation for cabmen, but in the context of the entire journal, it does suggest that she considers the information interesting and worth noting, and perhaps worthy of further contemplation. In her journal Potter is not at all reticent about voicing her disapproval of individual artists, politicians, and public figures. The lack of negative commentary here points to at least neutrality where the fair compensation of cabmen is concerned.

The mice, like many of the workers in England from the late nineteenth century through to the first World War, look at the sumptuous lives of the upper classes and want a piece of it. After all, those material and even luxury goods enjoyed by the upper classes are not possible without the labor of the working classes, and the comfortable houses of the upper classes cannot be kept up without a force of servants. Those servants and their lives, of course, are largely invisible to their employers—just as the mice are invisible to the little girl, the governess, and the dolls. However, when the working classes/mice decide to agitate, the effects of that agitation are both visible and impossible to ignore. Potter herself witnessed riots, demonstrations, and even violence linked both to working-class agitation and to the struggle for Irish Home Rule, and as she grew older was increasingly responsible for hiring and managing the servants who ran Bolton Gardens. She had a certain amount of sympathy for the working classes, or at least a sense of fairness: they should be treated fairly, if not equally, with the upper classes. We have seen this sense of fairness at play in both *The Tailor of Gloucester* and *Squirrel Nutkin*, and it makes an appearance in *The Tale of Two Bad Mice* as well. This sense of fairness is consistent with her Unitarian upbringing and the Unitarian impulse toward equity and fairness for all, including workers, even if that impulse did not extend to raising the actual class status of workers.

It is this sense of fairness and the subtext of British class unrest that accounts for the ending of *Two Bad Mice*, as much as any desire Potter may have had to present an example of moral behavior to her readers. Social authority, in the form of the policeman doll, and domestic authority, in the form of the governess who sets mousetraps, are both ineffective against the desires of the mice. Just as Hunca Munca holds up her child to get a good look at the policeman, who is incapable of seeing that mice have again invaded the house he is supposed to be guarding, Tom Thumb explains the workings of the mousetrap to his offspring so that they will not be caught in it. But Potter goes on to tell us "they were not so very very naughty after all, because Tom Thumb paid for everything he broke" (*Bad Mice*, 56). He pays, however, with a "crooked sixpence," which he has not earned but found under the hearth rug. Hunca Munca appears to pay for what she has taken more honestly, in kind, by coming in at dawn "with her dust-pan and her broom to sweep the Dollies' house!" (59). But is Hunca Munca really paying the dolls back or only playing at paying them back? We have already seen how inactive and sterile the lives of the dolls are: how much work can sweeping up after them be? There will be little dust, no dirty dishes, and no trash or garbage to deal with. The mice, in fact, are making a show of being respectful and of paying for what they have taken, but in fact the show covers up their continuing rebellion against middle-class authority, a rebellion that will continue into the next (larger) generation of mice children, if we are to believe the illustrations.

Potter, in *The Tale of Two Bad Mice*, wants to have her cake and eat it too. She approves of the domestic and social rebellion of the mice and of their desire for a comfortable home of their own. She disapproves of the sterility and emptiness of the dolls' lives, yet she understands the attractions of the dollhouse, the attractions of a comfortable domestic life based in part upon the labor of servants. At the time she is writing this novel, caught in her own rebellion against her parents, which occurs in the broader context of the rebellion of an entire class of disenfranchised people, Potter cannot help reflecting ambivalence in her little, apparently simple but very complex, story for children.

Despite Norman's death, Potter did find escape from Bolton Gardens through her earnings and the purchase of Hill Top in Sawrey, near Ambleside in Cumbria in 1905. Although to her parents she represented the purchase of Hill Top as an investment, it was more an emotional investment than it was an economic one, giving her freedom to escape London on her own, an excuse to separate herself from her parents, and a kind of artistic liberation. Some of her best books are set in the countryside around Sawrey or in the interior of Hill Top itself. If in *The Tale of Two Bad Mice* Potter is working through her difficulties in rebelling and leaving home, in the novels between 1905 and 1912 Potter explores the possibilities of newfound freedom to define domesticity for herself.

The first of the Sawrey books is *The Tale of Mrs. Tiggy-Winkle*, one of the last of the books for which Norman Warne would provide editorial advice. It is less assured than any of the novels that precede it and there seems to have been some discussion as to whether or not to produce it in a larger format (the final decision being to leave it in the smaller format), but in its way is as much a transitional work as *Two Bad Mice*. If the mouse book reflected Potter's conflicting attachment to home and desire to leave it, *Mrs. Tiggy-Winkle* shows Potter free from the conflicted interior domesticity of the earlier novel but unsure what to do with that freedom.

Mrs. Tiggy-Winkle has several aspects setting it apart from the earlier novels, aspects suggesting Potter's experimentation within the freedom she found in Cumbria. First, the novel concerns an animal unfamiliar to most children, both then and now: a hedgehog, the model for whom was one of Potter's own pet hedgehogs. The earlier animals—rabbits, mice, and squirrels—would be familiar to both urban and rural children, and are attractive, furry animals, soft to the touch and interesting to observe. Hedgehogs are another matter entirely. They might be familiar to rural children, but not to their urban cousins. Hedgehogs are certainly adorable to look at, but they are neither soft nor furry and hardly the sort of animal one would pick up to pet and cuddle. As Potter herself remarks, hedgehogs are covered with "prickles." They are also not very lively animals and less interesting to a human observer than the animals Potter previously portrayed.

Second, *Mrs. Tiggy-Winkle* has an unusually large human presence in the person of Lucie, who is constantly losing her handkerchiefs and her pinafores. Humans appeared before in Potter's books, indeed in all of them except *Squirrel Nutkin*, but they had largely been off-stage characters, and Potter generally drew them only from a distance, or in partial view—Mr. McGregor's hobnailed boot or his large hand, for example. Even the tailor in *The Tailor of Gloucester*, important though he is to the action of the tale, was given short shrift in the illustrations and spends most of his time in bed rather than in tailoring. *Mrs. Tiggy-Winkle* gives us a human as co-protagonist, the catalyst to the plot (such as it is), and forced Potter to include a number of face-forward portraits of Lucie. Of the twenty-three illustrations, sixteen include Lucie, and of these sixteen, eight present Lucie in a full-length frontal view. (Compare this to *The Tailor of Gloucester*, where the tailor appears in only seven of twenty-seven illustrations, and is never seen in a full-face view). Potter, who knew she had weaknesses drawing humans, who had struggled with a portrait of Mrs. McGregor in *Peter Rabbit*, and who showed the tailor in *The Tailor of Gloucester* only in partial and back views, here had the confidence to attempt inclusion of a human as an important character in her novel.

Third, in this novel Potter was more conscious than she has been of marketing techniques, including references to all of her previous novels both to give an inner consistency to the fantasy animal world she was creating and to remind readers who might not know of the earlier books that they do exist and are available for purchase. The endpapers, which since 1903 had included increasing references to prior Potter novels, also encourage readers to search out the earlier books.[8]

Although all of these new elements suggest Potter's growing confidence and willingness to stretch her artistic boundaries, like most new things, *Mrs. Tiggy-Winkle* is not perfect. Indeed, compared to Potter's earlier works its narrative line is quite weak. *The Tale of Two Bad Mice*, as we have seen, presents all sorts of ambiguities and possibilities for the reader; there is little of such ambiguity in *Mrs. Tiggy-Winkle*. It is a simple tale of linens lost and found, held together (as Ruth McDonald has suggested) by the appealing character of Mrs. Tiggy-Winkle herself, not by a narrative line. The only complications come with the narrative voice of the tale, but those complications arise more from uncertainty on Potter's part than they do from complexities within the text itself. Nonetheless, considered against the background of *Two Bad Mice*, the novel does present us with some further developments in the author's attitudes toward domesticity and class.

Mrs. Tiggy-Winkle is concerned with the domestic task of doing the laundry and was a tale Potter thought would particularly appeal to girls. It is a domestic novel that occurs largely outside human habitation, despite a number of views of the interior of Mrs. Tiggy-Winkle's house beneath the hill. We never see Lucie inside a human house; she is also a little girl who (like Peter Rabbit and Tom Kitten) sheds the clothing that links her to restraint and domesticity. Unlike Peter and Tom, however, she does not shed her clothes out of disobedience but out of forgetfulness, and is anxious to retrieve them, so anxious that she leaves the safety of the farmyard and heads up the hill to where she thinks she sees "some white things spread upon the grass."9

Here again we have ambiguity about the pleasures and comforts of domestic life—but with a difference. Whereas the mice in *Two Bad Mice* were tempted by the trappings of upper-middle-class urban life, Lucie is a farmer's child, one dressed in country fashion, one free to roam on her own through both farmyard and countryside. She has more freedom than the little girl who owns the dollhouse, but she is not entirely free, being bound up in late-Victorian pinafores and ruffles, ruffles she admires when she sees them beautifully ironed by Mrs. Tiggy-Winkle. Lucie wants to find her pinafore, the text suggests, not so much because she fears punishment if she does not find it, but because she is attached to this particular garment and would like it back in her possession. She is, in other words, attached to domesticity and to femininity. Lucie in some ways is reminiscent of the child Potter, who during summer holidays was free to roam the countryside, but who was generally confined by the conventional feminine clothing of late Victorian England.

When Lucie discovers Mrs. Tiggy-Winkle in her home, we find ourselves back in a miniature world like that of the dollhouse. But Mrs. Tiggy-Winkle's interior is a far more pleasant one. When Lucie steps inside, she finds "a nice clean kitchen with a flagged floor and wooden beams—just like any other farm kitchen. Only the ceiling was so low that Lucie's head nearly touched it; and the pots and pans were small, and so was everything there" (21). As in many farmhouses, the door opens directly onto the kitchen, the busiest and most social area of the house. The accompanying illustration is similar in composition to one in *The Roly-Poly Pudding* showing the doorway into Hill Top itself: everything is scaled to child or animal size. The dollhouse in *Two Bad Mice* was out of scale to the dolls, although the right scale for the mice. Here we have a cozy, country interior, one that has plenty of room for Lucie and makes her feel safe rather than claustrophobic. Ruth McDonald has commented that "One suspects that Potter found in Mrs. Tiggy many of the virtues she sought to pursue in her own life as a farmer and homeowner" (McDonald, 90–91).

This is one of the keys to *Mrs. Tiggy-Winkle*, which is the first of Potter's books to give her a chance to portray country life as opposed to city life, useful life as opposed to a life of show. Whereas the dollhouse was stuffed with merely decorative objects, everything we can see in Mrs. Tiggy-Winkle's abode has a purpose. Before we enter her house, we see her clotheslines built of "bracken stems, with lines of plaited rushes, and a heap of tiny clothes pins" (18). The illustrations of the interior of the house show not a single object that is merely decorative. Instead we get simple, sturdy wooden tables covered with blankets, acting as ironing boards; a sideboard filled with everyday china; a plain clock on the wall (as opposed to the gilded clock in *Two Bad Mice*); laundry and dishtowels hung from the ceiling; everyday objects on the mantelpiece; and a roaring fire in the fireplace, as opposed to the "crinkly paper" fire in *Two Bad Mice*—a fire before which hedgehog and girl can share a cup of real tea. Mrs. Tiggy-Winkle's house is alive with purpose, filled with the tools of her trade, and the laundress barely stops working, even while she talks to Lucie. She takes time out for a single cup of tea—only hospitable when a guest comes calling—but as soon as tea is done, she and Lucie are off to deliver the newly laundered clothes to their owners.

Potter admires not only the pleasant, utilitarian house that Mrs. Tiggy inhabits, but also admires her work and her skill. Here again is Potter's interest in the working classes who were often ignored and disenfranchised, but also a great deal of respect and admiration for the work of the laundress, which shows in both text and illustration. Within the text, Potter is careful to use the exact language of laundering. Mrs. Tiggy-Winkle not only irons but "goffers" Lucie's pinafore, thus gaining from Lucie the exclamation, "Oh that *is* lovely!" (33). She also knows the causes of wear and tear on items she is given to clean—Henny Penny's scratching and wearing out of her stockings and the birds' spillage of currant wine. She knows the laundry marks (actually the splashes of paint farmers use to mark their sheep) of all the sheep farms in the area. Potter carefully explains all of this to the reader, through Mrs. Tiggy's own words, showing respect for the complexities of the trade and encouraging the child reader to consider how much work goes into keeping clothes presentable. The illustrations go even further, showing us a very busy and competent laundress who checks her irons, folds and airs when she isn't ironing, pays close attention to her work, and does her best to make up for the mistakes of clients who persist in wearing and staining and losing their clothing. Mrs. Tiggy is fairly irresistible as a character, despite her prickles.

Carole Scott has suggested that *Mrs. Tiggy-Winkle* shows how Lucie discovers the way clothing presents "people's basic natures and how it blurs the dividing line between the natural and the social animal," and further that the treatment of the animals' clothing in the book shows that "the animal's *natural covering* [*sic*] is being viewed as its clothing, whereas in other cases, like Peter Rabbit's blue coat, or Mrs. Tiggy-Winkle's own clothes, they are clearly inspired by human wardrobes."[10] Scott seems to suggest that in Mrs. Tiggy-Winkle there is a kind of continuum of outer-self, inner-self, expressed through clothing. We have the entirely human Lucie, who is distressed when she loses her pinafore and handkerchief, two items that Scott rightly observes are not necessary for Lucie to appear entirely clothed. She is still a civilized little farm girl in a dress, jacket, sturdy shoes, and so forth, but losing the pinafore and the handkerchief suggests that she is losing at least some of the civility of human life, and specifically of *adult* human life. Children, by and large, are not as careful of their clothing as are adults, who provide children with pinafores to keep the more expensive dresses clean and free of stains and other damage. Children also do not feel the need to reach for handkerchiefs when they need to blow their noses—but adults encourage them to do so. Mrs. Tiggy-Winkle herself is at the middle point of the continuum. She is an animal, but she is clothed (until the end) in human clothing, and cares about the presentation of the clothes left in her care. Her essential animal nature cannot be entirely restrained, however: her prickles stick out from beneath her clothing, and in the end she sheds human clothing altogether and runs away on all fours, a complete hedgehog. Furthermore, although real hedgehogs can be held in the palm of one's hand, Potter illustrates Mrs. Tiggy as being child-sized, on a par with Lucie. On the far end of the continuum are the animals who have left their clothing—Henny Penny's yellow stockings, cock-robin's red vest—for Mrs. Tiggy to launder. As Scott points out, Potter suggests that the natural coverings of animals are, in fact, clothing. Hence, just as pinafores indicate something of human nature, the natural coverings of animals indicate their animal nature.

This all seems very tidy, but in fact is not. Had Potter been consciously working toward some sort of clarification of the interaction of clothing with the social and animal selves of both humans and animals, she would have remained consistent and shown us animals who left only their natural coverings behind to be laundered. She does not: one of the items in her care is Peter Rabbit's blue jacket, "very much shrunk" (*Tiggy-Winkle*, 45). Here Potter has let her marketing concerns overtake her artistic sensibilities. Peter was the most famous and most popular of her characters, and inserting him into this story must have been calculated both to remind readers that yes, they are reading a book by Beatrix Potter, and also that they can go back and reread or buy for the first time a book about Peter. Peter's blue jacket, as early as the year of *Peter Rabbit's* publication, had become iconic. Here, however, the icon gets in the way of any coherent theme concerning clothing and its uses by both humans and animals.

Turning to Lucie for a moment, if the shedding of clothes is often a prelude to the shedding of social conventions and the abandonment of innocence for experience (as Scott suggests), then Lucie ought to shed some of her civilized human self (the adult side of her personality) for a childlike expression of self in the book, but she does not. True, she leaves the safety of the farmyard for the adventure and excitement of traveling up the mountainside in search of her missing laundry—but she is in search of icons of adult life and propriety, not of childhood glee and adventure. She is, in fact, a proper little girl, one comfortable taking tea with her hostess and knowing enough not to ask rude questions about the "hairpins" sticking out from underneath Mrs. Tiggy's clothes. The knowledge she gains of the world—that lambs can shed their coats, robins their vests—is knowledge not of herself or her own world, but knowledge of the animal world.

Furthermore, Potter undercuts the knowledge Lucie gains by showing us, in the end, Mrs. Tiggy without her clothing: "And *how* small she had grown—and *how* brown—and covered with PRICKLES! Why! Mrs. Tiggy-Winkle was nothing but a HEDGEHOG" (59, Potter's emphasis). Unlike the other animals, Mrs. Tiggy apparently cannot shed her coat for cleaning, or chooses not to. If the other animals in the tale reveal something of their humanity by giving up their coverings to the laundress, the laundress reveals her animal nature by shedding human clothes for her prickly natural self. Potter goes on, in a parenthetical closing paragraph, to tell us that some people think Lucie was dreaming, Alice-like, but if that were the case Lucie would not have found her clean clothes. Furthermore, the narrator claims to be personally acquainted with Mrs. Tiggy.

What are we to make of this? Here is Potter attempting to expand her artistic horizons, but once she has launched herself into new territory she seems unsure how to navigate. The authorial intrusion in that last paragraph is not typical of Potter at her best. She has certainly intruded before (at the end of *The Tailor of Gloucester* and *Squirrel Nutkin*, for example) but generally in a sentence or an aside, not in an entire paragraph that serves as the epilogue of the book. She seems uncertain of her own fantasy here, unsure that it is believable. The same kind of uncertainty shows up in the weak narrative line. *Mrs. Tiggy* is analogous to the comedy sketch that should have stayed at joke length, but is unwisely stretched into ten minutes of tepid comedy. The idea of the animals shedding their clothing to be laundered is full of possibilities for amusing illustrations—the most amusing perhaps being those limp yellow stockings of Henny Penny—but there is no strong, forward-moving narrative line to grasp the reader's attention. McDonald is right: the story is held together by Mrs. Tiggy herself, both by her comic language and the endearing illustrations of her at work.

Potter was unsure about much in her life at the time she finished work on *Mrs. Tiggy-Winkle*: marriage to Norman was a dream unfulfilled; she had made a bold move in purchasing her own property far from London and now had to figure out how to manage both it and her disapproving parents; she had lost her strongest editorial guide. *Mrs. Tiggy-Winkle* is the result of these uncertainties. It is not a bad book, which Potter is largely incapable of producing, but it was not entirely successful in what it set out to achieve. She is more successful with her next book, *The Pie and the Patty-Pan*, yet another domestic novel, which also gives us Potter working with new material, making changes in her approach, and proceeding with much more confidence.

The Tale of the Pie and the Patty-Pan[11] is the first of the Sawrey books to have a recognizable village setting, and in it Potter has reconciled both her ambiguities regarding domesticity and her uncertainties about tackling new subject matter and new artistic challenges. There are two immediately obvious differences in this text from Potter's previous books. First, her protagonists are for the first time domestic animals, a dog and a cat. She wrote about wild animals again, but for the first time seems comfortable addressing the lives of domestic animals. Second, this is the first of her novels to intersperse small black-and-white sketches with full-color illustrations, a technique she will use again in other of the Sawrey books (*Ginger and Pickles* and *The Roly-Poly Pudding*) and to great effect in *The Tale of Mr. Tod*. There is also a further difference, less obvious to the contemporary reader of the tale: *The Pie and the Patty-Pan* was originally printed in a larger-format size (177 mm by 138 mm) than the earlier books, thus giving Potter more room for the illustrations, room she took advantage of.

Thematically there are some new things in the book as well. Once again we have a domestic novel, but this time we have some bourgeois domestic animals with social aspirations, aspirations that land both animals in some pie-deep trouble. The social comedy that existed in *The Tale of Two Bad Mice* is back, but this time with less irony, more amusement, and a kind of lovingness toward the absurdities of village life. Just one year after the publication of *The Pie and the Patty-Pan*, Potter writes to Millie Warne, Norman's sister, that in Sawrey, "I hear that Jo Taylor is having a furious quarrel with somebody else, . . . There are several rows going on! but I am not in any of them at present—though much inclined!" (*Letters*, 146) and a few years later she comments that "the little town seems nothing but gossip and cards" (224). One can sense, in *The Pie and the Patty-Pan*, Potter's delight at finding herself part of a village community, with all of its exasperations; her pleasure in learning the social rules of village life and of having at last a place she could call a home of her own.

Our protagonists are a tabby-cat called Ribby (alias Mrs. Ribston) and her friend Duchess, a black Pomeranian. The two animals appear faintly ridiculous from the start. Here they are, living cheek by furry jowl in a small village, following the complex social rituals of a class (and largely an urban class) entirely unsuited to a small village community. In this tiny village where one cannot leave one's home without literally bumping into one's neighbor in the street, Ribby composes a careful letter of invitation to tea, to be delivered by the postman. Ribby is willing to pay postage to deliver a letter to a home mere doors away from her own for the sake of appearing formal and proper. Ribby may have reason to be anxious about the social niceties because she is inviting someone named "Duchess" to tea, and Duchess is not just any dog, but a pure-bred Pomeranian. Ribby herself is an ordinary domestic house cat—not a Persian or a Siamese or some other representative of the higher echelon of the cat kingdom. There is from the beginning of the story a subtle kind of class rivalry, which is comic because when we come right down to it, both of the animals are *domestic* animals, pets, and in the real world at any rate they are subject to the whims of human owners. They are both, in a sense, of a lower social order within the human world.

The two animals lack the independence of wild animals in the early Potter books. Potter is aware that there are constraints upon the independence of her wild animal characters because in her woods and fields and urban homes wild animals live side by side with humans, and the interaction between the two is not always positive: Mr. McGregor battles against Peter and his cousins; the humans in *Two Bad Mice* want to destroy the mouse characters. Once Potter decides to write about domestic as opposed to wild animals, however, she opens up an entirely new level of social satire for herself. Once we are squarely in the domestic world—there are only minor appearances by wild animals in *The Pie and the Patty-Pan*—Potter can have enormous fun with human foibles, embodied in the dog and the cat protagonists of the book. Even the fact that she has chosen the prototypical animal kingdom foes—dog and cat—clues the reader in that all will not be well beneath the polite social surface of the book.

The slightly different social status of Ribby and Duchess—and slight differences loom large in small villages—can be seen both through the details in the illustrations and through the culinary details Potter presents the reader. Ribby is shown in a small black-and-white illustration writing her invitation, and we see Duchess reading it in a full-color garden. What we can see of Ribby's house in the first illustration suggests that she is comfortable but not living in anything like the splendor of the dolls in the dollhouse of *Two Bad Mice*. She appears to be writing at her kitchen table, not at a special desk or in a study. She has decorated the room with a row of potted geraniums and we can just make out the interior wall, which appears to be unplastered stone. This is a comfortable interior with a comfortable mistress who has the leisure time to write tea invitations with a feathered quill pen. The other interior views of Mrs. Ribby's house further emphasize the comfort, but not elegance, of her abode. She has a big country kitchen fireplace, but also a double-oven coal or wood-burning stove, a family portrait of a cat on the wall, and a "fur" hearth rug in the form of a lambskin throw. There is solid country comfort in Mrs. Ribby's house, but not much elegance.

We do not get as complete a view of the interior of Duchess' house, but we are treated to a black-and-white sketch of her brushing her "beautiful black coat" in front of a vanity mirror. The details in the sketch suggest that Duchess is of a slightly higher social status than Ribby, or at least has pretensions of belonging to such a class. She has space devoted in her house to the pursuit of beauty. Her dresser has a ruffled skirt and a vanity mirror (aptly named) that tilts for a better view. She has a comb and a brush—plain-backed and not silver—but also a small jar of what is probably meant to be a cosmetic cream of some sort. Duchess certainly is vain, particularly of her shiny black coat, which she chooses not to hide beneath human clothing, adorning herself only with a blue ribbon. That Duchess remains unclothed does not suggest her inferior social status, but rather her superior status. She need not depend on the outer trappings of garments to show her (literally) better breeding: she is who she is by virtue of birth, not by virtue of her earned wealth or status. Potter gives a further sly reminder of Duchess' better breeding by giving her a blue ribbon: Duchess, after all, is a blue-blooded dog, or top dog, if you will.

For Potter, of course, social status is both problematic and the source of much fun. Potter was no fan of social pretension nor of the simply decorative. The Pomeranian Duchess is both pretentious and decorative. She is not a working dog (like Kep in *Jemima Puddleduck*), nor even a spaniel who at least was bred to work, even if it no longer does. She is entirely decorative, with no purpose beyond that of providing a pleasing appearance and pleasant company. Her decorative and nonutilitarian nature is further emphasized by Potter's use of domestic garden flowers to set off Duchess' black coat and by Duchess's complete failure at doing the one job she has set herself, which is to replace the mouse pie with her own ham-and-veal pie. But whereas pretension and uselessness came in for sharp attack in *Two Bad Mice*, here the criticism is downplayed and amusement at the foibles of two silly and social animals is in the forefront.

The lovely color illustrations for this book further underline Potter's humorous take on social pretension. When Duchess receives the invitation to tea she is in such a hurry to open and peruse it that she apparently has been waiting at the gate for the postman (who can be seen in the background continuing on his rounds), and she rips open the invitation immediately, leaving the rest of her post on the garden path. She is so intent on the contents of the invitation that she has failed to close the garden gate. On the village street beyond the fence we can see not only the postman, but another tradesman on his rounds, and two children at play. Clearly the rest of the world is an active and busy place, but we see Duchess at full stop and full attention, greedily reading an invitation to a formal tea party for two to be given by someone she no doubt sees on a daily basis. Potter frames the dog in a glorious profusion of cottage flowers, not in a kitchen garden, despite the culinary focus of the story. Each of the full-color illustrations devoted entirely to Duchess, illustrations that were larger than any previous Potter illustrations, shows her completely framed in decorative flowers, and when we see her leaving her front door on her way out with the ham-and-veal pie we can see that her door has a fancy fanlight, cornice, and pilasters—hardly an ordinary cottage door— and that her front garden, the one the neighbors are most likely to see, is filled with Turk's Bells, a nonnative lily, rather than the common English flowers that predominate in the back garden. Duchess clearly cares about appearances, both her own and her house's.

The invitation and the reply to it receive a great deal of attention from Potter. Ribby tries hard to strike the right social tone in her note, referring to her friend as "my dear Duchess" and promising something tasty to eat at tea, which Duchess shall have all to herself. But Ribby's attempts at social propriety are somewhat undercut by her boast of having a pie dish with a "pink rim" and her statement that she herself will be content to eat muffins, a statement that rings suspiciously of false modesty. Hostesses, of course, should always make sure guests have the tastiest morsels, but they should not draw attention to the fact that they are doing so.

Duchess's reply is equally polite, stating that she will come "with much pleasure at a quarter past four," promising to be punctual, and ending with a comment about the promised delicious food: "I hope it isn't mouse?" (12). Like Ribby, Duchess knows the formula for polite social correspondence but has a hard time sticking to it. If hostesses should not draw attention to their self-sacrificing ways, guests should not demand certain foods from their hostesses or complain about what it is they are served. Duchess thinks better of her closing line, scratches it out, and changes it to "I hope it will be fine" (14), which is an improvement but not much of one: "I'm certain it will be fine" would be more polite. Duchess is quite worried about having to eat mouse pie, knowing she will have to eat it "because it is a party" (14) and one does not refuse food from one's host. She therefore concocts a plan to replace the dreaded mouse pie with her own ham-and-veal pie when Ribby is out buying muffins. The worries about food are further made comic when the reader realizes that the supposedly genteel fare to be served is actually hearty country-fare of muffins and pie, not the tea cake and cucumber sandwiches someone of the urban upper classes or even the landed gentry might serve.

Ribby and Duchess are not the only village inhabitants with firm ideas concerning social propriety. When Ribby goes out to buy items for the tea party, she stops at the store run by Cousin Tabitha Twitchit. Potter tells us that the two cats indulge in some "pleasant gossip" (25), but once Ribby has left, Tabitha is "disdainful afterwards in conversation—'A little *dog* indeed! Just as if there were no CATS in Sawrey!'" (25). The gossip has turned less pleasant, and Tabitha cloaks her displeasure and jealousy at not being invited to the party herself by disparaging the entire class of dogs, not merely Duchess. By the end of the story, when Ribby is running through the village to find the doctor for the ailing Duchess, Tabitha Twitchit says, satisfied with her social acumen and with the disastrous end to a party to which she has not been invited, "I *knew* they would over-eat themselves!" (50). And of course the entire village is also entertained by the outcome of the tea party, as social pretension is overturned by animal appetite and a confusion of pies.

There are further hints, before the party begins in earnest, that the surface of social propriety and pretension may hide other less proper attitudes and actions. Ribby worries that Duchess may choke if the bones are not removed from the mouse pie, "because Duchess did nearly choke herself with a fish-bone last time I gave a party. She eats a little fast—rather big mouthfuls" (18). There are two items of interest here. First, Ribby is obviously the sort of hostess who thinks more of her own comforts than those of her guests. She chooses to serve the dog Duchess fish and mouse, items traditionally on the cat menu, not the dog menu.

Furthermore, even though Duchess has poor table manners (manners that, amusingly, are true of dogs in general), she is "a most genteel and elegant little dog; infinitely superior company to Cousin Tabitha Twitchit" (18). The word "superior" here is used ironically. Potter means the reader to understand that "superior" means both "preferable to" and "higher in status." Duchess is both, and she is preferable because she is higher in status. She has been invited not because Ribby enjoys her company, but because she wants to make a social statement and perhaps even wants to annoy her cousin Tabitha Twitchit.

But Ribby may not be quite as genteel as she pretends to be, despite the lilac silk gown she dons for the party. Once she has left the house for the shops, Duchess lets herself in to replace the mouse pie with the ham-and-veal pie. She has difficulty discovering where Ribby has put her mouse pie, however, not realizing that Ribby has a double oven. Duchess's pie goes into the top oven, and she searches the house for the detested mouse pie: "I have looked all over the house. . . . I cannot think what she has done with it" (28). Potter treats us to a full-color illustration of Duchess on the hunt for the pie. This is the only portrait of Duchess not framed by flowers, but Potter compensates by showing us Duchess lifting herself up higher by standing on flower-patterned pillows with a trail of potted ivy and geranium in the background. Ribby does not have the profusion of purely decorative flowers that the superior Duchess has. What is more interesting is where Duchess has chosen to look. She stands on her hind legs in front of a cupboard that apparently is kept locked, because we can see the key in the keyhole. Inside the cupboard we can see some china on the bottom shelf—but on the top shelf is a row of bottles that look suspiciously like wine and cordial bottles. No wonder Ribby keeps the cupboard locked; it contains unladylike evidence of alcohol in the house. Duchess herself is not as genteel and well-bred as we are initially led to believe because she has let herself into a neighbor's house unasked and has searched through private property in order to avoid eating mouse-pie.

Thirty-two of the novel's sixty pages go by before the comic tea party actually gets underway, thirty-two pages where Potter sets up her joke as elaborately and comically as any director of a screwball comedy. Duchess has "run" through the village streets in her eagerness to get to the party and thus has to "wait a little while in the lane that leads down to Ribby's house" (32) before she can knock on the door at a quarter past four "to the minute" with "a most genteel little tap-tappity" (33), Duchess inquires (of Ribby herself, as Ribby has no servant), "Is Mrs. Ribston at home?" and presents her hostess with a bouquet of flowers in appreciation of her hospitality.

It takes only a few minutes of conversation, once the tea party is underway, for social pretensions to unravel further. Duchess first says, "Do not talk about food, my dear Ribby," goes on to compliment the tea-cloth, and then says, "Is it done to a turn? Is it still in the oven?" (36). The food she has not wanted to talk about is the mouse-and-bacon pie, but she can't resist bringing up pie a moment later because she is thinking about her own ham-and-veal pie, which she herself has put into Ribby's oven. The animals both collect themselves and Ribby offers tea, asking Duchess "Do you take sugar, my dear Duchess?" to which Duchess responds that yes, she does, "and may I have a lump upon my nose?" (36). Ribby complies, we see a small black-and-white illustration of Duchess on her hind legs with a lump of sugar on her nose, but she soon drops it because she thinks she smells the ham-and-veal pie. This causes Duchess to scramble under the tea table in search of her sugar while Ribby takes the pie out of the oven.

Potter has very neatly distracted Duchess from seeing which pie is coming from the oven while leaving the reader in on the joke and waiting to see if Duchess is going to catch on to it. She also shows how difficult it is for Duchess, at this point, to maintain her dignified ways: her animal appetites assert themselves, and the instant they do she is in trouble. Her impatient desire for ham-and-veal causes her manners to deteriorate, as does her desire for sugar. The closer she gets to food the more doglike she becomes. And her comic foil, the cat, becomes more and more genteel. The two animals struggle for balance in social graces, but if one succeeds, the other fails: each, at differing points in the story, becomes a comic foil for the other, although in the end Duchess—the more pretentious of the two—comes off the worst.

The meal is finally on the table, and the ever-polite Ribby says "I will first cut the pie for you; I am going to have muffin and marmalade," to which Duchess replies, "Do you really prefer muffin? Mind the patty-pan!" (39), warning her of the small implement baked into pies to facilitate cutting of slices. Here is the same kind of polite conversation, undercut by subtle selfishness, that we saw earlier in the story. Ribby draws attention to her self-sacrifice, and Duchess appears to caution Ribby for her own good, but in reality is concerned that she herself will unwittingly be served the patty-pan which she baked into the ham-and-veal pie. The animals share some more polite conversation while they pass the "toothsome" pie and muffins, and while the reader is treated to some of Duchess's interior monologue. She is impressed by how small the pieces in the pie are, not remembering mincing them so fine. She does not yet realize, of course, that she is eating mouse-and-bacon. We also get Ribby's interior thoughts, which run to how quickly Duchess is eating, while she herself "buttered her fifth muffin" (41).

The comedy gets into full swing when Duchess becomes alarmed that she cannot find the patty-pan that she knows she put into her pie, unaware that she has just consumed Ribby's entire mouse-and-bacon pie. The humor again is based both on animal and human behavior. Dogs, notorious for gulping their food, can hardly have time to taste it, and Duchess's' dislike of mouse-and-bacon pie is obviously an irrational prejudice and not based on her actual ability or desire to eat such a pie. On the human level, Duchess is a parody of hypochondriacs and hystericals because she goes into a panic thinking that she has swallowed the patty-pan. Ribby, getting more and more proper, says " 'I disapprove of tin arti-cles in puddings and pies. It is most undesirable—(especially when people swal-low in lumps!)' she added in a lower voice" (44). She has good reason not to like objects in her pies, because her "Great-aunt Squintina . . . died of a thimble in a Christmas plum-pudding" (45). Duchess gets more and more hysterical the more Ribby insists that there is no patty-pan, that she owns only four, and they are all in the cupboard. Duchess sets up a "howl" and exclaims, "I shall die! I shall die! I have swallowed a patty-pan!" (45). The reader knows first that Duchess has not swallowed a patty-pan because she has not eaten her own pie, and second that if Duchess is feeling ill it is because she has wolfed down an entire pie in a very short period of time.

Ribby, ever the good hostess, although quite an exasperated one at this point, says "Shall I run for the doctor," although in the same breath she says "I will just lock up the spoons," suggesting that she doesn't altogether trust Duchess not to steal the silverware. Ribby goes off to find Dr. Maggoty, a magpie who exclaims in conundrums, and as they head back to Ribby's house the doctor "hopped so fast that Ribby had to run. It was most conspicuous. All the village could see that Ribby was fetching the doctor" (50). The social comedy has now spread from the interior of Ribby's house to the village streets, and poor Ribby, who wants only to be considered a proper hostess, finds she is making a spectacle of herself and causing village gossip. Worse, she causes the spurned cousin Tabitha Twitchet to say, "I *knew* they would over-eat themselves" (50). Ribby is becoming the butt of local village gossip, which is the last thing she intended when planning her ele-gant tea party.

Meanwhile, Duchess discovers her own pie is still in the top oven in the kitchen, and realizing she is in an awkward position decides to put it in the back-yard "and say nothing about it" so that she may collect it on her way home (54). When she slips back for her pie she discovers it has been eaten by Dr. Maggoty and three jack-daws, so she runs home "feeling uncommonly silly" (38). When she comes out to wash up after the party, Ribby discovers the smashed pie dish and a patty-pan. She never puts two-and-two together, but says to herself, "Did you ever see the like! so there really was a patty-pan? . . . Next time I want to give a party—I will invite Cousin Tabitha Twitchit!" (60).

The comic resolution of the story puts Duchess firmly in her place and con-vinces Ribby that she is better off with her own kind, and not with pursuing the likes of the socially pretentious Duchess. It is, ironically, Tabitha Twitchit, a working woman in the village, who is the beneficiary of the action of the tea party: she will be asked to the next party. But of course, the social comedy will not be over even then, since Tabitha now feels superior to her cousin Ribby, who had to make a spectacle of herself by chasing after the doctor.

The illustrations in *The Pie and the Patty-Pan* benefit from the larger format of the book, although some of the detail is lost in contemporary printings of the tale, now published in the standard format of 139 mm by 104 mm. Potter can include more detail of gardens and of the village streets and can devote more attention to the backgrounds of her drawings, giving the reader a greater sense of depth and of the busyness of the village, helping to underline the villagers' attention to the activities of neighbors. The garden backgrounds are detailed enough that we can make out the species of flowers: clematis over Ribby's doorway, lupine and pinks and lilies in Duchess's garden. The village appears in only two illustrations, first as background to the color illustration of Duchess opening the invitation and then as setting in a black-and-white sketch of Tabitha Twitchit watching Ribby and Dr. Maggoty run down the street. Both illustrations give the impression of a small busy village filled with curious inhabitants. The color illustration shows us the busy village street at work and at play and the black-and-white sketch shows a number of curious canine and feline inhabitants watching the magpie and Ribby—including Tabitha Twitchit, standing by her doorway knitting as she spies out the village activity.

All three of these books, *The Tale of Two Bad Mice*, *The Tale of Mrs. Tiggy-Winkle*, and *The Tale of the Pie and the Patty-Pan*, show Potter struggling with expanding her horizons as an artist just as her major artistic guide, Norman Warne, disappears from her life. They are all three social comedies of one sort or another. *Mrs. Tiggy-Winkle* may not seem like a social comedy at first glance, but it is a kind of social comedy in reverse. Instead of seeing the pretensions of the animals who wear the clothes Mrs. Tiggy launders, we see the hard work that goes into keeping the animals properly clothed and looking presentable—and are aware, however subliminally, that the animals without their clothes are faintly ridiculous. Potter moves into the realm of social comedy, a realm she will stay in fairly consistently for the rest of her career, at a time when she could afford to laugh publicly at the pretensions of a certain class of people, a class she herself came from but was repudiating as she made her own money, bought her own property, and became a hardworking country woman. In many ways, Potter's entire life can be seen as socially downward, or certainly would have been seen so by her parents. Here she was, a well-off London woman with a well-connected family, moving into the business world, making money from her writing, and ultimately moving into the world of the rural farmer. She wrote several more stories about wild animals, at least one of which (*Jeremy Fisher*) was been in the planning stages while Norman Warne was alive, but even her wild animals became more domesticated. Her concerns, increasingly, were with the lives of country farm animals and village people, just as these became the focus of her own life.

Notes

1. Ruth K. McDonald, *Beatrix Potter* (Boston: Twayne, 1986), 71.
2. Beatrix Potter, *The Tale of Two Bad Mice* (London: Warne, 1904; 1987), 9. Unless otherwise noted, all text references are from the 1987 edition.

3. Judy Taylor, ed., *Beatrix Potter's Letters* (London: Warne, 1989), 93.

4. Judy Taylor, *Beatrix Potter: Artist, Storyteller, and Countrywoman* (London: Warne, 1986), 166.

5. Neville Kirk, *Change, Continuity and Class: Labour in British Society 1850–1920* (Manchester: Manchester University Press, 1998), 193.

6. Donald Read, *England 1868–1914: The Age of Urban Democracy* (London: Longman, 1994), 354.

7. Leslie Linder, ed. *The Journal of Beatrix Potter from 1881 to 1897* (London: Warne, 1966), 125.

8. See Leslie Linder, *The Writings of Beatrix Potter* (London: Warne, 1971) for a helpful discussion of the history of the endpapers. The endpapers currently in use combine the papers first used for *The Tale of the Flopsy Bunnies* and *The Tale of Mrs. Tittlemouse* and include references to eleven of Potter's novels.

9. Beatrix Potter, *The Tale of Mrs. Tiggy-Winkle* (London: Warne, 1905; 1987), 13. Unless otherwise noted, all text references are to the 1987 edition.

10. Carole Scott, "Between Me and the World: Clothes as Mediator between Self and Society in the Work of Beatrix Potter," *Lion and Unicorn* 16 (1992): 192–98.

11. Beatrix Potter, *The Tale of the Pie and the Patty-Pan* (London: Warne, 1905; 1987). Unless otherwise noted, all text references are to the 1987 edition.

4

Dangers and Delights of Domesticity

The Pie and the Patty-Pan was the first of Potter's books to have a Sawrey setting and the first to show her delight in her new home in the Lake District. Three other novels, *The Tale of Tom Kitten* (1907), *The Tale of Samuel Whiskers, or the Roly-Poly Pudding* (1908), and *The Tale of Jemima Puddleduck* (1908) are also set in Sawrey and more specifically at Hill Top, Potter's beloved farm.[1] But in these three novels, as Potter moves both literally and metaphorically into her own domestic space, some of the anxieties of domesticity, some of the dangers of the independent yet domestic life, percolate beneath the surface of the comedies she sets in her own backyard. The Sawrey books, taken together, show Potter at the height of both her narrative and her artistic powers. Her confidence in herself and her work seems to have been fed by the confidence she gained through owning Hill Top and becoming a farmer and is reflected not only in the increasing specificity of the illustrations, the freer use of color, and the openness of the background spaces, but also in her insistence that, like *The Pie and the Patty-Pan*, at least one other of the Sawrey books, *The Roly-Poly Pudding*, should have a larger than usual format. Her drawings were becoming more expansive; they were becoming more numerous in the books that used small black-and-white illustrations alongside the color illustrations; and the greater detail in them (particularly of garden plants and household interiors) demanded a larger page size. Her books were expanding just as her personal horizons were expanding, despite Norman's death.

The Tale of Tom Kitten (1907), like *The Pie and the Patty-Pan*, is a comedy of manners, but a simpler comedy. The level of humor in the latter book is better suited for an older, perhaps even an adult audience, but the humor of *Tom Kitten* is at a child's level, although there is plenty to amuse an adult as well. The narrative line here is simpler: the kittens are dressed up for company and supposed to stay tidy, but fail; they are banished from the adult tea party, and their mother must make excuses for them and avoid embarrassing herself at the same time. There is no complicated double narrative line here, as there is in *The Pie and the Patty-Pan*, although the reader is certainly aware that Tabitha Twitchit is making preparations for the tea party as the kittens romp in the garden. All the reader need know is that preparations are underway, so the illustrations provide no detail. The only actions of the mother cat the reader need see are Tabitha Twitchit's brushing, combing, and dressing her children. The novel's attention is placed squarely on the kittens themselves, who behave as amusingly as all kittens do.

The narrative voice sets up the entire problem in the second sentence of the novel, when we are told the kittens had "dear little fur coats of their own; and they tumbled about the doorstep and played in the dust."[2] Their mother refuses to see her kittens as they really are, refuses to see that they are properly clothed already and that their natural behavior is to play in dust and get themselves dirty. Real cats, after all, know how to clean themselves. Even if these are kittens and still need to be washed by their mother, it is natural for them to tumble and play and not mind the dirt and dust and cobwebs they are likely to encounter in their adventures. These kittens are also tumbling about the "doorstep," and the illustration shows them more out of the house than in it, indicating the kittens' restlessness with domestic life within the house.

Tabitha Twitchit, on the other hand, is committed not only to domesticity but to absurd formalities and unrealistic expectations of what domestic life should be. Potter devotes six illustrations to the mother cat collecting, washing, brushing, combing, and dressing the reluctant kittens, all the while dressed up for the tea party in a lilac gown that looks suspiciously like the one her cousin Ribby wore while serving tea to Duchess. She ought to wear a common housedress while engaged in making her energetic children presentable for company, but apparently feels a need for formality even while performing domestic chores.

All of the kittens are resistant: Moppet struggles against her mother's washcloth; Moppet and Tom tease their sister and try to engage her in play while she is being brushed; and Tom, "very naughty," goes so far as to scratch when his mother attempts to comb his tail and whiskers, two very sensitive parts of a cat's anatomy. Tom's resistance continues in the next illustration, while his mother takes "all sorts of elegant uncomfortable clothes out of a chest of drawers" in order to dress him up (18). Tom is on all fours, his back half-arched and his tail down, in a typically resistant cat posture. Poor Tom is about to be literally sewn into his clothes, the buttons having burst over his growing body. Like his predecessor Peter, he is the only child character with a human name, and like Peter he is stuffed uncomfortably into suffocating clothing.

The kittens are finally "unwisely" turned out into the garden by their mother, who wants them out of the way while she makes hot buttered toast for the party. Her last words to the kittens are an admonition to keep their clothes clean, to stay on their hind legs, and to keep away from four specific dangers of dirt—an impossible set of commands for the kittens to follow because each and every one of them violates kitten nature: kittens do not belong in clothes and cannot keep them clean; kittens cannot walk on their hind legs; kittens are naturally curious and drawn to things like hens and ducks and pigsties. The illustration of Tabitha Twitchit in the doorway emphasizes, in Potter's ironic way, both her sternness as a parent and the essential wrongness of her actions. We see her threaten her children with a toasting fork, a gesture underlining her authority, but the fork bears some resemblance to the trident held by the traditional figure of the devil, suggesting that the cat's approach to discipline is not entirely acceptable.

Ruth McDonald has noted that Tom's sisters can turn their pinafores around to free their legs to go on all fours, and have an easier time of climbing the garden wall. Tom, however, is dressed in clothes that make him look "like a cross between Little Lord Fauntleroy and Tom Sawyer on his way to church."[3] The fussiness of Tom's clothes is important not just to the comedy of the tale but to what Potter is suggesting about domesticity, and particularly domesticity for boys. Indeed Tom does look something like Fauntleroy. There is a frill around his collar and he wears a very feminine straw garden hat—not a boater or a more masculine cap, but a wide, soft-brimmed straw hat bedecked with a blue ribbon to match his suit. Tabitha Twitchit, not unlike many turn-of-the-century mothers, is making an attempt to feminize her son, to make him both look more feminine through his clothing and to force him into more restricted behavior by putting him into restrictive clothing—the way girls were expected to wear restrictive clothing that limited their movements. Tabitha Twitchit not only wants her kittens to behave in ridiculously inappropriate human ways, but she wants them to behave like adult humans, and more specifically adult female humans. In other words, she wants her children—including the male Tom, whose very name indicates his masculine sex—to be just like her, an overly proper adult cat who imitates human social behaviors.

Tabitha Twitchit, comic though she is, is also a kind of demon-mother figure, waving that toasting fork at her children. All of her actions are meant to restrict her children: she holds them still while she brushes them, she buttons them into too-tight clothes, she wants to restrict them to adult behaviors, she tries to restrict their garden adventures to specific areas. Although this is the first book in which Potter uses the interior of her own Hill Top as the model for the cats' house, she does not lavish the kind of loving attention on the interior as she does in its sequel, *The Roly-Poly Pudding*. Of the five illustrations showing Tabitha Twitchit cleaning her kittens, only two show any detail of the interior of the house, and our view is restricted to a single room. We have one brief glimpse of the stairwell as the mother cat takes her offspring upstairs for cleaning, and the only other interiors of the house are the doorway scene where Tabitha Twitchit welcomes her guest and two views of the bedroom where the kittens are banished, and which they put into complete disarray. The majority of the book takes place out of doors, in the garden and the farmyard, and we can often see glimpses of the Cumbrian hills and open sky in the background.

The yearning in this book is for freedom from domesticity, or more specifically for freedom from the absurd conventions of domesticity and proper society, conventions that were largely upheld (if not invented by) women, and conventions with which Potter is impatient. When Tabitha Twitchit discovers her disheveled children "on the wall with no clothes on" (46), Potter not only comments on Victorian prudishness about the body but also underscores Tabitha Twitchit's unwillingness to see her kittens for what they are—kittens who really are clothed, as that second sentence about their "dear little fur coats" has already told us. The mother cat is, quite literally, blinded by social convention to see what is not present (nudity) and not to see what is present (fully natural and perfectly acceptable kittens). She is so distraught by the kittens that she "smack[s]" them and tells them "you are not fit to be seen; I am affronted" (49). Tabitha Twitchit takes personally the behavior of her kittens, as if they had purposefully plotted to embarrass their mother and disrupt her tea party.

Tabitha Twitchit realistically portrays the behavior and feelings of some parents, who do indeed take as a personal affront various behaviors of their children, much of which has to do with the way children (particularly adolescents) choose to clothe themselves. She is also so clearly out of line with reality and concerned with social propriety that Potter uses her to criticize what she had always despised: false fronts, false courtesy, and speech that was less than plain. Her critique continues once Tabitha Twitchit welcomes her guests, to whom she tells a "polite" social lie of which the narrator clearly does not approve: "I am sorry to say she told her friends that they were in bed with the measles; which was not true" (50). And of course the friends must politely go along with the lie, despite the "very extraordinary noises over-head, which disturbed the dignity and repose of the tea party" (53).

All of the words Potter associates with Tabitha Twitchit—the "fine company" (10) she expects; the "elegant" (18) clothes she provides for her children; the way she is "affronted" (49) by their nudity; the "dignity and repose" (53) of the tea party, speak to her formality, her stiffness, her falseness to her own cat nature. The words associated with the kittens—their "dear" fur coats (9), the way they "skip and jump" (26) up the garden wall, the way Tom "break[s] the ferns" in his struggle to join his sisters—speak to the essential and natural expression of their cat natures. More significantly, we learn what the kittens are all about—not through their words but through their actions: it is the two wonderful illustrations of the romping kittens at the end of the story that tell us how destructive they are, not the words used to describe that destruction. Their mother, on the other hand, like all social and artificial creatures, is defined by her words (often false or falsely polite) and to a lesser extent by her elegant outfit.

The two final illustrations also provide sharp commentary on the nature of both domesticity and gender. In the first of the two illustrations we see what is clearly Tabitha Twitchit's proper and feminine bedroom. There is a chaste single bed with white covers, but it is made fancy and feminine by deep pink bed-hangings. Laid out on the bed before the kittens arrive, are a dressing gown and some other items of clothing, now lying in a heap on the floor. They are in a heap because the kittens, all of them, are busy romping destructively. One kitten is crouched on top of the canopy, making it sag alarmingly; another is clawing the canopy curtain from behind; and Tom is trying on mother's blue bonnet.

They are, in fact, destroying emblems of both domesticity and femininity. Bedrooms and kitchens are the two most feminine rooms in most houses, and Potter emphasizes the femininity of this bedroom by having the deep pink of the canopy dominate the illustration and by showing the heap of feminine clothes the kittens have knocked to the floor. All of the kittens—girl kittens and Tom alike—are engaged in destroying their mother's feminine bedroom, just as they threaten to destroy the feminine domestic ritual of the tea party downstairs. Indeed, if Potter has shown attempts at feminizing Tom earlier in the novel, she now shows that Tom has successfully evaded those attempts and further has infected his sisters with masculine qualities of energy and action. Their activities are a triumph of masculine behavior, which overturns their mother's excessive, formal, and pretentious domesticity and femininity.

By the time Tabitha Twitchit comes upstairs to discover the source of the noises, the room is in even greater disarray. One of the bed-hangings has been pulled from its rod; the bed is completely unmade and the pillow has nearly vanished beneath the bed; there is a larger pile of clothing on the floor; the slippers have moved nearly 180 degrees. Two of the kittens hide beneath the bed coverings but Tom remains in the open, trying to look innocent beneath his mother's blue bonnet. That bonnet, in fact, is being worn in a rather defiant fashion. Tom has, after all, shed the clothing his mother insisted he wear, clothing that tries to feminize him. Here he voluntarily dons a feminine garment, but the key word is *voluntarily*. He puts on the bonnet to mock femininity, not to imitate it. Appropriating the bonnet as he destroys his mother's bedroom, Tom is appropriating not femininity but maternal power, and mocks his startled and disapproving mother at the door with the extent of the destruction he and his sisters have caused. They have not only destroyed the bedroom and its marks of femininity, but have also destroyed the "dignity and repose" of the tea party, of the very polite gathering of female adult cats downstairs. The destruction upstairs suggests not only the destruction of some of the conventions of domestic life, but also the superiority of energy and activity over the quiet and passivity of the female tea party. The kittens in the bedroom, quite literally, are superior and above the female cats below.

Potter herself was not a feminist in any recognizable way, although she defied traditional gender behavior and was aware of the prejudice she would face in certain spheres if her gender were known. She was a woman who brooked no nonsense and was more often to be found tramping the fields or working in the pig sty than she was doing domestic chores or making social visits. One Sawrey acquaintance told of how Potter described a meeting with a tramp on the road, who said to her," 'It's gay weather for the likes of thee and me, missus,' and she roared and laughed as she told us about it. But if you had seen her; she had a pair of old Wellingtons on, a mackintosh too big for her, and a sort of soft, floppy hat. She was like someone on the run."[4] Potter also knew her letters to the editor would be taken more seriously if she signed herself "H. B. Heelis," disguising both her gender and her celebrity. She had no patience for ridiculous social rituals with little purpose beyond passing the time and sorting out the social hierarchies. Her idea of a good time, at least after she married William Heelis, was to spend the day hiking around the sheep fields and in the evening going to watch the villagers do country dancing—an energetic social activity that had purpose, unlike tea parties. For Potter the confining aspects of her life were connected with the constrictive behavior not only of her own mother, but also of most of the women of her time and class. Although she did not find it easy to defy these conventions in life, her books show her skewering them with great glee.

Potter's glee in defying convention is demonstrated by the way she finally disposes of the kittens's clothing. The comic and sly ducks (including Jemima Puddle-Duck, soon to have her own book) appear beneath the garden wall and pick up the girls' clothing and put it on themselves. The kittens fall off the wall laughing, and ask Mr. Drake Puddle-Duck to help them button Tom into his clothes. The duck advances in a "slow sideways manner" (41) and puts the clothes on himself, rather than on Tom, making himself look ridiculous. The ducks abscond with the clothes, but when they go into a pond (as ducks will), the clothes "all came off directly, because there were no buttons" (56). This is Potter's final comment on the uselessness of party clothes: they are inappropriate for everyone because they are not "natural." Not only do the clothes impede the natural activities of the kittens, they make ducks look ridiculous and, when put into the natural environment of the pond, disappear completely, sinking to the bottom never to be seen again. Nature, both duck nature and cat nature, triumphs in the end of this small story.

The sequel to Tom Kitten's story is the darker *Roly-Poly Pudding* (1908), another tale of the dangers of domestic life and one in which Tom is in greater danger than he was in his first story—this time the danger is brought on largely by his own activities. He gets into difficulties because his mother, who wants to do her baking in peace, tries to lock Tom and his sisters in the cupboard while she goes about her business, once again trying to confine them in domestic spaces. Tom cannot be found, and although Moppet and Mittens are put in the cupboard, they manage to escape and hide in a flour barrel and a jar. Tom looks for a hiding place and finds "a nice convenient place" (36) in the kitchen chimney.

The complications of the tale begin early on. Once again, Tom wants to avoid the claustrophobia of domesticity. His mother's idea of control this time is to lock him in a cupboard, rather than to lock him into his clothes. (He is the only kitten wearing a jacket, but it is unbuttoned and much too small—he bursts out of its domestic confines just as he did in the earlier story). Tom wants nothing to do with the cupboard, nor does he want anything to do with baking, which is as conventional a symbol of domesticity as one could want. Yet the route of Tom's escape is, ironically, an even stronger emblem of domesticity: the kitchen fireplace, the hearth and chimney that traditionally signify home. By trying to escape the domestic world of his mother, Tom vanishes into a literally darker domestic world, both in the vast chimney of the fireplace and in the nightmare domestic world inhabited by the rats, who have plans to turn Tom into a roly-poly pudding for dinner. If the rats have their way Tom will literally be consumed by domesticity: he will be turned into the baked goods he originally was trying to flee.

In *The Roly-Poly Pudding* Potter returns to and expands the double-narrative line she first explored in *The Tailor of Gloucester* and later in *The Pie and the Patty-Pan*, and also returns to the idea of a secret life within the walls of a house, a theme that first appeared in *Tailor* and is further explored in *The Tale of Two Bad Mice*. She also returns to the alternation of color and black-and-white illustrations, a method she first used in *The Pie and the Patty-Pan* and generally a sign of a more complex narrative line in the later novels. In *The Roly-Poly Pudding* the double narrative reaches its most complex and effective form. The entire tale turns on the double-sided nature of domesticity, both its delights and its dangers. Potter shows us the literal double-edged nature of domesticity by showing us what exists both within and behind the walls of the house, in the mirror images of Tabitha's baking and the rats' plans for baking. There is also the double-nature of animal life existing side by side with human life, shown both by Potter's brief appearance in the action of the novel itself and by Farmer Potatoes's appearance in the story. There is the double nature of the house itself, whose walls both surround cat life and contain rat life. There is, indeed, layer upon layer of domesticity in this novel, ranging down to the spider inhabiting the attic who critically contemplates the knots confining Tom. Potter suggests that domestic life is richer and more complex than we might have imagined, and that it can be dark and yet cozy at the same time.

Potter emphasizes the dual nature of domesticity by combining black-and-white and color illustrations. She does not reserve the black-and-white illustrations for the darker tale of the rats, but instead gives nearly equal time to both cats and rats in both the color and the black-and-white illustrations: there are five color illustrations (including the frontispiece) of the adult cats by themselves; four of the adult rats by themselves; three of Tom by himself; and three of Tom and the rats together. Adult cats, kittens, rats, and John Joiner the carpenter receive about the same attention in the small black-and-white illustrations, and at the end of Tom's adventure we see adults, kittens, and carpenter together in the kitchen as Tom is being washed clean of butter. Humans also occupy two of the full-color illustrations. There is a small drawing of Potter herself observing the rats stealing her wheelbarrow (which we know was made for her by the dog-carpenter John Joiner), and a large drawing of Farmer Potatoes in his barn, frustrated by the presence of rats. The duality of domesticity exists on both animal and human levels and those levels are shown as interacting in both positive and negative ways in the novel.

Mrs. Tabitha Twitchit does not seem to have fared well with her kittens since *The Tale of Tom Kitten*. Having learned that sending them into the garden to behave will only lead to trouble, she now attempts to shut them into a cupboard but neglects to lock the door, allowing the kittens to escape. Tom, who caused so much trouble in the first novel, has learned to avoid his mother before she has a chance to confine him in either clothes or cupboards, and Tabitha must spend the first part of the novel going "up and down all over the house, mewing for Tom Kitten"[5] with no success. Furthermore, her active kittens seem to have increased her general level of anxiety. She becomes "more and more distracted" (14) when she cannot find her son; she is crying when she answers the door to Mrs. Ribby and says to her, "What a thing it is to have an unruly family!" (20). Tabitha says "tearfully" that her house is "infested with rats" and that "The rats get upon my nerves, Cousin Ribby" (25). It is not Tabitha but the practical Mrs. Ribby, whose nerves have not been shattered by an "unruly family," who has the useful suggestion of calling in John Joiner when they hear the ominous roly-poly sounds from beneath the attic floor. Domesticity, first in the form of elegant tea parties and then in the form of the difficulties of baking and parenting, have made Tabitha into a nervous and ineffectual cat.

Tom will also end up nervous and ineffectual by the end of the story, done in by the dark domesticity behind the walls of the house, although as we shall see the ending of the tale is more complicated than it appears on first reading. Tom's first mistake is to try to escape domesticity by using an emblem of domesticity as his escape route, only to find the chimney is more confining than the house and the rats more confining than anything he could have imagined in his worst nightmares. Tom is first presented as being quite a clever cat, "balancing himself upon the iron bar where the kettle hangs" (38) when he first leaps into a chimney that is "wide enough inside for a man to stand up and walk about" (36), and then landing "on a ledge high up inside the chimney" (39) before he begins his explorations through flues that increasingly narrow and constrict. But the reader knows already he is not as clever as he seems, because he has gone up the chimney just after the fire has been laid, and smoke begins to rise. "Tom Kitten coughed and choked with the smoke. . . . He made up his mind to climb right to the top, and get out on the slates, and try to catch sparrows" (41). He is in literal danger of suffocating, a more serious state of affairs than the more metaphoric suffocation he suffered in his party clothes in the first novel. In the first novel he escapes domestic confinement by venturing into the garden; here he also looks to the out-of-doors for freedom. He wants to escape suffocation by climbing up to the roof, to fresh air, freedom, and the chance to practice his predatory skills upon the sparrows.

Poor Tom never reaches the roof, but Potter provides us with a lovely illustration of the view from the roof, where we can see flowering fruit trees, the roofs of farm buildings, and the lane twisting away through the countryside to the hills and blue sky beyond. Potter is showing us the joys of the outside world, the freedom of the open lane, the glories of fresh air and springtime, all of which Tom longs for but cannot reach, trapped as he is first in the chimney and then in twine and dough. It is as if the author is providing us with a visual image of Tom's fantasy of the unattainable joys of life outside the house. Tom's nightmare journey through the chimney and behind the walls is made more nightmarish by its juxtaposition with the airy illustration of life outside.

Tom is concerned that he cannot go back down the chimney, even though he is beginning to wish to as his journey becomes more difficult and dangerous. He worries that if he slips "I might fall in the fire and singe my beautiful tail and my little blue jacket" (41). These are significant worries on Tom's part. He worries that his adventure is beginning to threaten both his natural kitten self, symbolized by his tail, and also his more domesticated self, symbolized by the blue jacket (a jacket similar to Peter's iconic blue jacket). In other words, the totality of Tom's self is threatened by the position he has put himself in and will be threatened further as soon as he falls into the rats' lair, where he loses his jacket altogether and his tail nearly vanishes beneath the stolen dough.

Before showing us Tom in the paws of the rats, however, Potter builds suspense about the kitten's fate in several ways. She has already shown us the rats stealing dough from the kitchen, so that we know who the villains are and what they are up to. She then shows us Tom in two small black-and-white drawings that emphasize the claustrophobia of his journey through increasingly dark and narrow spaces. When the illustrations open up to a full-color picture of Tom we are not much relieved because Tom is shown having discovered some rather large and gnawed-upon mutton bones, which he finds "funny" as he notices a strong smell "something like mouse; only it is dreadfully strong" (44). Tom finally escapes the chimney when he falls through a hole, but he has fallen into mortal danger. He lands in the rats' territory, in "a place that he had never seen before, although he had lived all his life in the house" (49).

Potter's sentence here is significant. Tom should know the nature of the house he has inhabited all his life—after all, how complicated can the house be? Yet the house holds secrets, as all houses hold secrets. We have seen Potter play with this idea before, first in the tailor's house, which contains a secret world of mice who are at war with Simpkin the cat; then in the tale of Tom Thumb and Hunca Munca, who lead a secret life behind the wainscoting in the nursery and who invade the nursery to plunder the dollhouse for their own ends. Yet in *The Tailor of Gloucester* most of the secret activity happens not in the tailor's house, but in his shop. We do not see the secret life of mice living behind the walls of his house, but rather the secret lives of mice living in *other* houses in Gloucester and in the tailor's shop. In *Two Bad Mice* we have views of both the mouse home behind the wainscoting and the dollhouse, which we know exists within the larger confines of a human home. In this novel Potter more clearly shows the secret nature of life behind the walls, but there is still a clear distinction between dollhouse and mouse house. The two are not intertwined, but rather exist side by side. Not until *The Roly-Poly Pudding* do we see the secret and open natures of home and domesticity completely intertwined. In fact it is difficult to tell where one ends and the other begins. The rats literally live within the walls of the house, their house *is* the human house: the boundary is hard to discern.

Potter herself had to keep all kinds of secrets in Bolton Gardens. She lived, for all intents and purposes, a secret life in the third-floor nursery. She kept many of her pets secret from her parents; she crept out at night to collect and hide fungi; she published her first drawings without parental knowledge; she had secret correspondence with Charlie McIntosh about fungi and worked secretly on her scientific paper; she became engaged to Norman Warne before her parents knew what she was up to; she pretended to buy Hill Top as a financial investment, when in truth it was an investment in her own independence. Potter was no stranger to secrets, particularly secrets kept within houses. When she turned to writing her children's books, her own secrets, desires, and fears were transformed into the secrets, desires, and fears of her animal characters. In many ways the illustrated books are a coded version of Potter's interior life.

The question, then, is what secrets, desires, and fears is Potter expressing in *The Roly-Poly Pudding*, a novel written after she established herself as at least a part-time inhabitant of Sawrey—after she made substantial progress in breaking away from Bolton Gardens and the control her parents wielded over her life. We might expect to find Potter less concerned with "coding" her life at this point, but Potter's anxieties about domesticity now shift from Bolton Gardens to Sawrey. Many of the secrets, desires, and fears in the Sawrey books are easy to discern and are linked to Potter's new role as homesteader and farmer. Hill Top was infested with rats, who led a secret life behind the four-foot thick walls of the house. Potter's desire was to rid herself of these rats, although at first she was reluctant to kill them, having had pet rats as a child. Her fears, no doubt, were at least partially the fears of every new homeowner: that she won't be up to the task, that the house she has bought has secret and dangerous flaws, that it won't turn out to be the perfect house of her dreams.

But other secrets and fears are hidden in the text, just as the lives of the rats are hidden behind the walls of the house. Potter had indeed taken an important step in independence by buying Hill Top and by spending increasing amounts of time in Sawrey rather than in London. This cannot have been easy for her, and in fact must have been somewhat terrifying. Potter had always been shy and had always had difficulty dealing with strangers, and here she was, embarking on a real estate deal that involved working with an attorney she did not (at first) know; hiring farmhands and caretakers for her new property and learning to manage it, in part, from a distance; and having to work herself into the fabric of village life. She had desired a home of her own for years, yet the process of obtaining it had its difficulties and must have provided many anxious moments and periods of doubt. It is at this point in her life that one most acutely misses the journal, which ended in 1897.

One must piece together her thoughts about her new life from comments in her letters. Hill Top held many challenges, as she comments to Millie Warne in 1906 when she says that the first thing she did when arriving at Hill Top "was to go through the back kitchen ceiling. I don't think I ran any risk, it went down whole-sale so it was not scratchy to my stockings, and the rafters were too near together to permit my slipping through. The joiner & plasterer were much alarmed & hauled me out. I was very much amused."[6] She also notes that "I thought my property was looking extremely ugly when I arrived I was quite glad you weren't there! . . . I have told the farmer to plant potatos [*sic*] all over [the field] this season, as I don't feel inclined to pay any more wages at present for altering it. It reminds me of the confusion about making colour-blocks one third smaller. The lawn is too big!" (*Letters*, 140). Her comment here is especially telling: she makes a conscious connection between the work she has done in designing books to the work she is has begun in designing a farmstead and its house. The move to Sawrey inspired some of Potter's best work, but it also ultimately leads to her marriage and the abandonment of writing books for children. Even before she becomes engaged to William Heelis, however, her attention is drawn more and more into farming rather than writing.

She writes to Millie Warne in 1907 of her plans for the garden at Sawrey, giving great detail about the "splendid phloxes" that will "look nice between the laurels while the laurels are small" (146), and in an illustrated letter to the young Louie Warne in 1907 can't keep herself from commenting that the pigs have "got rings in their noses to prevent them from digging holes in the field, but at present they are shut up in their little house because the field is so wet. It rains every day—whatever shall we do for hay! There is a little bit cut and it is sopping wet" (152). Even in an illustrated letter to a child friend, Potter can't help veering off into the practicalities of her new life as farmer.

The delights of her house and independence clearly far outweigh her fears. This can be seen in *The Roly-Poly Pudding* both in the attention the illustrations pay to the house's interior—which is Hill Top's interior, down to the furnish-ings—and in the successful banishment of the rats at the end of the tale. The house and the powers of domestic house-and-rat cleaning triumph at the end. This, of course, suggests Potter's own victory over the rats at Hill Top and also her victory over (most) of her fears about the enormity of her venture into inde-pendence. By the end of the book she has claimed a home of her own.

The interiors of the house are lovingly drawn by Potter. Visitors to Hill Top today are invariably struck by the accuracy of the illustrations of *Roly-Poly Pud-ding*. The interiors are drawn to cat scale, not human scale, but beyond that are instantly recognizable. She wrote in 1907, again to Millie, that "Another room has been got straight, the front kitchen—or hall, as I call it. I have not meddled with the fireplace, I don't dislike it, and besides it is wanted for the next book [*The Roly-Poly Pudding*]. I have got a pretty dresser with plates on it & some old fashioned chairs" (155), all of which can still be seen both at Hill Top and in the pages of *The Roly-Poly Pudding*. Potter lavishes a great deal of attention on the interior of the house. We can see the individual plates upon the dresser and the bowl of peonies that graces it; we see the rugs upon the floors and the red curtains on the landing window; the details of curtains and ceilings and furniture in the full view of the kitchen once Tom has been rescued. It is as if Potter has learned her house through drawing it, from all angles and points of view. She once said that she had to draw whatever she saw, and here she can't stop looking at her new home, and hence can't stop drawing it. One learns to truly see if one sketches—and Potter truly sees, and allows the reader to see, her home in this book. Indeed, she opens her home to the viewer, even if she disguises it as a cat's home. To some extent she drops her guard and opens up her "secret" home to the outside world. She can't help herself, she is so in love with it.

Tom, however, is less and less in love with the house the more he tries to escape it. The spaces he is trapped in grow narrower and narrower and "confusing" as "One flue seemed to lead into another" (*Roly-Poly*, 44) and he is forced to "squeeze" through a hole and drag himself "along a most uncomfortably tight passage where there was scarcely any light" (46). As if to emphasize Tom's constraints, Potter abandons Tom behind the wall and shows the reader an interior view of an empty and spacious attic with a tiny asterisk on the baseboard to show where Tom is trapped. And he stays trapped until he falls free of the chimney into a pile of rags that Samuel Whiskers uses as his bed, and the startled rat confronts Tom "chattering his teeth" (49) in an all-too-realistic and aggressive ratlike fashion. Tom hardly has time to enjoy being freed from the flues before he is even more tightly confined by the rats.

Before Tom knows what is happening, Anna Maria rushes up, pulls his coat off, and ties him up "with string in very hard knots" as Samuel Whiskers demands "a kitten dumpling roly-poly pudding for my dinner" (52). The two rats argue about the proper way to cook such a dumpling, sounding like any quarreling married couple, before they race off to steal butter and rolling pin, leaving Tom to squirm and mew for help, but no one hears him. The full-color illustration of Tom tied up in knots is truly piteous. The poor kitten is on his back, vulnerable, with his powerful hind legs tightly tied, and although his mouth is open and we can see his sharp teeth he is totally incapable of either finding help for himself or of using his teeth to cut his bonds. His only company is a spider who critically examines his knots, of which it is a judge "because it had a habit of tying up unfortunate blue-bottles. It did not offer to assist him" (60). The rats, when they return, are comic in a horrifying kind of way. The horror lies in the disconnection between their barbaric desire to wrap up a live kitten in dough and bake it and their very formal and polite speech. Their language has an archaic and polite tone to it, even while they are discussing the edibility of kittens. Samuel Whiskers "inquires," "Will not the string be very indigestible, Anna Maria?" (62), and when the rats hear sounds of John Joiner's saw, Samuel Whiskers says," We are discovered and interrupted, Anna Maria. . . . I fear that we shall be obliged to leave this pudding" (66). The language of the rats, and particularly of the greedy and over-stuffed Samuel Whiskers, is as polite as that of Duchess and Ribby in *The Pie and the Patty-Pan* and serves much the same purpose. In both cases falsely polite and formal language disguises animal appetite and animal behavior. The rats, like Duchess and Ribby and Tabitha Twitchit, speak in euphemisms. They "borrow" objects from the humans when in fact they are stealing.

In all of the Sawrey books up to this time, Potter was concerned with the false surface of social interaction, a surface that lies over the earthier and more complicated true nature of the lives of the animals. Although recognition of the false politeness of much human social interaction had preoccupied Potter since the days of the journal, once she was in Sawrey and more independent of the formalities of London life she tackled the theme more overtly. Life in the village must have sharpened her eye for this. She was living with villagers who had a solid sense of hierarchy and social niceties, who at the same time slaughtered animals, plucked chickens, and lived a mere breath away from the rhythms of life in both woods and pastures. Potter herself increasingly led such a double life, a woman who had money and position, yet at the same time tramped the fields with her hired hands and helped with the sheep and the chickens. She must have had comic moments of polite conversation while inspecting birthing sheep and sick chickens.

For Potter the social niceties are usually connected with women, who in her lifetime were the arbiters of taste and social convention. Thus it is the female characters who come in for the most criticism in her novels, and it is from females and feminine behavior that her male characters wish to flee. They are not fleeing women so much as they are fleeing the propriety and domestic virtues associated with women, which is certainly the case for Tom Kitten in his two stories. Yet the ending of *The Roly-Poly Pudding* is complex, particularly where Tom's fate is concerned. He manages to escape the rats with the help of John Joiner and the anxious adult female cats, but his desire to escape the confines of the house ironically leaves him incapable of ever leaving it. The last we see of Tom is in a small black-and-white drawing, where he is backed into a corner, his tail brushed out in alarm, facing off with a startled-looking mouse, while the text tells us that "Tom Kitten has always been afraid of a rat; he never durst face anything that is bigger than—A Mouse" (81–82). The illustration shows us that even a mouse unnerves Tom. His sisters, on the other hand, "have grown up into very good rat-catchers" (78) who hang "dozens and dozens" (80) of rat tails on the barn door to advertise their skill. The sisters are accorded a full-color illustration at the end, where they are shown out in the farmyard successfully stalking and catching rats.

The ending of the novel is suggestive. Tom is the one who has most earnestly attempted to flee domesticity, who in both books seems determined to escape being feminized by his mother. Yet in the end he is more trapped in the female domestic space of the house than are his sisters. His sisters also want to escape confinement—in the first novel they have burst out of their clothing even before Tom bursts out of his, and here they escape the cupboard in which their mother has confined them with little difficulty. Yet at the same time the sisters in *The Tale of Tom Kitten* uphold femininity; they encourage the ducks to help dress Tom back into his clothes, and in *The Roly-Poly Pudding* they find hiding places in the domestic spaces of flour barrel and dairy pan. When they discover dough they want to use it to make muffins for themselves, to engage in traditional female behavior. But the sisters are the ones who escape confinement to the house, while Tom does not.

Tom's problem is, quite literally, that he is too big for his britches. He wants to leave home far before he has the skills to do so; he suffers from the sin of pride, if you will. In climbing the chimney in this book, in scaling garden walls and taking over the upstairs bedroom in the earlier book, he is quite literally reaching beyond his grasp. His desire to leave domesticity behind is not the problem—all children and small animals wish to leave home, but if one leaves home before one is ready, danger and potential death may be waiting. This is the theme Potter first struck in *Peter Rabbit* (which has an equally contradictory ending) and it continues to surface in many of her books, even once she herself has left home for Sawrey. Tom's sisters know enough to stay at home until they have the rat-catching skills to leave safely, and when they try to escape their mother's ministrations they do not try to escape the house altogether, but instead choose to hide in domestic objects and by so doing are able to see what the rats are up to and to help the adult cats rescue Tom. They are incapable of rescuing their brother by themselves, are terrified of the rats at their age, and know it. But because they know it, they will live to a courageous adulthood and become champion rat catchers.

This reading of *The Roly-Poly Pudding* is strengthened when we consider it in conjunction with *The Tale of Tom Kitten*. In the earlier novel the girl kittens do not resist their mother when she tries to clean them (although they do harass their brother); they head out into the garden because their mother has sent them there; and they lose their clothes by accident. Indeed, they are willing accomplices of their mother in trying to get Tom back into his clothes, but they are also Tom's accomplices when they romp wildly in the bedroom, although they hide from Tabitha when she appears at the door while Tom boldly faces her. The girl kittens are adventuresome in this earlier novel, but only within the confines of the house, and even there they take care. In the second novel they are more resistant to their mother—they and Tom seem a bit older than they do in the first book—yet again they know their limitations and therefore suffer no ill effects from their mild rebellion, unlike their brother.

Potter is on the side of rebellion in these two books about the cats, as she usually is, but her allegiance is a complicated one. It appears that one must know when to rebel, not only how to rebel, in order to be successful, and if you mistime your rebellion you may never be able to leave the confines of home. Significantly in these two books, Tom never fully escapes feminization and domesticity, while his sisters, whose rebellion has been quieter and who have been willing to bide their time, take on as adults some of the masculine attributes of aggression and entrepreneurship that one would more commonly expect from Tom. Obvious rebellion can backfire; quieter rebellion may win the day. Potter's own life followed this pattern, ultimately making it possible for her to support herself and move to Sawrey.

In 1908 Potter's books move out of the house at Hill Top and into the farmyard in *The Tale of Jemima Puddleduck*, which again gives us interaction among three separate groups of characters: the human farmers, the domesticated duck and dogs, and the wild fox. As in the two cat books, we have a mother figure here in Jemima (and in the secondary character of the farmwife), and again she is treated with comic irony. But Jemima's failings are rather different than Tabitha's. For one thing she does not yet have her own ducklings, but only a deep desire for them. By the end of the tale, however, the reader understands why the farmer's wife wants to take the duck's eggs away from her: Jemima is a foolish duck and would make a foolish mother. Indeed, she is not really a grown-up duck, mature enough to handle the responsibilities of motherhood. Jemima's foolishness and lack of maturity may be laid at the feet of selective breeding. She is, after all, a domesticated duck, lacking the natural caution and protective coloring of her wild cousins. Yet not all of her wildness has been bred from her: she still desires a quiet, private place to lay her eggs, and she wants to hatch them herself. She is dangerously caught between her wild self and her domestic self, and as we shall see she is not entirely suited to either role.

In *Jemima Puddleduck* the illustrations are the key to the irony and to the story's events, more so than they have been in the other Sawrey books, and the irony is botanic. When Potter gives us an illustration of Jemima trying to hide her eggs from the farmer's wife and her son, we can see that she is hiding them beneath rhubarb leaves. The rhubarb stems provide some needed color in a monochromatic illustration, but the color could just as easily have been provided by campion flowers or some other plant—however, Potter specifically chooses rhubarb. Rhubarb is an early clue to the deep ironies of the story. Rhubarb, as gardeners know, provides in its stems a kind of tart sweetness that makes for good pies—but the leaves of rhubarb are highly poisonous. It is also a deep-rooted plant nearly impossible to eradicate once a patch is established. The contradictory nature of the plant underlines both Jemima's contradictory nature and its persistence despite lessons to the contrary. Her desire to mother her own ducklings might be seen as "sweet" or positive, but it is also dangerous or "poisonous" to her very life when it sends her out of the farmyard and into nature to find a proper nesting place. Her desire for her own nest and her own ducklings is never eradicated in the novel, and it never leads to an entirely satisfactory ending for her.

The farmer's wife is a human mirror of some of the contradictions of Jemima's nature. We have first seen the farmer's wife feeding her poultry, looking like a good human "mother" to her livestock, and the illustration with the rhubarb includes both the mother (looking on approvingly) and her son, who is finding and collecting Jemima's eggs as quickly as she can hide them. The farmer's wife thinks she is doing good by saving eggs she is sure Jemima will abandon; but of course she is saving eggs and ducks for the purpose either of eating the eggs or raising ducklings for slaughter, which puts her in the same class as the fox. She is apparently a good human mother—supervising her children's chores—but not a good "duck mother," if by that term we mean someone who cares for and nurtures ducks for their own well-being, not for her own. But the farmwife is not condemned for her behavior, nor treated as a villain, as is the fox. She is performing what for her, in the human world, are natural behaviors. The difficulty is that the values of the human world do not coexist easily with those of the animal world. The fox, too, is behaving like a natural predator, but is punished because his natural desires conflict with human desires, which are clearly at the top of the hierarchy in this tale. Potter the farmer understood all too well that while domestic and wild animals might be admired and respected, they existed primarily to be useful to the farmer, and if not useful they must be eradicated.

When Jemima flees the farmyard for life over the hills, where she hopes to raise her ducklings in peace, Potter draws her "wearing a shawl and a poke bonnet."[7] There are layers of comedy and irony here. To begin with, Jemima thinks she is doing the proper thing by dressing up to go traveling, although the reader knows that ducks do not wear clothes and that for a duck who wants to escape to the wild, donning clothes is doubly ridiculous. Why would she wear domestic, human clothing when she is fleeing the domesticated, human world? Like both Peter Rabbit and Tom Kitten, Jemima looks constricted in her clothes, her shawl wrapped tightly around her wings in the first two illustrations, before she bursts free to run and flap her wings and take off over the treetops. Although she thinks she is flying into the wild blue yonder she ends up landing "rather heavily" (22) in a clearing in the woods, a clearing that has been made by people rather than by natural forces. She has not escaped so very far after all, and in fact she has "escaped" into greater danger than she faced in the farmyard, although she is blissfully unaware of this.

The reader is not unaware, however. Jemima first fancies "a tree-stump amongst some tall foxgloves" (22) as a nesting place, but is soon startled to find an "elegantly dressed gentleman" with "prick ears" and "sandy-coloured whiskers" sitting upon the stump. The accompanying illustration gives pride of place to the foxgloves, which dominate the picture. Like rhubarb, foxgloves have a contradictory nature. They both provide the basis for an important heart medication (digitalis—the botanic name for the foxglove Potter illustrates is *digitalis purpurea*) and provide a poison: too much digitalis will kill you, as a number of mystery writers over the years have known and taken advantage of. Although we must turn the page to be certain, the "gentleman" among the foxgloves is indeed a fox, a traditional predator of farmyard fowl. The text never defines the gentleman as a fox, but the illustrations make his identity perfectly clear.

There is a complicated interplay in this novel between the wild world and the domestic world. Jemima is a domesticated duck whose ancestors have been brought into the farmyard from the wild, to which Jemima wishes to flee. The farmyard itself was at one time wild land and is still attached to some woodlands, although those woodlands are being harvested and used by the humans who now own them. The foxgloves in the clearing are wild flowers but also flowers that have been domesticated and are often featured in English cottage gardens. The fox himself is a wild canid (whereas Kep the collie is a domesticated canid), but is also the kind of wild animal that has adapted to living in close proximity to humans— and to the fowl they raise, which are easier hunting than wild fowl. Even though *Jemima Puddleduck* takes place almost entirely in the out-of-doors, and we never once see the interior of the human house, the tensions in this novel are as domestic as they were in the two cat books. In the cat books the tension is between the natural state of kittens and the false social state in which Tabitha wants to place them, and the ironies concern social proprieties. Here the tension has little to do with instilling false propriety into natural beings, but rather with the tensions between the domestic and the wild, the urge to stay at home and leave home, and the dangers inherent in both actions. In different ways both the cat books and the duck book explore the difficulties and dangers of navigating domesticity.

Jemima Puddleduck, in a loose sense, is a retelling of "Little Red Riding Hood," a tale Potter illustrated in 1894 with a human Red and a very naturalistic and sly-looking fox taking the place of the wolf. Here the fairy tale is much more important than it was the first time Potter alluded to it in *Peter Rabbit*. Both "Little Red Riding Hood" and *Jemima Puddleduck* are tales about appetite, temptation, and foolish behavior, and in both works the appetites that fuel the tales have dual natures. "Little Red Riding Hood" has the heroine head into the woods to bring food and drink to her sick grandmother, but because she fails to listen to her mother's admonitions she is lured by a wolf, and comes to either a frightening end (last-minute rescue by the woodsman) or an altogether bad end (Red is a meal for the wolf and there is no rescue). Whether one reads a version of the Grimm "Little Red Riding Hood" or the older and sterner Perrault version, there are undercurrents of physical appetite present, and perhaps even sexual appetite. Red is delivering food but she herself becomes food for the hungry wolf, and Red finds the wolf attractive because he is silver-tongued and good-looking. Jemima, Potter's stand-in for Little Red Riding Hood, does not have sexual appetites, but she does have a kind of maternal appetite. The fox, of course, is just as greedy as the wolf in the original tale, but here the fox wants to eat both duck and ducklings, not grandma and Red. Jemima and her eggs become stand-ins for the grandmother and Red.

Jemima lacks a mother-figure to warn her away from dangers in the woods, although to some degree the farmer's wife and Jemima's cousin Rebeccah fulfill this role. The farmer's wife does not specifically forbid Jemima to leave the farmyard—there is not that level of interaction between the human and the animal worlds—but all of her actions serve to confine and protect the duck. Jemima, like Red, refuses to submit to domestic confines and heads off into the dangerous but attractive woods. There she meets the villain, transformed by Potter from a wolf into a fox. This makes perfect sense because wolves have long since vanished from England but foxes have not, and Potter was a farmer, well acquainted with the wily nature of foxes and their appetites for domestic fowl.

The fox shares with his wolf cousin in the original story an ability to hide his bestial nature beneath a polite and gentlemanly exterior. Potter consistently refers to her fox as a "gentleman" and he is dressed much like an English country gentleman, in plus-fours, jacket, and vest. When Jemima discovers him sitting on the stump he is reading a newspaper, for all the world like a gentleman at his club or in his comfortable country study. His identification as a gentleman also links the fox with laziness or at least with leisure. He has all the time in the world, time to read the paper instead of hunting, perhaps because he knows there are penned-up chickens and ducks at Jemima's farm, and now his life has become even easier because the prey has conveniently come to the predator.

The fox is the first male villain Potter has presented the reader, with the exception of Samuel Whiskers, who shares the role of villain with his wife. The male villains, like all the negative characters in Potter's books, present false social fronts that disguise their bestial natures. The fox in *Jemima Puddleduck* is not only male but is a gentleman of leisure. Throughout the body of her work Potter has had little patience for those who lack industry—think of the dolls in *Two Bad Mice*. In *Jemima Puddleduck* the fox's lack of industry is worsened by his duplicity and his thieving ways. He is literally living off the labor of farmers, and in the end some of the "farmers" (embodied in the farm dogs) will drive him out. Potter's disapproval of the fox has to do with both his lack of industry and his social class.

The fox, apparently polite and accommodating, listens to Jemima's wish for a safe place to raise her ducklings and offers her his woodshed, which is a "very retired, dismal-looking house amongst the foxgloves" built of "faggots and turf," with "two broken pails, one on top of another, by way of a chimney" (29). Jemima happily follows the fox to his woodshed, paying no attention to either its rather bleak appearance nor to the bushy tail of the fox, which she can now see clearly for the first time. She ignores the physical evidence in front of her eyes and instead pays attention to the superficial qualities of dress and speech, actions that will have dire consequences for her.

When Jemima enters the shed she discovers that it is "almost quite full of feathers—it was almost suffocating; but it was comfortable and very soft" (33). Jemima thinks she has found domestic safety, the perfect spot to lay and hatch her eggs. She makes the nearly fatal mistake of not asking where all the feathers in her bed came from. She is literally building a nest on the dead bodies of other fowl as foolish and unfortunate as she. She has fled one domestic space that she felt to be too confining and dangerous, only to find herself in a place that seems safely enclosed but in fact is even more dangerous than the farmyard, and is indeed a kind of trap. The farmer's wife only wants Jemima's eggs, not Jemima herself (or at least, she doesn't want her for the roasting pan immediately); the fox wants to have an omelet accompanied by roast duck, and the sooner the better.

As Jemima prepares her nest, the fox remains "polite" and seems "almost sorry to let Jemima go home for the night," promising to "take great care of her nest" because "he loved eggs and ducklings; he should be proud to see a fine nest-ful in his wood-shed" (34). The very dry ironic humor here goes right past Jemima, who does not understand that the "love" the fox professes for all things duck has to do with his love for the taste of ducks and their eggs. The humor does not go past the reader, however, who has been encouraged from the moment we meet the fox to laugh at Jemima's silliness and, if not to be on the fox's side, to recognize the fact that he is more clever than Jemima, and we are meant to have a grudging admiration for his cleverness. This, of course, is not unlike the English attitude toward real foxes, who are a nuisance and regularly hunted, but who also have the respect of farmers and hunters for their ability to escape more frequently than they are caught. We know we are being encouraged to identify with the fox because, in the illustrations, the fox seems to be winking at the reader and letting the reader in on the joke to which Jemima is oblivious. When Jemima enters the woodshed the fox looks not at her, but out at the reader, giving us a wink and holding his hand to his mouth as if to control his mirth and self-satisfaction at his own cleverness. The reader—who is never told directly that the "sandy-whiskered gentleman" is a fox—is given enough information to figure this out, and to figure it out long before Jemima has even begun to wonder. Potter lets the fox out of the bag when she shows him, without his gentlemanly attire, on all fours as he greed-ily turns over Jemima's nine eggs when she is not there in the woodshed. His true animal nature is clear to the reader, if not to Jemima.

The fox, like a true gentleman, asks Jemima to a dinner party for two and asks her in language as proper as that in Ribby's invitation to Duchess: "Madam . . . before you commence your tedious sitting, I intend to give you a treat. Let us have a dinner-party all to ourselves!" (38). He then goes on to politely request that Jemima bring the herbs for an omelet—herbs that are also used to flavor duck stuffing, which the fox nearly mentions out loud. Jemima, the out-of-patience narrator tells us, "was a simpleton: not even the mention of sage and onions made her suspicious" (41). She cheerfully goes back to the farm garden to collect the necessary vegetables and herbs to turn her eggs into omelet and herself into a roasted main course. Luckily for her she encounters Kep the collie, who is suspicious of her actions and questions her closely before he heads into the village to find some foxhound puppies to aid him in a rescue operation.

When Jemima returns with the herbs she feels "surprised, and uncomfortable" (49) at the suddenly abrupt speech of the previously polite fox. She does not become fearful until she hears the sound of "pattering feet" outside the woodshed and sees a "black nose" sniffing at the door before it is locked, at which point "Jemima became much alarmed" (50). The noises outside the shed are those of the rescuing Kep and his foxhound puppy allies, who have come to rid the woods of the troublesome fox. Again there is irony here, an irony pointing to a thin line between the domestic and the wild. Foxes and dogs are both canids, members of the dog family, yet the domesticated dog has been bred to be a helper to humankind and to be used in chasing down his wild cousin, the fox. Some of the wild predatory nature of canids has been kept in the domesticated dog, but now it is turned against its source, wild canid ancestors and cousins. The wild nature of the dog and its unnatural domesticated nature are suggested by the foxhound puppies, who become so excited by the hunt that when they gain access to the woodshed they "gobble" up all the eggs before Kep can stop them (54). They are puppies, after all, and not all the wildness has been trained out of them.

There is further irony in that the wild fox in this story has turned farmer, in a manner of speaking. Rather than exploit his wild predatory nature and go hunting for his food, the fox cleverly takes to enticing and fattening up farmyard fowl to save himself the trouble of hunting wild prey. It might not be stretching a point to say that the fox treats the farmyard as if it is tended by his own tenant farmers, thus making ducks his due. That Jemima is not his first victim is made clear to us by that pile of feathers in the woodshed and by the fox's practiced, silver words that are so effective upon poor simple Jemima. The domesticated world and the wild world not only coexist in this novel, but are intertwined in complex and ironic ways. Potter, who increasingly saw herself as farmer and countrywoman and not as writer, was well aware of these ironies and contradictions. *The Roly-Poly Pudding* gave us one version of the interaction between the wild and the domestic in the cats and rats, but *Jemima Puddleduck* is a more complex treatment of a similar theme. When Jemima is returned to the farmyard, she is allowed to retain her eggs—but only four of them hatch, thus fulfilling predictions by both her sister-in-law Rebeccah and the farmwife that she is a "bad sitter." Poor Jemima's nature as a domesticated wild animal leaves her constantly confused and torn: should she behave like a tame duck or a wild one? When she brings her domestic nature into the wilderness, she barely survives and her eggs do not. When she brings her wild nature into the barnyard and broods her own eggs, she survives, but the majority of the eggs do not. Poor Jemima can find no easy place for herself in the world.

The true winner in this tale is the farmer's wife. She regains her lost duck and rids herself of the predatory fox. It is domesticated wildness and the human world that win in the end of the story. In an oblique way, Potter is arguing for the primacy of a well-ordered home and the pragmatism of farm life over the fantasy lives of animals: Jemima is returned to her proper place in the farmyard. She was to repeat this pattern in her own life, as farming and Sawrey replaced the fantasy animals as a central element in her life.

The last of the important Sawrey books was *Ginger and Pickles* (1909) in which Potter turns full circle to come back to the village life she portrayed in *The Pie and the Patty-Pan*. While not as specifically or concretely about domestic life as the earlier Sawrey books, *Ginger and Pickles* does concern itself with the necessities of domestic life, in the form of candles and soap and other items one must purchase at the village store. And although *Ginger and Pickles* does not have either the complexity of narrative or irony of the earlier novels, it does have some of both, and it, too, shows Potter stretching herself artistically.

The plot of the story is simple enough. Ginger, a tom cat, and Pickles, a terrier, run one of two village stores, and theirs is the more popular because they extend credit, whereas Mrs. Tabitha Twitchit (whom we have seen in three previous books) insists upon cash at her store. Naturally, Ginger and Pickles have the more popular establishment. The ironies of the tale concern the ironies of predatory animals (cat and terrier) running a store for the convenience of what would ordinarily be prey for them (rats, mice, and rabbits, among others), yet being unable to make a living because they do not understand the consequences of running a business on unlimited customer credit. The two store proprietors have become human enough to wear clothes and to run a store complete with weights, measures, and books kept in pounds sterling, human enough to want to make their living from commerce rather than from hunting. Yet they have only a hazy idea of how to run such a business and are constantly tempted by the nature of their customers. Ginger asks Pickles to wait on the mice when they appear in the store, because, "I cannot bear to see them going out at the door carrying their little parcels."[8] Pickles replies that "it would never do to eat our own customers; they would leave us and go to Tabitha Twitchit's," to which Ginger answers "gloomily," "On the contrary, they would go nowhere" (16). Here is the core of the tale's irony: each animal has the ability to make its own "living" by catching and devouring natural prey, but each denies animal nature in attempting to run a very human village shop, thus starving themselves and helping their customers live comfortably and cost free. By abandoning their animal nature they find themselves having to resort to eating their own stores and hiding from policemen and rates collectors.

In all of the Sawrey books, Potter rings changes on the conflict between the domestic and the wild, between the natural instincts of animals and their domestication. She plays with these themes as a way of working out some of her own difficulties in taming her nature to the domestic life and of figuring out how to lead what, to her, was a natural life as an independent countrywoman rather than a dependent city dweller. Whereas in the earlier Sawrey books she focuses on the silliness of social conventions or the dangers lurking in old farmhouses, here she focuses on the nature of village life and gives us far more detail about it than she did in *The Pie and the Patty-Pan*. She does something else, as well: she brings into her fictionalized Sawrey village store nearly all the characters she has written about previously, as if she is bringing them home with her to Sawrey and incorporating them into her new life there.

The very first characters we see, in a black-and-white illustration, are Lucinda and Jane from *The Tale of Two Bad Mice*, who are standing just outside the "little small shop just the right size for Dolls" (11). Succeeding pages show us Samuel Whiskers in his green coat standing at the counter; Jeremy Fisher trying on a new pair of galoshes and Peter Ptolemy waiting for service; Peter and his sisters waiting their turn; Squirrel Nutkin pilfering nuts from outside the store; Jemima and her ducklings talking to Sally Henny Penny while the mice from *The Tale of Two Bad Mice* converse to one side; and finally the troublesome policeman who wants money for dog licenses and taxes is the very same policeman doll from *The Tale of Two Bad Mice*. The reader might see the incorporation of these characters into a new (and very loosely organized) tale as shameless promotion of the earlier texts, but such an interpretation would be unfair. For one thing, the endpapers for this book are not the usual framework of intertwined Potter characters from other books, nor the endpapers of later books with Potter characters looking at billboards advertising Potter books. These are, rather, amusing illustrations of mice trying to extricate themselves from bottles, while other characters play with the scales. The mice seem to be taking advantage of store goods while the proprietor has gone away—getting trapped in bottles while trying to pilfer the contents, then pilfering twine to extricate themselves; Jeremy Fisher and Ptolemy Tortoise fiddle with the scales while the owners are not paying attention. The endpapers relate to the present volume, not previous volumes.

More important, however, is the fact that Potter's narrative voice never comments upon the activities of the customers in their prior adventures. There is no authorial intrusion to remind us of Jemima's headlong rush into the woods or Jeremy's near escape from the trout. In fact, a reader unfamiliar with Potter's earlier work could look at *Ginger and Pickles* as an entirely self-contained world. Those who do know the earlier work would recognize the significance of some of the details in the illustrations. For example, Mrs. Tiggy-Winkle is buying a bar of soap, and the reader who knows her story would recognize that in *The Tale of Mrs. Tiggy-Winkle* the hedgehog ran out of laundering soap. Jeremy Fisher must try on new galoshes because the fish he was able to escape swallowed his old ones. These are details to delight someone who already knows the stories, not details meant to entice new readers to discover older texts.

The second clue that we are not meant to see *Ginger and Pickles* as simply an exercise in self-promotion is the care Potter has taken with her illustrations and the way she has stretched herself as an artist. Yes, she is drawing old characters, but she puts them into entirely new situations and an entirely new setting, the exquisitely drawn and detailed village shop. Potter's palette here is richer than it has been since *The Tailor of Gloucester*. The second full-color illustration in the text gives us, in the same frame, the green of Samuel Whiskers' coat, the blue of Peter's jacket, the very deep pink of his sisters' cloaks, and the orangey-tan of both Jeremy's stockinged legs and Ginger's striped coat. This is more color, on a single page, than we have seen almost anywhere else in Potter's work. Additionally, the play of light is quite sophisticated in this illustration. The interior of the shop might have been dark and fairly dismal, but the combination of the color of the animals' clothing and the light streaming in from the deep-set window opens the illustration up. The window, in fact, has been our invitation into the shop in the first place. The frontispiece shows three cats peering longingly through the window into the shop, and we see them from the viewpoint of someone inside the shop. The light on the street and cats is brilliant; Potter shows us this not only with her nearly all-white background but also with the beautiful reflections on the bottles in the shop window. The second (black-and-white) illustration shows us the two dolls gazing longingly into the window, and only in the third illustration is the viewer drawn into the store, into that profusion of customers and color, to luxuriate in what has tempted all of the characters so far. The story was first published in the larger format of *The Pie and the Patty-Pan*, and more space again gives Potter room to expand both the content of her art and also its technique.

Potter was also interested here in giving a kind of rapid sketch of village politics and society, as centered in the village store, which of course (along with the post office, perhaps) is the center of village life, where people of all walks and all religions and all opinions converge. The story is an encapsulated version of capitalist culture as played out in a small village setting. In the tale's beginning there are two shops in competition with one another. Ginger and Pickles have more customers, but no profit, because they extend unlimited credit. Tabitha Twitchit has fewer customers but a profitable business, because she refuses to extend credit. The instant Ginger and Pickles decide they must close their business, Tabitha Twitchit raises her prices by a half-penny and still refuses to give credit. The narrator helpfully points out that "Of course there are the tradesmen's carts" but that "a person cannot live on 'seed wigs' and sponge-cake and butterbuns" (48)—there is a need for a village store that sells a variety of necessities such as candles and galoshes. The dormouse family begins a business to compete with Tabitha Twitchit, but they are not serious businesspeople: the business is run out of their home, their candles melt in warm weather, and Mr. John Dormouse stays in bed when complained to, "which is not the way to carry on a retail business" (34). The story finally ends when Sally Henny Penny reopens Ginger and Pickles's store with a "Grand co-operative Jumble!" (57). The reopening attracts much attention, and the chicken gets "rather flustered" when trying to count out change (difficult, after all, for an animal with claws instead of hands or feet), but she "insists on being paid cash" and is "quite harmless" (59). Sally Henny Penny will succeed where Ginger and Pickles did not because she insists on being paid cash and she does not find her customers palatable as food. Furthermore, the customers will benefit because Tabitha Twitchit now has serious competition.

McDonald sees the end of *Ginger and Pickles* as one long coda, the longest coda in the books so far. The reader discovers in the course of twenty pages or so what happens after Ginger and Pickles must close their shop. However, in many ways, the end of the story is not a coda about the characters but rather a coda about social and political issues that were close to Potter's heart. One of these issues, free trade, is played upon amusingly, if glancingly, in the ending of *Ginger and Pickles*. The policeman doll, whom Pickles fears has come to deliver a summons, is rather sharply attacked by Potter. Ginger encourages the barking Pickles to "Bite him, Pickles, bite him! . . . He's only a German doll!" (36). The important qualifier here is *German*. The book is written before the start of the First World War, and the epithet "German" is not based on political fears of the Germans and their uniformed authority, but rather on the issue of free trade. Potter had run-ins with copyright infringement and with German toymakers early on in her career as a writer of children's books and a designer of children's toys. Warne had failed to register the copyright for *Peter Rabbit* in America and hence the book was pirated, Potter receiving no royalties for its American publication.[9] Potter remained philosophical over this issue, but she was less so when it came to German manufacturers and toymakers. In 1908 she wrote to Harold Warne concerning an agreement to turn some of her animal characters into china figurines, telling Harold, "I should not care to offer them to the German people. I hope you will be able to get rid of them" (*Letters*, 157). Two years later, in 1910, Potter was engaged in a campaign to create posters for a Unionist campaign for tariff reform; Judy Taylor notes that Potter felt strongly antagonistic toward Free Trade. She had failed to find a British manufacturer for the *Peter Rabbit* doll and was infuriated to find shops filled with cheap and unauthorized German versions. Taylor notes that Potter created a number of posters she referred to as her "Camberwell Beauties," one of which featured a doll made in Camberwell, "leaning against a gravestone marking the death of the South London Toy Trade, 'killed by Free Trade with Germany.' "[10] Again she wrote to Warne, objecting to the management of her "sideshow" projects by a Mr. Hughes, whom she "should *not* [Potter's emphasis] myself choose to employ," because he is "strongly pro German & has *no desire* to save English patents" (180; Potter's emphasis).

Potter is unable to keep herself from commenting on the free trade issue in *Ginger and Pickles*, which was written at about the time that she was busily engaged in a campaign against free trade. Amusingly, however, she packages her criticism of free trade in a little book that is more literally about "free trade"— Ginger and Pickles are engaged in free trade in the sense that they give away merchandise for free. Potter shows, in this book, the dangers of extending credit as well as the dangers of free trade in its more political sense, thus ironically conflating a moral and economic lesson for children with a moral and economic lesson for adults.

The unusual endpapers for this book also comment on its economic themes. The front endpapers show one mouse trapped in the bottom of a big bottle and another group of mice extending a lifeline of twine down to it. These are clever and resourceful mice in more ways than one. It appears that they have not only been "shopping" at the store but also helping themselves after hours. The bottle is empty, making the mice's attempt at thievery fruitless, but there is a handy roll of twine nearby, which the mice may "borrow" to rescue their companion. The closing endpapers give us both mice and the characters from Jeremy Fisher playing with the store's scales, scales that have had a prominent position in the early illustrated pages of *Ginger and Pickles*. The scales suggest justice on one hand, and fair trade on the other: weights and measures need to be accurate so that one does not cheat one's customers nor oneself. Potter had had firsthand experience with such scales. She writes to Millie Warne in 1905, during a trip to her newly acquired Hill Top Farm, that "every body who traded was to send in their weights & measures to be tested," and "horrible to relate" hers are returned with a note that they are out of register. "Fortunately I have been cheating myself, the dish that held the butter had some enamel chipped off it, so we have been selling about 1/2 ounce over the pound. If it had been the other way round I should probably have been fined" (134). In *Ginger and Pickles* the endpapers suggest that the scales have been played with and that whatever trade is going on in the store is unbalanced, as are Ginger and Pickles's account books.

Potter, after she moves to Sawrey, is increasingly interested in working out problems of the interaction between wild and domestic, or between natural and social behaviors. This is certainly one of the appeals of her books for child readers, who themselves are caught between delightful natural behaviors (running around without clothes, getting dirty in the mud, ignoring parental rules) and needlesome social behaviors (getting dressed up for relatives and company, having to take baths, obeying silly adult rules like saying 'thank you'). But like all of the truly great writers for children—Grahame, Lewis, Carroll, Sendak, and others—the stories speak to both adults and to children. All adults still have something of the child buried in them, though the child may be buried deep, just as all domesticated animals have something of the wild still in them. And all adults have, from time to time, a desire to break away from the social conventions and to behave in a more natural if less polite fashion.

For Potter, these age-old themes also had a personal dimension. She came to them at a time when she had fled what was to her a far too constrictive and restrictive social and family world for the freer world of country life, a world hundreds of miles from London, from daily carriage rides and annoying calls and tea parties. But like the animals about whom she wrote, she could not entirely abandon that constrictive world, which of course had shaped her. She did not move permanently to the Lake District until after her marriage to William Heelis, a marriage of which her parents disapproved; even after marriage she found herself frequently traveling to Bolton Gardens to cope with her mother's various domestic difficulties. After her father died in 1914 and her mother was alone and elderly, Potter moved her to the Lake District—but makes sure to keep Lake Windermere between the two of them. As letters from the period indicate, her mother's demands continued to place restrictions on Potter, restrictions with which the dutiful daughter did her best to abide. Potter had, since childhood, seen the natural world as her escape from the overly domesticated world of Bolton Gardens, but the natural world held its difficulties as well. The two worlds come together in the major Sawrey books, often to comic effect, but always with a darker undertone. Like Jemima and Tom, Potter had to negotiate a life between the domestic and the natural or wild. There were dangers and delights in both—finding the balance was the trick.

Notes

1. The other major book of this period is *The Tale of Jeremy Fisher* (1906), which is not specifically set in Sawrey and will be discussed in the following chapter.
2. Beatrix Potter, *The Tale of Tom Kitten* (London: Warne, 1907; 1987), 9. Unless otherwise noted, all text references are to the 1987 edition.
3. Ruth K. McDonald, *Beatrix Potter* (Boston: Twayne, 1986), 100.
4. Judy Taylor, *Beatrix Potter: Artist, Storyteller and Countrywoman* (London: Warne, 1986), 167.
5. Beatrix Potter, *The Tale of Samuel Whiskers, or The Roly-Poly Pudding* (London: Warne, 1908; 1987), 14. Unless otherwise noted, all text references are to the 1987 edition.
6. Judy Taylor, ed., *Beatrix Potter's Letters* (London: Warne, 1992), 147.
7. Beatrix Potter, *The Tale of Jemima Puddleduck* (London: Warne, 1908; 1987), 14. Unless otherwise noted, all text references are to the 1987 edition.
8. Beatrix Potter, *The Tale of Ginger and Pickles* (London: Warne, 1909; 1987), 15. Unless otherwise noted, all text references are to the 1987 edition.
9. See Potter's letter to Norman Warne of April 30, 1903, in *Letters*, 74.
10. See Leslie Linder, *A History of the Writings of Beatrix Potter* (London: Warne, 1971), 398–401 for a discussion of these posters, including two reproductions of them.

5

Interlude: Mining the Past

Technically, *The Tale of Jeremy Fisher* (1906) is one of the Sawrey books, but unlike the other books of this period it was not directly inspired by the Lake District. Potter had been intent on writing something with a frog as the main character since at least 1894, when she approached the publishers Ernest Nister & Co. with nine illustrations for a little booklet called *A Frog He Would A-Fishing Go*; they offered her an unsatisfactory sum, which she successfully negotiated upward to her satisfaction.[1] Later she bought back the rights to the illustrations, and she and Norman had been discussing the possibility of a frog book in early 1905 when Potter wrote to Norman to say, "I wonder if you will care for either of these [the draft texts of *Jeremy Fisher* and *The Pie and the Patty-Pan*]," although at the time she was still working on *Mrs. Tiggy-Winkle*. She added in a postscript: "I'm afraid you don't like frogs but it would make pretty pictures with water-forget-me-nots, lilies, etc." (*Letters*, 112). When she finally did the illustrations for the book, she changed the original background from the River Tay in Scotland to Esthwaite Water in the Lakes.[2] The illustrations are indeed lovely, showing Potter's skill as both a naturalist and as a fantasist.

A somewhat later and little-known work, *The Tale of Mrs. Tittlemouse* (1910), is a land-based rather than a water-based story, but in many ways it is a logical work to examine in tandem with *Jeremy Fisher*. Both novels, although dating from the Sawrey years, look back to an earlier period in Potter's artistic development: *Jeremy Fisher* to her early years as a card illustrator, and *Mrs. Tittlemouse* to her experiments with drawing microscopic views of nature. Potter never threw anything away—her letters are filled with references to older sketches that can be recycled for newer books—and we should not be surprised that earlier interests and earlier sketches show up in later books. (By the time

Potter came to the two nursery rhyme books at the very end of her career, she used recycled illustrations almost exclusively). Interestingly, however, the major themes of domestic life and the importance of class divisions remain in these two novels, although treated very differently.

As we shall see, after about 1910, Potter's interests were shifting away from the writing of children's stories. They had begun to shift as soon as she bought Hill Top in 1905, but her new status as landowner, village inhabitant, and more-or-less independent woman at first inspired her and gave her material for some of her best work. But as the novelty of Sawrey life wore off, the practicalities of farming and of local and national politics began to preoccupy her, and she began to find the writing of children's stories tiresome. For all intents and purposes, she gave up writing original stories entirely after her marriage to William Heelis in 1913. By 1925 she wrote to a child friend, "No more bunny books! . . . I cannot paint very well, with being obliged to wear strong spectacles. I drew a picture of Peter and Cottontail for the 'Invalid Children' [a charitable cause], I would like you to have a copy of it" (*Letters*, 292). Her artistic talents were increasingly used for social and political causes.

However, in 1906 Potter is still at the height of her powers, and the illustrations for *Jeremy Fisher* are proof of this. Potter has gone back to vignetting her illustrations, as she did for *Peter Rabbit*, and here she has much more scope to show her talent as a watercolorist than she did in her first rabbit book. The paintings are delicate and transparent, so much so that we can see the shadowy form of the trout beneath Jeremy's lily-pad boat and his webbed feet beneath the water as he gratefully climbs up the bank after his adventure. These may be miniature watercolors, but they show complete mastery of the medium. Potter further shows mastery of composition by easily shifting both point of view and perspective in the illustrations. We sometimes see Jeremy in close-up, as we do in the first illustration of him sitting by the doorstep of his "little damp house";[3] sometimes from a distance, as he punts his lily-pad boat across the pond; sometimes from below, as when we see the water beetle nibbling on his galoshes (galoshes that have realistic nubble painted on the soles). Potter's palette is more limited in these illustrations than it has been in earlier books, restricted as she is to mostly browns and greens, but the variety of the composition gives more than sufficient interest to the illustrations, as of course do the fantasy elements of the characters' dress and accountrements.

Jeremy's tale is one of gentlemanly leisure. He is dressed, like the characters in *The Tailor of Gloucester*, in Regency-era clothing, down to delicate little pumps into which Jeremy manages to stuff his rather large webbed feet. The joke here, of course, is that Regency fashion emphasized the elegance of leg and foot, and while frogs have appropriately long and graceful legs, their feet destroy the effect. Potter gets around this by having Jeremy, for the majority of the story, wear footwear disguising the large webbed nature of his feet. Jeremy is perfectly aware of his elegant legs, sitting with gracefully crossed legs and delicately pointed toes in order to draw attention to his best features.

When we first see Jeremy we understand him to be a frog of leisure. He is sitting out-of-doors, reading the newspaper, framed by leaded-glass windows, and watched by a mayfly. He is not only a gentleman with enough leisure time to enjoy the morning newspaper (and to ignore a potential meal), but also a gentleman who can afford a country home "amongst the buttercups at the edge of a pond" (9). His clothes mark him as gentleman and not as farmer, as does his fishing kit (special mackintosh and galoshes, wicker creel, pole, and private boat). This is a frog who fishes for amusement rather than for his livelihood, much as gentlemen of Potter's acquaintance went to Scotland to fish for salmon for sport. That Jeremy is not entirely serious about his fishing is indicated by his tackle, which includes "the dearest little red float" (22), a float admired for its appearance rather than its usefulness, which with Potter is always a sign of impending trouble. When Jeremy becomes bored with fishing he takes a rest and eats the lunch he brought, a "butterfly sandwich" (26), a suitably fancy sandwich for a gentleman frog.

But if Jeremy is a gentleman he is somewhat out of his depth in the wider world of the pond, a world that contains wild creatures that pose an immediate threat to his obliviously happy, upper-class life. The first threat is the water beetle who nibbles on his galoshes, a water beetle Potter draws with scrupulous scientific accuracy and no anthropomorphism at all. The threat to Jeremy is a threat to his "unnatural" life as gentleman by the natural denizens of his pond world. Jeremy merely pulls his legs out of reach of the beetle and goes on eating his sandwich, not the least bit interested in or concerned about a lower form of life (in the biological sense) who must search and hunt for its dinner. His attitude is perfectly consistent with that of an upper-class gentleman who pays no attention to how the lower classes must work to earn their own sandwiches. Whereas in earlier works, like *The Tailor of Gloucester* and *The Tale of Squirrel Nutkin*, references to class are, if not immediately obvious, at least not entirely buried within the text, here Potter merely makes reference to a lower *biological* form with no human attributes whatsoever. The reader is not encouraged to read Jeremy's encounter with the beetle as anything other than a natural occurrence within the pond world. In this book Potter is not consciously (or perhaps even subconsciously) thinking of class hierarchy. However, she still has hierarchy on her mind, as we can see not only in Jeremy's encounters with various forms of wildlife, but also in his choice of dinner partners at the end of the tale. After all, Jeremy is a gentleman and hierarchy matters to gentlemen.

Water beetles are merely a nuisance, but Jeremy hears a rustling among the reeds of the pond and worries that there might be water rats nearby, saying to himself, "I think I had better get away from here" (30). Water rats, of course, like frogs for their dinners when they can catch them, and Potter shows us that Jeremy is not imagining the threat. She gives us a watercolor of two rats, again absolutely natural-looking rats, one swimming in the water and the other nibbling on a reed. The rats are framed by lily pads and buttercups, visually suggesting that even the picturesque pond hides danger and threat, even to as gentlemanly a frog as Jeremy. Potter continues to escalate the threats to Jeremy, first when he mistakenly lands a sharp little stickleback too big for him to handle and on whose spines he injures his fingers; and finally when he encounters a very large trout who swallows Jeremy and releases him only because he does not like the taste of the mackintosh, letting Jeremy go with the loss only of his galoshes rather than the loss of his life.

All of the threats to Jeremy are made by animals who, unlike the frog, are portrayed realistically: there is no sense that they have human qualities, despite the fact that the stickleback is called Jack Sharp by Potter. The illustrations of the animals who threaten Jeremy could as easily appear in a scientific journal of the period as in a children's novel, and are clearly linked to Potter's many drawings and paintings from nature.[4] Even the trout, who in the end gulps down Jeremy Fisher, is painted realistically, with little minnows fleeing from its swift passage and with Jeremy so small in his mouth that one has to look twice to see that he is really there. The use of scale here emphasizes both the size and danger of the trout—who is much larger than any of the earlier threats to Jeremy—and the ridiculous nature of Jeremy, who has a sense of self-importance but who is really quite small, even in the miniature world of the pond. Indeed, a joke that a naturalist might see in the story is that Jeremy is merely a common English frog (*rana temporaria*) and not of special, gentlemanly stock at all. He has a misplaced sense of self-importance, and Potter at least temporarily deflates him during his fishing adventure.

Jeremy's encounter with the trout is reminiscent of Jonah's encounter with the whale. Jonah was a Hebrew prophet who was thrown overboard for disobedience to God, swallowed by a large fish or whale, and disgorged three days later. A further biblical connection to the tale may well be Jeremy's name, a play on "jeremiad;" his indeed is a tale of woe and lamentation. But Potter's touch is quite light here, and comic. *Jeremy Fisher*, unlike *Peter Rabbit*, cannot be read as any sort of moral tale. Like Peter, Jeremy is merely fulfilling his nature, but unlike Peter, Jeremy is not trespassing on anyone else's territory, nor is he stealing from anyone. Despite his Regency clothing, he is acting the way real frogs act and for the majority of the story he is part of the natural world, not part of a fantasy world of "damp little houses" for frogs. The only moral he learns is that fishing can be dangerous, and he isn't sure he wants to pursue it as a hobby any longer. Furthermore, whereas Peter's human clothing is very nearly the cause of his demise, Jeremy's human mackintosh is what saves him from the trout: it is his denial of his frog-nature that saves him, although his un-galoshed webbed feet allow him to swim quickly away from the dangerous trout. If he isn't really a frog he can't really be food for the trout.

Potter's entire approach to Jeremy is unusual, in that Jeremy does not come in for as much censure as the nonindustrious characters in her novels often do, nor does he pay much of a price for taking on human characteristics. By the end of his adventure, Jeremy manages to replace his tattered mackintosh with a handsome red jacket (about the only spot of bright color in the book) and to throw a dinner party for some friends. Fittingly, his friends are other pond denizens, Sir Isaac Newton, a crested newt (*triturus vulgaris*) with a "black and gold waistcoat" (54) clearly inspired by the natural coloration of these newts, and Mr. Alderman Ptolemy Tortoise. Jeremy's friends are other males of the upper class, a scientist and a politician. They dress for dinner, Sir Isaac more than Mr. Ptolemy Tortoise, who (as Ruth McDonald points out) wears his shell the way an eccentric Englishman might wear an outsized overcoat (97). They sit down to a table spread with a tablecloth, to dishes served on silver platters. Jeremy serves "roasted grasshopper with lady-bird sauce" (59), a gourmet delight from a frog's point of view. There is no mention of servants in the story, but the table and the nature of the meal certainly suggest that servants are somewhere in the background, invisible but necessary.

Carole Scott noted that "Potter's ambivalence about the dictates of proper society, a society whose power she both sought and resented, is expressed in the clothing that she gives her animals; sometimes dress is the mark of social class, which can be empowering and restrictive, sometimes it is just a simple covering."[5] In *Jeremy Fisher* the clothing is certainly a mark of social class. Even Jeremy's mackintosh, which might be seen as a working-class item of clothing, is the sort of temporary countrywear a gentleman would don in the rain. The dinner guests show their social class not only through their fancy dress (in the newt's case), but also in the heavy medallion of political office that Ptolemy Tortoise has around his neck. Potter certainly made sharp critiques of middle- and upper-class life in earlier books, particularly in *The Tale of Two Bad Mice*, but here her ambivalence shows: her amusement at the foibles of the upper class outweighs her annoyance at their uselessness. The comic, light-hearted nature of the social comedy is similar to that in *The Pie and the Patty-Pan*, which was conceived at about the same time and has the same forgiving attitude toward etiquette and propriety. Once Potter moved to Sawrey, she seems much less judgmental in her appraisal of English social life, willing to accept the silliness of the aspiring middle class as well as the eccentricities of the upper classes. Perhaps she has the last laugh in *Jeremy Fisher* because the frog is so clearly from a past time period, and not from the present: the world he is a part of is now long gone, Potter suggests.

The Tale of Mrs. Tittlemouse (1910)[6] also looks backward, both artistically and thematically. Here the concern is not with clothing so much as it is with the difficulties of domestic life, a theme upon which Potter has already rung many changes. Potter explores this theme through a tale of a compulsively tidy little wood mouse whose home is constantly invaded by insects and other uninvited guests. The insects are drawn with the same microscopic detail and accuracy as the water beetle in *Jeremy Fisher* and the various insects in Potter's naturalistic drawings done from views through her brother's microscope in the 1880s.

The first part of the tale emphasizes the extensive nature and the tidiness of Mrs. Tittlemouse's domain. There are "yards and yards of sandy passages" (10) and many storerooms for nuts and seeds, all consistent with the habitat of real wood mice, although Mrs. Tittlemouse wears a dress and overskirt and is obsessively tidy: she keeps a dust brush and dust pan by her bedside, at the ready. The text describes her as "a most terribly tidy particular little mouse, always sweeping and dusting the soft sandy floors" (14). The job of keeping the sandy floors in order is not made any easier by the constant invasion of insects. First there is a beetle with "little dirty feet" (14), then a ladybug, a spider, and finally bees who have set up home in an abandoned storeroom, a home made of "untidy dry moss" (26). All of these insects are drawn with scientific accuracy, down to the hairs on the legs of the spider and the mandibles on the ladybug. None of the invaders has human language or characteristics, although Mrs. Tittlemouse does. As in *The Tale of Jeremy Fisher*, the enemy animals are purely animal with no human characteristics whatsoever, with the exception of the neighboring toad who shows up later in the story.

Whereas *Jeremy Fisher* is an outdoor tale, giving us only two interior views of Jeremy's house, *The Tale of Mrs. Tittlemouse* is an entirely indoor tale, giving us no exterior views at all. Although it is also a comic story, the comedy has much more underlying anxiety than we find in *Jeremy Fisher*, despite the fact that Jeremy is in danger of his life and Mrs. Tittlemouse is in danger only of dirt. There is in this tale a sense not so much of the coziness of a miniature household, but almost a desperate sense of needing to keep that household free of invaders and outsiders. Mrs. Tittlemouse is as concerned with the proprieties of middle-class life as were Lucinda and Jane in *Two Bad Mice*, and like the dolls, has that life disrupted by invaders, but here Potter is on the side of the invaded rather than the invaders.

Some of Mrs. Tittlemouse's anxiety may reflect Potter's own unhappiness about her notoriety as a writer and what McDonald refers to as "the intrusiveness of English visitors" to Sawrey (20). "Many assumed a familiarity Potter found presumptuous; others treated her as yet another holiday sight to be consumed during their summer vacations" (20). Potter herself wrote in a letter in 1939 that she "hat[ed] publicity" (*Letters*, 406). Potter was always proprietary about Hill Top and its surrounding property, and although during the second World War she gave Hill Top over to some friends made homeless by air raids and was generous in loaning her land to the Girl Guides for camping, she was always careful about setting boundaries and removing items she cared about into safekeeping. She was, once married, grateful to be known as "Mrs. Heelis" and not "Miss Potter" because her married name gave her a certain anonymity. Potter, once she had a home of her own, was jealous about keeping it to and for herself, and some of that jealousy is projected onto Mrs. Tittlemouse's anxiety about the sanctity of her home. She is not a hermit—she gives a party at the end of the tale—but she wants and needs to be in control of the guest list and the activities of the party: Mr. Jackson the messy toad is specifically excluded.

There is a kind of nightmarish quality to the action of this little story: the poor mouse cannot stay a step ahead of the insect invaders. When she finally gives up on the bees, she finds Mr. Jackson (a large, wet toad) sitting uninvited by her fireplace, "twiddling his thumbs and smiling, with his feet on the fender" (30), making himself entirely at home. Mrs. Tittlemouse has a house of her own but she seems to have no control over who may inhabit the house: she is trapped within, fighting off invaders from without, with hardly a moment to breathe. Ironically, the home that should make her feel safe is instead making her both anxious and even claustrophobic. It is one thing to feel safe and cozy at home, but another to feel one cannot leave home for an instant, for fear of who might invade and take over.

Despite her unhappiness at her uninvited guests, Mrs. Tittlemouse cannot keep herself from attempting to live up to social expectations. Although she is annoyed at Mr. Jackson's appearance and goes around mopping up after him, she never complains and in fact asks the toad to dinner—where he has the temerity to complain that he has no teeth with which to eat cherrystones and that he does not care for thistledown, either. What he wants is honey, and he proceeds to rudely inspect first the cupboards and then the rest of Mrs. Tittlemouse's house until he discovers the bees that the mouse has not yet been able to dislodge. As he hunts for honey he disturbs both a butterfly and some "creepy-crawly people" in the plate rack (42), but is eventually successful in finding the bees and the honey. While Mrs. Tittlemouse hides, Mr. Jackson dislodges the bees' nest, helps himself to honey, and goes away with the rest of the invaders, leaving behind "untidiness" that was "something dreadful" (49), leading Mrs. Tittlemouse to a two-week-long cleaning frenzy.

The story ends with Mrs. Tittlemouse giving a party for five other mice, and it appears to be a lively and successful party. The illustration of the mice dancing is as lovely in line, if not in detail, as many of Potter's earlier, better work: the mice are graceful, light on their feet, and dancing away in tiny pumps and filmy little dresses. They drink honeydew from acorn cups and obligingly pass some to Mr. Jackson, who cannot come to the party because he cannot squeeze through the door, either because he ate too much honey or because Mrs. Tittlemouse has narrowed her entryway in order to keep him out. In either case, propriety is restored at the end of the tale, invaders kept at bay, and Mrs. Tittlemouse can show off her clean and tidy house to her well-behaved mouse guests.

The narrative line of this story is not very complex, nor do the illustrations enhance the tale of the mouse to any great degree. The interest in the illustrations is not in the human qualities of either the wood mouse or the toad, but in the microscopic accuracy of the insect drawings. In *The Tale of Jeremy Fisher* the scientific nature of the drawings enhanced our understanding of the frog's place in the world and underscored the serious threat to life and limb that lies just beneath the surface of the comedy in that tale. The one microscopic view in that book, of the beetle nibbling on Jeremy's galoshes, is from the perspective of the beetle itself, and we see it only in relation to the toe of Jeremy's foot, thus keeping more or less to the natural scale of the animals. In *Mrs. Tittlemouse* the insects seem to be drawn for their own sake and are often out of scale to the mouse and her world, or they seem to change scale unrealistically. The ladybug, for instance, appears far larger than Mrs. Tittlemouse, and this is not entirely due to the perspective of the drawing. More distressingly, the spider at first appears to be nearly as large as Mrs. Tittlemouse herself, but on the following page appears much smaller as it lowers itself from the window on its thread. The bees are nearly as large as the mouse and then nearly as large as the toad, although the toad is clearly meant to be larger than the mouse.

Potter is uncharacteristically careless here, and there are two explanations. First, she is intent on showing her skill with drawing from nature and on using sketches from earlier notebooks, and she does show that skill: the Red Admiral butterfly perched upon the sugar cubes is as detailed and beautiful as any of the nature drawings from the 1880s. But skill as a nature artist and skill as a fantasy artist, although related, are two entirely different things, and they do not match up very well in this text. In *Jeremy Fisher* the naturalistic animals were, in nature, enemies of the frog; here the insects are, in nature, cohabitants of the hedge with the mice. There is no natural enmity between mouse and insect, and thus no obvious reason for the contrast of humanized mouse and natural insects. The issue is further complicated by the toad, who *is* portrayed as having human characteristics, but the reader is uncertain why. Is this last invader meant to be seen as the most invasive of all, suggesting that invasion by an equal (insofar as the toad and mouse are both anthropomorphized) is more serious than invasion by inferiors? The toad *does* rid the house of its bee invaders, even if he leaves a mess behind. Are we then to see him as a helpful, if untidy, creature? If so, why is he excluded from the party? Potter's lack of clarity here speaks to a lack of attention and care on her part. In works like *Peter Rabbit* and *The Tale of Two Bad Mice*, the ambiguities of the tales' endings add to the richness of the work. In *Mrs. Tittlemouse* the ambiguities detract rather than add to the tale's meaning.

The other explanation for the mismatched nature of the illustrations and the general lack of a cohesive worldview in this tale (despite its references to themes common to Potter's earlier works) is that by 1910 she was tiring of producing children's books and was more interested in pursuing her life as a farmer. By 1910 Potter's letters to Harold Warne were filled with requests for money against royalties, complaints about the lack of prompt reporting of sales of her books, and comments about the purchase of yet more property in the Lakes. Her letter to Harold late in 1909 is typical: "Can I have another cheque? If convenient I should like £40 to pay into the country bank this week . . . to get rid of part of the loan for my new fields" (*Letters*, 170). She needed money to further her property purchases, and was more concerned about profit margin than she was about total number of books sold. In July of 1910 she wrote to Warne that "I do not see any advantage of having immense sales without a fair profit—if Harrod's [*sic*] for instance would not pay 9d, for my part I would have let Harrods go without it" (182). Her letters to Millie, at the same time, say nothing about the books she is writing but give detailed accounts of farm life, telling Millie that the farm business "is mostly sheep sales," that "There is actually a frozen meat butcher started at Windermere selling mutton at 6 1/2d," and that she "was pleased the butter did well at the Dairy Show" (185). The complaints about money continued, culminating in Harold's arrest for forgery in 1917 and Potter's attempts both to protect her own copyrights and finances and to help protect the firm that had nurtured her and her books for years. She increasingly looked back to old sketches and ideas, not forward to new ones, and although she frequently blamed failing eyesight for her inability to start or finish books on time, it is clear from letters that her preoccupation with farm matters in Sawrey was at least as responsible for the decline in both output and quality of her work from about 1906 onwards. By 1919 she wrote to Harold Warne, "you don't suppose I shall be able to continue these d . . . d little books when I am dead and buried! I am tired of doing them and my eyes are wearing out" (259). The use of an expletive, even if somewhat disguised by the ellipsis, is uncharacteristic of Potter and suggestive of the depth of her exasperation with Warne and Company.

Another preoccupation for Potter during this period was local politics. Yet as we saw in *Ginger and Pickles* and in some of her letters, Potter was distressed by the impact of cheap German imported toys upon the British toy market. As the journal entries attest, Potter was strongly anti-Free Trade long before she had any personal interest in the issue. Her political opinions predate her self-interest. Potter first became aware of the impact of free trade through her difficulties in finding a British manufacturer for the Peter Rabbit dolls she had designed. Leslie Linder writes that Potter "therefore felt strongly that Free Trade should be abolished and some form of tariff reform brought in; and with the 1910 Election in sight, busied herself with propaganda in favor of tariff reform, which amongst other things was one of the issues of this election."[7] Potter expended a great deal of energy, both artistic and political, in campaigning against Free Trade. She drew a number of large posters (about 280 mm by 215 mm in size) with captions such as "Here Lies the Camberwell Wax Doll Killed by Free Trade With Germany," the illustration for which is a limp doll posed against a tombstone (Linder, 398–99). She also wrote verses like the following, quoted by Linder:

> When a Workman ain't got any Wages—
> Now what is the good of 'cheap' bread?
> While you argues and talks and rampages—
> Poor Camberwell Dolly lies dead!

(LINDER, 399)

Camberwell was the site of the British doll manufacturing trade, which was very nearly destroyed by free trade with Germany. Free trade allowed German dolls to be imported at very favorable tariff rates, rates so favorable as to undercut the British market.

Potter was also concerned about trade and tariff issues with the United States, concern that would be one of the reasons she chose, late in her career, to publish several books in the United States alone, with the Philadelphia publisher David McKay. She wrote in a pamphlet in 1910

> There has always been very great difficulty about English books in the United States. The States are enormously rich and protected by heavy tariffs. We have no tariff by means of which we might bring the States to reason. They simply laugh at us. My most successful book [*Peter Rabbit*] has been pirated and reprinted by American printers who have never sent me a halfpenny. (quoted in Linder, 402)

For Potter, free trade and tariffs were personal as well as political issues. However, it is telling that she was concerned not only with the effects on her her own finances but with the conditions of the British working classes. The working-class language of the verse quoted previously is one indication of her desire to ally herself with working-class concerns; she wrote in the 1910 pamphlet that "British factories and work-people are restricted—most properly—by the Factory Acts. We are fighting foreign competition with one arm tied, so long as there is no import duty" (Linder, 402). Here Potter concluded that legislation to protect the rights and conditions of workers were "proper." The problem lay not with the British workers but with British foreign trade policy.

Potter's political concerns extended to issues that were of importance not only to herself or to the urban working classes, but also to farmers. Potter was no gentlewoman farmer, solely dependent upon farm managers and tenant farmers to work her land. She was intimately involved in both the daily chores of buying, selling, and keeping livestock, as well as in the larger issues that affected the daily lives of farmers. One of the issues of local import preoccupying her in 1910 was a shortage of horses and possible government interference with their supply. She wrote to Wilfred Evans in February of 1910, on the subject of pamphleteering on Free Trade, that "It is useless to talk to farmers about *dolls*. But if there *is* a subject which enrages us—it is meddling with our horses!" (*Letters*, 176; Potter's emphasis). The pronoun here shows Potter allying herself with farmers, counting herself as one among them. She goes on to say that the previous week it became clear in the House of Commons "that we have rendered our horses liable to requisition in case of necessity during war. . . . What the Unionists have advocated for a long time is a proper system of reserve horses, earmarked & registered for a very small retaining fee. I would willingly keep a yeomanry horse. But to seize the very scanty present stock would bring agriculture to a standstill" (176) She goes on to say she has written a letter that she would like to send Evans for publication but wants to sign it "N. Lancs," "as a female farmer is silly on paper; though well informed, being in a neighborhood much devoted to horse breeding, *when it paid*" (176; Potter's emphasis).

Potter may have left London for the countryside, but she never lost interest in or contact with political doings in Parliament. In her pamphlet concerning Free Trade she ended by noting

> My grandfather was a Radical member of Carlisle, a colleague of Bright and Cobden. In those days the working man had not the Franchise. It is nonsense to pretend that the old bad days of the Corn Laws can ever come back, now that the people have votes. The working man can safely give Tariff Reform a trial without being frightened by the bogey of dear bread. (quoted in Linder, 403)

Late in life she commented that John Bright was an old family friend, "impressive by strength of character" and "obstinate as a mule" (*Letters*, 353), characteristics that would have appealed to Potter's sense of resistance and rebellion. She notes that after Bright's death his own business "was completely ruined by foreign competition," yet he "believed that all the world would be converted to Free Trade; that's the rub" (353). Tariffs and Free Trade were consuming issues in the elections of 1910 and as Peter Marsh has noted, when Salisbury left office in 1892 (just about the time Potter began publishing her novels) "the commercial leadership of Europe passed incontestably to Germany."[8] Furthermore, "What hastened Britain's descent . . . was the unilateral pursuit of free trade" (Marsh, 209), a pursuit hastened by Gladstone's policies—Gladstone, Potter's perennial political nemesis. Potter's concerns about free trade were not entirely personal or based on her own individual experiences: Free Trade was an issue hotly debated in 1910.

Yet Potter is always a pragmatist, not bound so much by party loyalty or loyalty to a particular politician as to the practical economic outcomes of policy. She thought that the government's scheme to requisition horses might be better handled by the Unionists—the same party that was advocating Free Trade. She felt she could have an effect on the outcome of both the Free Trade issue and the horse-requisitioning problem by making solid political and economic arguments, only rarely relying on her celebrity as a children's author, understanding that her kind of celebrity would undermine rather than enhance her arguments. Only rarely, and only when her own literary work supplied a good example with which she could argue about Free Trade, does she mention her publications.

Even though women did not yet have the vote in England, Potter certainly felt she could wield influence over public and political matters. Her pamphleteering and letter writing was not the work of a female crank—although her caution about revealing her gender in print shows that she is well aware that she might be characterized as such—but of a serious female professional who expected her arguments to carry weight and sway public opinion. She had some success. She had more than a thousand pamphlets about the horse issue printed up and distributed, with a return address of "Messrs Evans," the printers. She did not expect many replies to her pamphlet but was pleased to receive some letters in response, including a letter of appreciation from the Printers' Association.

Another local issue incensing Potter during this period was the intrusion of "flying machines" into the Lake District. She wrote to Millie Warne in December of 1911 that there was a disturbance that

> moved me to bad language. There is a beastly fly-swimming spluttering aeroplane careering up & down over Windermere; it makes a noise like 10 million bluebottles. . . . [I]f others are built—or indeed this one—[it] will very much spoil the Lake. It has been buzzing up & down for hours today, and it has already caused a horse to bolt & smashed a tradesman's cart. (*Letters*, 192)

Her complaints were not confined to letters to Millie; there was at least one long complaining letter published in *Country Life*, in which she argued that "A more inappropriate place for experimenting with flying machines could scarcely be chosen,"[9] an argument supported by the editor, who wrote that "Admiration [for the aeroplane] cannot prevent us from sympathising with the protest made by Mrs Potter" (Taylor 125). Potter also drew up a petition against the airplanes, hoping publishers would support her because they recognized the name "Beatrix Potter" and that farmers would support her because they would support "H. B. Potter *farmer*" (quoted in Taylor, 126, emphasis in original).

As if Free Trade, horse requisitioning, and the intrusion of airplanes weren't enough to distract Potter from her children's books, she was beginning to have difficulties with her publisher, Warne and Company—difficulties that would culminate in Harold Warne's arrest and imprisonment for forgery in 1917. She had been asking for checks against royalties as soon as she began to purchase land in Sawrey and environs, but she was increasingly irritated by a lack of accounting on Warne's part. The publishers had always been scrupulous about keeping Potter apprised of even minute details about printing, but their financial statements were becoming increasingly erratic. In 1911 Potter wrote to Fruing Warne (Harold was out of town) to ask

> Would you mind telling me—without sentiment—& I trust without the slightest irritation—does FW&Co mean to pay the first installment of the 1910 royalities in Aug or Sept? . . . I am not short. I am not of the opinion that the circulation of the books is smaller than it ought to be . . . [Harold's] letters are enough to drive anybody mad . . . it is very annoying that he always thinks I am complaining about the amount of the money, whenever I ask about the date. . . . The difficulty of getting cheques at the time promised has sometimes rather perplexed and alarmed me. (*Letters*, 188)

Potter was right to be perplexed and alarmed, for Harold was raiding the publishing accounts to pay for another family business that was in economic difficulties, eventually forging checks and nearly bringing not only the publishing company but his entire extended family to the brink of financial ruin.

Given all of these worries, it is not surprising that both *Mrs. Tittlemouse* and the novel that followed it, *The Tale of Timmy Tiptoes* (1911),[10] were well below the usual standards of Potter's work. Potter was concerned with reaching the lucrative American market, despite high tariffs on imported British books, and so decided to write a story that might appeal more to her growing American audience than to her British audience. As Judy Taylor points out, *The Tale of Timmy Tiptoes* introduces "characters that would be easily recognisable by American children who, after all, had never had the opportunity of even seeing a hedgehog" (Taylor, 123). The characters include gray squirrels, chipmunks, and a black bear, all of which would (theoretically, at any rate) be recognizable by American children. The bear is certainly an unusual animal choice for Potter and one she could not have drawn from nature, which at least partially accounts for its stiffness in the illustrations: it is nearly as stiff as Potter's human figures tend to be. Potter noted in the manuscript version that the bear was "Intended to represent the American black bear" (Taylor, 123), and while it is recognizably a bear, it lacks any of the clumsy gracefulness of bears and any of their human qualities (bears, after all, can stand and even walk for brief periods on two legs), qualities Potter could only have realized from seeing bears in the wild, for which there was no opportunity in England.

Ruth McDonald has pointed to a number of difficulties with this book, noting its unclear sense of audience as a possible explanation. She observes that the treatment of the chipmunks' marital discord is not characteristic of Potter and that the chipmunks' story disrupts the main story of the squirrels. The uncertainty of audience is due not only to Potter's unfamiliarity with American children and their interests, but also with her increasing unfamiliarity with children altogether. The Moore children, for whom she wrote the earliest of her illustrated stories, were now grown, and Potter seems not to have replaced them with other local children, although she did continue to write letters to child fans who wrote to her. Potter's uncertainty about audience is also ironically linked to her attempts to write for a specific commercial audience, something that never led Potter to her best work. This is apparent in *The Story of a Fierce Bad Rabbit* (1906) and *The Tale of Miss Moppet* (1906), which were early attempts to write books for clearly defined, very young audiences. Both these little books attempted to appear more like toys than books, first being published in a panoramic foldout form contained in an envelope, not in boards. This proved to be one of Potter's rare poor business decisions because booksellers found the wallet format difficult to deal with in their stores. Both little books were eventually republished in the familiar small format in 1916. Another possible reason for the relative unpopularity of *Fierce Bad Rabbit*, at least, was its overt moralizing and the relative stiffness not only of the human hunter but also of the rabbits. Furthermore, the rabbits in this book bear little resemblance to the more adorable rabbits in the books featuring Peter and his kin. *Miss Moppet* was somewhat more successful: the illustrations are more fluid and the storyline more humorous and less moralistic. Potter, in an attempt to write the kind of moral tale common in the Victorian era, fails to capture the reader's imagination in either story or in pictures.

Much the same thing happened in *Timmy Tiptoes*, even though the narrative line is less moralistic. In both *Fierce Bad Rabbit* and *Timmy Tiptoes*, Potter is thinking of audience first and story second, which is generally fatal to a writer. In *Timmy Tiptoes* her preoccupation with North American animals led her to lose control first of the plot and then of the illustrations. In some ways the plot can be seen as a kind of *pourquoi* story in which we get an explanation of why squirrels hide nuts and what happens when they hibernate. There is a connection to the first of Potter's squirrel books, *The Tale of Squirrel Nutkin*, which gives the reader an explanation of how a particular squirrel lost his tail and of how squirrels collect nuts for the winter. The two squirrel books further share a preoccupation with rhymes and riddles. Nutkin irritates Old Brown with his series of riddles and rhymes, and Timmy gets chased by other squirrels because they have listened to the birds singing "Who's bin digging-up *my* nuts? Who's-been-digging-up *my* nuts?" (21; Potter's emphasis). The riddles in the first squirrel book add up to an amusing game for the child reader and also illuminate Nutkin's character; here, they simply provide an almost mechanical way to move the action of the story forward, just as both the convenient storm and the appearance of the bear act as *deus ex machina* to move both squirrel and chipmunk back to their wives.

In *Mrs. Tittlemouse*, Potter combined animals with and without human characteristics, with no apparent logic behind the difference, and we find the same problem in *Timmy Tiptoes*. The central squirrel and chipmunk characters wear human clothing, while the angry and jealous squirrels and the bear do not. Although this may be an attempt on Potter's part to separate the anthropmorphized squirrels from the natural ones, the attempt fails on both narrative and artistic grounds. In terms of the narrative, all the squirrels are engaged in the natural actions of collecting nuts and it is unclear how Timmy is acting any differently than his fellow squirrels, except that he has a wife. Married or not, they still live in a nest high in a tree, not in a cozy little "house" somewhere. In other words, there is no clear delineation between natural and personified squirrel nature. Timmy and Goody blur the distinctions. Second, Potter is inconsistent in her portrayal of Timmy and his red jacket. We are told on one page that he hangs his jacket up before he collects nuts, but on succeeding pages he is wearing his jacket while he is chased by the other squirrels. He is apparently without his jacket when he is stuffed down the tree hole, but is wearing it when we see him portrayed at the bottom of the hole. The red jacket seems to appear and disappear according to whether or not Potter feels she needs more color in a given illustration, not according to its importance to Timmy's character or to the plot. Here is yet another indication that Potter is not letting the story find its own shape but is forcing shape upon it to suit external forces, to the detriment of the story.

Potter's apparent lack of interest in the story, or at least her artistic disengagement from it, shows in the overall quality of the illustrations as well. If one did not know Potter's previous output, one would be hard put to find much of interest in this little tale. McDonald compares the squirrels to stuffed animals dressed in dolls' clothing. The story also marks the end of Potter's book-a-year output. Despite a couple of very fine books yet to come, her books decrease in number and the length of time between books increases dramatically. Warne could no longer count on a book a year from Potter.

Potter still had two books to write before her marriage to William Heelis in 1913: *The Tale of Mr. Tod* (1912) and *The Tale of Pigling Bland* (1913), both of which are comfortably back in Sawrey territory. The first is of the same high caliber as Potter's earlier works, with *Pigling Bland* nearly as good. After this point in Potter's career, she wrote only one more text for which she did original illustrations, as opposed to raiding earlier sketches (*The Tale of Johnny Town Mouse,* 1918), but even this text, like *Apply Dapply's Nursery Rhymes* and *Cecily Parsley's Nursery Rhymes,* depends on someone else's story and is not an original story of her own. Her marriage effectively marked the end of her career as a children's writer, just as the original move to Sawrey marked the beginning of her most productive years and original work. But as both *Tod* and *Pigling Bland* show, Potter was becoming tired of writing nice books for nice children.

Notes

1. Judy Taylor, ed. *Beatrix Potter's Letters* (London: Warne, 1989), 28.
2. Ruth K. McDonald, *Beatrix Potter* (Boston: Twayne, 1986), 96.
3. Beatrix Potter, *The Tale of Jeremy Fisher* (London: Warne, 1906; 1995), 9. Unless otherwise noted, all text references are to the 1995 edition.

4. See both Enid and Leslie Linder, eds., *The Art of Beatrix Potter* (London: Warne, 1955; 1972) and Anne Stevenson Hobbs, *Beatrix Potter's Art* (London: Warne, 1989) for reproductions of some of Potter's naturalistic animal studies. She specifically sketched fish, lizards, newts, and tortoises in the 1880s.

5. Carole Scott, "Clothed in Nature or Nature Clothed," *Children's Literature* 22 (1994): 86.

6. Beatrix Potter, *The Tale of Mrs. Tittlemouse* (London: Warne, 1910; 1987). Unless otherwise noted, text references are to the 1987 edition.

7. Leslie Linder, *A History of the Writings of Beatrix Potter* (London: Warne, 1971), 398.

8. Peter T. Marsh, *Bargaining on Europe: Britain and the First Common Market, 1860–92* (New Haven: Yale University Press, 1999), 173.

9. Quoted in Judy Taylor, *Beatrix Potter: Artist, Storyteller, and Countrywoman* (London: Warne, 1986), 125.

10. Beatrix Potter, *The Tale of Timmy Tiptoes* (London: Warne, 1911; 1987).

6

Into the Sunset

The last two major Potter works—the last two with both original stories and new illustrations—were *The Tale of Mr. Tod* (1912) and *The Tale of Pigling Bland* (1913). Both are fairly long narratives meant for older readers; both combine pen-and-ink sketches with color plates; both have as central characters a pair of animals. The pair in *Mr. Tod* are a disagreeable pair, a fox and a badger, sworn enemies; while the pair in *Pigling Bland* are two of Potter's most endearing characters, a pair of pigs who dance off into the sunset together. One novel ends in violence and destruction, the other with dancing and freedom. Each, in its way, underscores the best that Potter accomplished in her career as a writer, even if each has weaknesses.

The Tale of Mr. Tod can, in some ways, be seen as the culmination of the story of Peter Rabbit, begun back in 1893 with the illustrated letter to Noël Moore. Old Mr. Bouncer, the rescuer of Peter and Benjamin in *The Tale of Benjamin Bunny*, appears here as a doddering grandfather, while Peter and Benjamin themselves must rescue the missing baby rabbits, leaving Benjamin's wife Flopsy at home to argue with her father-in-law and fret over the fate of her children. Despite this, the rabbits in *Mr. Tod* are not the main characters. In fact, they spend the majority of the book either locked in a cold oven (in the case of the baby rabbits); buried in a tunnel (in the case of Peter and Benjamin); or offstage and off-page, in the case of Flopsy and Mr. Bouncer. Potter begins the novel by telling the reader that she is going to tell a tale of "two disagreeable people," Mr. Tod and Tommy Brock,[1] and the first five pages of the story are devoted to telling us about their disagreeable habits, with only incidental mention of the rabbits. In fact, Potter could have lost the rabbits altogether from this narrative and still kept the central conflict of fox and badger intact, and certainly could have given us the final battle without needing to filter it through the perceptions of the rabbits. The rabbits function as a means to an end in the story, not as an end in themselves.

This, of course, is fitting because the rabbits provided Potter herself with a means to an end, with the financial means to escape her own family and buy property in Sawrey. As we already saw in Chapter Two, Potter's interest in the rabbits and their story lessened from novel to novel, until in *The Tale of the Flopsy Bunnies* the rabbits are barely differentiated one from the other. By *Mr. Tod* the rabbits were completely subsidiary characters with Potter's interest having shifted to the more robust, energetic, and problematic fox and badger. Her interests shifted from the domestic to the wild, although she went back to domestic animals in *Pigling Bland*. *Mr. Tod* is the book in which Potter said farewell to the rabbits and their timidity, and although she does not approve of Mr. Tod and Tommy Brock, her text does have a grudging admiration for the two of them and an appreciation for their natures. Potter metaphorically buried her rabbit-past with Peter and Benjamin in that tunnel, moving forward into the dark habitations of badger and fox.

Warne was well aware of the darkness of this novel, which is at least as dark as *The Roly-Poly Pudding*. The publisher objected to the original opening of the story, which was to be, "I am quite tired of making goody goody books about nice people. I will make a story about two disagreeable people, called Tommy Brock and Mr. Tod."[2] Warne's objection was probably at least in part due to the tone of that rejected opening sentence, which is as impatient and forthright as Potter's own letters, lacking any of the subtle irony of earlier texts. Indeed, the rejected opening sentence is quite similar in tone to the sharp letter Potter wrote in response to Warne's objections about the manuscript, which reads in part, "you are a great deal too much afraid of the public for whom I have never cared one tuppenny-button. I am *sure* that it is that attitude of mind which has enabled me to keep up the series"[3] (Potter's emphasis). Potter, of course, cared about the public in the sense that she wanted to sell books and make money, but her greatest books were written more for herself or for a specific child of her acquaintance, not for a more generally conceptualized audience. The publishers worried that the public would not care much for *Mr. Tod*. It was the longest of Potter's manuscripts to date; it was short on the by-then iconic rabbits and long on predatory animals with sharp teeth and nasty habits. Potter, however, prevailed, giving us sharply realized characters that allow her to limn some of her major thematic preoccupations.

The first of those preoccupations is with the dangers of domestic life and also with its attractions. By 1912 Potter is well settled in Sawrey; she has gotten close enough to William Heelis to be more than friends and was to marry him in 1913. She is still, however, tied to her parents, both of whom were still living, and both of whom objected to the engagement to William Heelis—although their objections soon evaporated in face of the surprising news that Bertram had himself been secretly married for several years. She could not have felt entirely safe in her domestic circumstances during the writing of *Mr. Tod,* the conception of which began some years before its completion and publication in 1912. Her growing attraction to William Heelis must have brought up painful memories of Norman Warne, both about his death and about her parents' strenuous objections to her engagement. Some of the same ambivalences about domesticity and its dangers that were apparent in the earlier novels made a sharp reappearance here, for the last time in Potter's literary career.

The opening of the novel is obsessed with houses and housing. We learn that Mr. Tod is of a "wandering habit" (*Mr. Tod,* 11) and that he moves from house to house, from a "stick house in the coppice" to a "pollard willow" to an "earth amongst the rocks at the top of Bull Banks," and that in fact he "had half a dozen houses, but he was seldom at home" (12). This wealth of houses, however, does not translate into a full and safe domestic life for Mr. Tod. For one thing he is a bachelor: there is no Mrs. Tod here. For another, when Mr. Tod is absent from home, "The houses were not always empty" because "sometimes Tommy Brock moved *in*; (without asking leave)" (13; Potter's emphasis). The uncomfortable-sounding houses of Mr. Tod and the homeless state of Tommy Brock are contrasted with the rabbit burrow, where the baby rabbits "lay in a fluffy bed of rabbit wool and hay, in a shallow burrow, separate from the main rabbit hole" (16). Here the babies are wrapped and warm and kept away from the main entrance of the burrow, hidden safe inside from predators. Except, of course, that the rabbit left in charge of them for the day, old Mr. Bouncer, "had forgotten them" and invites Tommy Brock in to share some wine and a cigar (16). The rabbit burrow, which at first seems so cozy and protective, turns out to be no protection at all from the predatory badger, and has its nightmare equivalent later in the story when Peter and Benjamin must hide in the tunnel beneath Mr. Tod's house.

There is no safe domicile in this novel and when disaster strikes for any of its characters, it strikes indoors, not outdoors. When the novel opens, Mr. Tod is living in his stick house and Benjamin hears a plate drop and break inside. We learn much later in the story that Mr. Tod is particularly annoyed at having broken this plate because "it was a china plate, the last of the dinner service that had belonged to his grandmother, old Vixen Tod" (45). Even before Mr. Tod discovers his home has been invaded, before he and Tommy Brock have a wild fight destroying that home entirely, we have its destruction foreshadowed by the breaking of the plate, which is a link to an apparently civilized and feminine past, to a home somewhere in Mr. Tod's family that had good china to eat on and probably the good manners to go with it. But that is in the past, and Mr. Tod's present is concerned with protecting his homes from the invasion of the likes of Tommy Brock, who himself is apparently homeless and merely appropriates the dwellings of others.

Our first view of Mr. Tod's house, the house he keeps locked and (he hopes) free from badger invasion, is not a promising one. Benjamin and Peter, who have tracked Tommy Brock to Mr. Tod's house, peer at a house that "was something between a cave, a prison, and a tumble-down pig-stye. . . . The setting sun made the window panes glow like red flame; but the kitchen fire was not alight" (33). This is a nightmare version of the cottage-in-the-woods of fairy tales, a cottage that is not full of false promises, like the candy cottage of "Hansel and Gretel," but is quite clearly a hellish, lifeless place, akin to Baba Yaga's house of bones in the Russian tale of "Vasilisa the Beautiful." Indeed, a few pages later the rabbits discover that there "were many unpleasant things lying about, that had much better have been buried; rabbit bones and skulls, and chickens' legs and other horrors" (38). These details underline the appropriateness of Mr. Tod's name, "tod" being German for "death," after all. The interior of the house is nearly as dark as the out-of-doors, but what Benjamin and Peter can see from the window is not encouraging. Just as the cold hearth suggests a lifeless house, the items on the kitchen table suggest not so much a warm and comfortable meal to come as they do murder and dismemberment. The rabbits see "an immense empty pie-dish of blue willow pattern, and a large carving knife and fork, and a chopper" (34). There is no sign of the baby rabbits, but clearly they have not yet been killed and eaten, so the adult rabbits have some hope of rescuing them, although enormous obstacles lie in their way.

Here again, as in nearly every one of Potter's novels, is the theme of the eater and the eaten, the threat of being consumed by a predator either human or animal. This is the theme that appeared in her first published book, *Peter Rabbit*; it is echoed again here with the reference to rabbit pie, which is of course the fate of Peter's father, and the threat facing the rabbits in the other two books about them as well. Jemima may end up as roast duck for the fox, Tom Kitten may meet his fate as a roly-poly pudding for the rats, Squirrel Nutkin may be eaten by the owl, and so on. Of all of Potter's books to date, only *The Tale of Mrs. Tiggy Winkle*, *The Tale of Tom Kitten*, and *The Tale of Mrs. Tittlemouse* are free of overt treatment of this theme. *Tom Kitten* and *Mrs. Tittlemouse* do not present the protagonists with the threat of being eaten, but they are presented with the threat of being consumed by either the unreasonable demands of a parent or the unceasing work created by unwanted guests.

Being consumed—by a predator, by an invader, or by a claustrophobia-inducing house—is a lifelong preoccupation of Potter. Metaphorically, Potter felt constrained and consumed by her parents' demands, as well as the demands of class and gender, and it was only through her books that she was able to express this constraint and to break free of it, not only metaphorically but actually. The books gave her both the confidence and the money to buy her own property and, eventually, to defy her parents to marry and construct a home of her own.

There are several other important aspects to the story up to this point. Once again we see Potter weaving together a triple-stranded narrative: the narrative of the rabbits and their fate; the narrative of Tommy Brock and what he is up to; and the narrative of Mr. Tod and his doings. All three of these narratives come together in the ominous house in the woods where Mr. Tod (not knowing about the rabbits hidden in his oven) tries to dislodge Tommy Brock, while the adult rabbits attempt to rescue the babies. As in other of Potter's longer narratives, notably *The Tale of the Roly-Poly Pudding* and *The Tale of the Pie and the Patty-Pan*, Potter skillfully uses multiple narrative lines to heighten suspense and keep the reader turning the pages. We do not know the fate of the baby rabbits until the adult rabbits find Tommy Brock at Mr. Tod's house; we do not know what Mr. Tod is doing while Tommy is headed toward his house; Mr. Tod does not know what awaits him at home, and so the reader does not know what to expect. The reader must worry about whether the baby rabbits will be rescued, whether the adult rescuers will be apprehended before they can save the babies, and what Mr. Tod will do when he discovers Tommy Brock. All of these worries neatly come together when all the protagonists are gathered at Mr. Tod's house.

Again, as in the other novels with longer narrative lines, the story is given to the reader in both a series of small pen-and-ink sketches and in a number of color plates. Here, however, Potter sets off the pen-and-ink illustrations, which are quite small, with a heavy black square outline, giving the pictures the look of old-fashioned woodblock prints and linking them to the framed color illustrations. The framing device gives the sketches more weight and importance than they had in earlier books. Furthermore, Potter shifts point-of-view in the small illustrations much the way a filmmaker might change point-of-view in setting up an establishing shot: the use of the small sketches is much more sophisticated than it has been in earlier books. For example, the two small illustrations of the kitchen on pages thirty-four and thirty-five give us the kitchen table and its implements not in one long view, but in two separate views, from different angles, moving from cooking preparations to eating preparations, and giving equal attention to both, rather than diluting attention by giving us one larger illustration. There are other times when Potter shifts the point-of-view between the small illustrations and the larger color ones. For example, we have on facing pages a large, close-up illustration of Mr. Tod walking through the woods with his walking stick, paired with a small black-and-white illustration of the same action seen from a distance, thus allowing Potter to suggest the large amount of territory Mr. Tod covers in his wanderings and his essential smallness in the largeness of the natural world. This shifting perspective and combined use of black-and-white and color further heightens the suspense of the story.

Potter's characters in this tale are a combination of the human and the animal, with the animal taking the foreground by the end of the tale. Mr. Tod is the first character Potter illustrates, in the frontispiece to the novel, where we see the fox heading alertly out his door, dressed in country tweeds and carrying a walking stick, his black legs masquerading as high boots. He has a predator's stance but the stance is ironic, given what the viewer can see in the background, which is a hunting print of a man on horseback with a pack of hounds, headed off in the same direction as Mr. Tod. Potter, from the very beginning of the tale, suggests that although Mr. Tod may be a predator he is also prey, and that dangers face him as well as the rabbits in this novel.

Mr. Tod's characteristics, as Potter gives them to us in the text and in the small black-and-white sketches on the opening pages, are natural rather than human characteristics. Potter emphasizes his foxy, musky smell, his habit of keeping various dens, and his terrorizing of rabbits and ducks, but Mr. Tod is merely a threatening and incidental character through the first half of the novel. We hear of his doings but see him only from a distance, although his presence as both title character and sole inhabitant of the frontispiece warns us that he will be an important character. Benjamin Bunny knows Mr. Tod is at home in his stick house because he can hear the fox, but neither he nor the reader sees him. The adult rabbits come upon his house on page thirty-one of the novel, but the house appears to be deserted: neither fox nor badger can be seen. Mr. Tod himself appears only as a tiny figure in the background of the black-and-white sketches until page forty-five, when although he is still restricted to a small sketch, we are now close enough to him to make out facial expressions. He does not appear in all of his brush-tailed glory until page forty-six, when he gets his first full-color illustration—Tommy Brock had his on page seventeen.

Even now that we are close to Mr. Tod and can see him dressed as a country gentleman, he still acts like a real fox and not an anthropomorphized one. He is annoyed by a screaming jay as he walks, so he "snapped at it, and barked" (48). When he arrives at his house, although he approaches the door with a rusty key, he also "sniffed and his whiskers bristled" (48). He can smell badger in the house, and Potter is careful to note that this smell "fortunately overpowered all smell of rabbit" (49–50). Mr. Tod discovers Tommy Brock sleeping in his bed (or pretending to sleep), and "For the next twenty minutes" he keeps creeping "cautiously" into the house and then slipping out to "[scratch] up the earth with fury" (51) even though he is afraid to tackle Tommy Brock and his teeth directly. Yes, the fox is disturbed that a badger has taken over his bed, but the fox is exhibiting behavior that a natural fox in the wild would exhibit at finding his den appropriated by an unwelcome visitor. In this case the den is a house with a "tester bed" in it, but the initial reaction of Mr. Tod to this invasion is a reaction his wild cousins would recognize.

Even when Mr. Tod begins to plot and plan how to safely dislodge Tommy Brock, the human traits he exhibits are linked to traditional fox traits that humans have personified for centuries. Mr. Tod would like to kill Tommy Brock—he appears in the bedroom with his walking-stick and the coal scuttle as potential weapons—but is too cautious of the ferocious nature of the badger to risk injury to himself by getting too close. Badgers are notoriously aggressive and persistent animals and are easily a match for foxes, which both Potter and Mr. Tod know. So Mr. Tod concocts a scheme to rig a bucket of water over the apparently somnolent badger, so that when he awakens he will be doused with cold water and will leave the house. Here Potter is playing with the traditional image of the fox as a schemer and a "sly one," a creature clever enough to think of a trick like this and a creature wise and sly enough to make sure that first and foremost his own skin is kept safe.

Celia Anderson pointed out that the portrayal of Mr. Tod links him to the figure of Reynard in the medieval French cycle of trickster tales. She argues that in the Aesop tales about foxes, the morals are rendered with a certain emotional neutrality, whereas in the Reynard tales there is often grudging admiration for the fox, and in their cousins, the Uncle Remus tales, the fox becomes the dupe of the superior trickster, Br'er Rabbit. Potter, Anderson argued, sees the fox characters of both *Jemima Puddleduck* and *Mr. Tod* as seeming to "inhabit a territory between the Aesopian and the Reynardian."[4] There is neutrality in that Mr. Tod is not entirely vanquished in the end—both he and Tommy Brock roll out of the house and out of the story still locked in battle—but there is a certain glee and admiration in Potter's portrayal of the cleverness of Mr. Tod's trick and his persistence in carrying it out, a persistence that extends to chewing his way through the rope holding the bucket, a procedure that takes "more than twenty minutes" (66). At the same time Mr. Tod is out-tricked by Tommy Brock, who has only been feigning sleep and is not in the bed when the bucket falls. In some ways Tommy Brock fulfills the Br'er Rabbit role of outwitting (or outfoxing) the trickster fox.

But what of the rabbits during all of this commotion? The horrifying opening of kidnapped, defenseless infant rabbits literally becomes buried in the text, buried beneath the story of the fox and the badger. Benjamin has taken off in search of his missing children, literally "tracking" the badger in a very un-rabbit-like way, and is joined in the search by his cousin Peter Rabbit. Both rabbits, like fox and badger, are dressed in human clothing. When they discover Mr. Tod's house and deduce that the baby rabbits are imprisoned inside a cold brick oven, they need to discover a way to get into the house and effect a rescue. After consultation, "Peter and Benjamin decided to dig a tunnel" under the house and to come up in the kitchen, which they hope has a dirt rather than a flagged floor (42). They dig for hours until they hear Mr. Tod bark at the annoying jay, when they "did the most foolish thing that they could have done. They rushed into their short new tunnel, and hid themselves at the top end of it, under Mr. Tod's kitchen floor" (44). Here the rabbits will remain until page seventy-three, with only two short, suspenseful mentions of them in the meantime.

The rabbits, too, are behaving in conventional rabbit ways, despite their human clothing and their human determination to track the missing rabbit children. They dig and tunnel until their claws are worn down and they resort to instinctual flight underground when the threatening fox appears—although this burrow has no escape exit, and can end only in the kitchen where the baby rabbits are already imprisoned and awaiting their fate. On the one hand we can see Potter losing some control over her narrative, not knowing what to do with the rabbits she started with, and thus burying them in a tunnel and in an oven until she can return her attention to them. The true suspense of the story is not whether or not the rabbits will be rescued, but whether or not the fox's trick will work and what its consequences will be. The suspense over the trick with the bucket—a trick guaranteed to tickle any schoolboy who might read the book, a trick worthy of the troublesome schoolboys in Kipling's *Stalky & Co.* (1899)—supercedes the suspense over the fate of the rabbits. For Potter the timid rabbits are pale and uninteresting characters in comparison to the energetic, if disagreeable, Mr. Tod and Tommy Brock. Villains, as both actors and writers know, are generally livelier and much more fun than "goody goody" characters, and Potter forgets the rabbits as she focuses on the more interesting predators.

And, of course, she was forgetting the rabbits in real life. She had tired of rabbits long before, was tired of writing books about them, and although they appear in *Mr. Tod*, they are only secondary. What is important is the great antagonism fox and badger have toward one another and how it is centered in a fight over a domicile rather than a fight over food. Who owns the home and who has a right to sleep in its bed is the central struggle in this novel. Homes are apparently worth fighting over, even if they are as disagreeable as Mr. Tod's homes are. Tommy Brock does not have a home of his own, wants one, and so steals one. Mr. Tod feels he should have the right to own many houses and to keep them to himself, whether or not he is actually in residence.

The emphasis on houses here dates nearly as far back in Potter's work as the theme of the eater and the eaten. Houses have always been problematic for Potter, particularly in *The Tale of Two Bad Mice*, *The Roly-Poly Pudding*, and *Mrs. Tittlemouse*. Houses tend to loom large in the writing of women—Wharton's *House of Mirth*, Austen's *Mansfield Park*, Brontë's Thornfield Hall in *Jane Eyre*—and for good reason: women's traditional responsibilities have been to the house and the domestic world, not to the wider world of city and town, of farm and field. Potter had been both trapped in houses (on the third floor of the house at Bolton Gardens) and liberated by houses, first her grandmother Jessy Crompton's country house, and then the holiday houses her parents rented in the countrysides of Scotland and the Lakes. Then there was cousin Caroline Hutton's house in Stroud, near Gloucester, the first house Potter visited without her parents. While Potter was quite aware of the constrictive nature of houses, she also understood that if one truly had a house of one's own it could be a source of independence and individuality. Her enormous pride and pleasure in purchasing, renovating, and furnishing Hill Top and then Castle Cottage, as well as her efforts to protect traditional Lake District farmhouses, speak to this. In *Mr. Tod* she once again destroys a house, as she did in *The Tale of Two Bad Mice*, but as in the earlier novel, the destruction of one home leads to the preservation and continuation of another.

The importance of houses and the conflict of eater and eaten are not the only of Potter's themes to appear in *Mr. Tod*. The novel also gives us yet another representation of hierarchy and struggle for power, struggle that again has an element of class struggle in it. In *Mr. Tod* the fox is clearly meant to be of a higher social class than the badger. He has associations with the British aristocracy, even if he is seen by the landed gentry as prey, not as equal—although of course one reason the fox is hunted is because he is seen as worthy prey for the landed gentry. Like the gentry with whom he is associated, Mr. Tod owns a number of houses. Like the gentry, he has associations with ancestors who had good china and knew how to use it. He dresses in country tweeds and carries a walking stick. He has the ability to move from house to house whenever he feels "out of humour" (47): Potter emphasizes that Mr. Tod's mobility has to do with mood and whim rather than necessity. In other words, many of Mr. Tod's characteristics and actions could as easily describe a member of the landed gentry as they could a fox.

Tommy Brock, on the other hand, is clearly of a lower social class than Mr. Tod. He has no honorific attached to his name. He is not a fastidious dresser like Mr. Tod, but instead "His clothes were very dirty . . . he always went to bed in his boots" (14). He tramps around the countryside setting mole traps and eating "wasp nests and frogs and worms" (13), food we can assume he does not eat from good china. Most importantly Tommy has no fixed abode but must find temporary lodgings where he can, usually in one of Mr. Tod's unused houses. Unlike the fox, who strikes terror in the rabbits, Tommy Brock has a passing acquaintance with the rabbits. The rabbits maintain a cautious relationship with him because he will only eat "very little young ones occasionally, when other food was really scarce" (14). Tommy, in other words, is opportunistic and takes from wherever he can in order to sustain himself, and is on comfortable social terms with the rabbits, who appear to be of the bourgeois or farming class.

Potter does not appear to be on Tommy's side or on Mr. Tod's, nor particularly on the rabbits' side in this story, although they are the only characters afforded a happy ending. She has given a portrayal of some of the complexities of a hierarchical, to some degree class-ridden society in which animosities sometimes stay literally underground and sometimes erupt into actual violence. The hierarchical society she describes in *Mr. Tod* is that of the countryside she inhabited, rather than of the village life she described in *Ginger and Pickles* and *The Pie and the Patty-Pan* or of the urban life of *Two Bad Mice*. She herself was not unlike Mr. Tod, accumulating more than one house and allying herself with the landowning classes, buying up more and more land in the Lakes to keep it from development. But when she tried to get signatures on her petition to ban airplanes from flying over Windermere in 1912 she noted that "the aristocrats won't sign. . . . I find radicals much more willing than conservatives" (*Letters*, 195). The radicals were much more likely to be either allied with or part of the working classes, and they were more sympathetic to Potter's attempts to keep Windermere pristine. She also had other similarities with the working-class Tommy Brock because she was herself a working countrywoman who was frequently seen tramping the fields in Wellington boots and clothing that made tramps take her for one of their own. Furthermore, she had some similarities with the rabbits as well because she remained a shy and retiring woman her entire life, although like the rabbits she had tough claws and knew how to use them.

In this context the fight between Tommy Brock and Mr. Tod is a class struggle for the right to own property. Tommy Brock wants property of his own and takes over that of Mr. Tod, who from Tommy's perspective doesn't have any use for it because he has more than one house. Mr. Tod, further up the class hierarchy than Tommy Brock, appreciates the threat the lower-status Tommy poses to life and property. Although Tommy always appears to be "grinning," as badgers often do, the grin is rather toothy and dangerous. The more Tommy Brock laughs and jokes, with either the rabbits or with Mr. Tod, the more dangerous he becomes. Any underclass can be seen as quaint or comic—witness the portrayals of costermongers or street sweepers in Great Britain, or of happy singing slaves in America—yet all underclasses, by their very nature, have the implicit ability to rise up in anger and topple those who have repressed them. Tommy's comic nature is threatening from the beginning of the story and becomes more so as it progresses. Furthermore, he has the ability to turn what appear to be the strengths of the upper class against itself: he tricks Mr. Tod more than Mr. Tod tricks him, outfoxing the fox. In Potter's own time the labouring classes used what had been upper-class privilege, primarily the voting franchise, to strengthen their position and, within Potter's lifetime, to create the Labour Party and to occasionally put working-class concerns at the center of British domestic debate.

What of the rabbits in this tale of hierarchy and struggle? Narratively they are a weakness in the story. Whereas the characters of Mr. Tod and Tommy Brock are drawn sharply and distinctly, the rabbit characters are fairly blurry. There is no particular continuity in the characteristics of Peter and Benjamin from their earlier stories to this one. The resourceful Peter of *Peter Rabbit*, who became timid and weak in *Benjamin Bunny* and who had metamorphosed into a farmer by *Flopsy Bunnies* is here resourceful once again, urging the more timid Benjamin to go into the house and release his children once the fox and badger have disappeared down the hill. "But Benjamin was frightened" and "Peter kept pushing him" (78). Peter is fulfilling the role Benjamin played in *Benjamin Bunny*, but Potter has never given us a hint as to why Peter is now brave and Benjamin, who has more at stake than Peter, is suddenly timid and ineffectual. Even after Benjamin rescues the babies he must ask Peter, "Can we get away? Shall we hide, Cousin Peter?" (81). The characters are inconsistent with some of their previous incarnations and are largely unconnected to the story of the fox and badger.

They are, nonetheless necessary to the story. At the end of the tale Mr. Tod's home is a complete ruin: "The crockery was smashed to atoms. The chairs were broken, and the window, and the clock fell with a crash, and there were handfuls of Mr. Tod's sandy whiskers. The vases fell off the mantelpiece, the canisters fell off the shelf; the kettle fell off the hob" (74–75). The two antagonists, still snarling and still locked in battle, have disappeared over the hill, leaving only wreckage and frightened rabbits in their wake: neither wins the domicile and the battle will continue, as Potter herself suggested in a letter to a young reader who enquired about the fate of the two characters. "I am sorry to tell you they are still quarreling . . . as for the end of the fight—Mr Tod had nearly half the hair pulled out of his brush . . . and 5 [*sic*] bad bites. . . . The only misfortune to Tommy Brock—he had his jacket torn & lost one of his boots" (*Letters*, 202). Tommy Brock, the working-class figure, seems to have gotten the best of the fight, at least temporarily, even if he is "nasty."

The rabbits go back to a restored home, where things have "not been quite comfortable" (79) in their absence. Flopsy and her father-in-law have been arguing over his role in the disappearance of the babies, to the point where Flopsy had "taken away his pipe and hidden his tobacco" and where Mr. Bouncer is "huddled up in a corner, barricaded with a chair" (80). Significantly, Flopsy is taking out her worries in housecleaning, "having a complete turn out and spring-cleaning, to relieve her feelings" (80). Her house has been invaded and robbed, so she immediately takes to cleaning and rearranging it in order to reassert her ownership of the home. This was Mrs. Tittlemouse's response to invaders as well. The image of Flopsy having just finished her cleaning is juxtaposed with a description of her husband nervously making his way through the dusty wreckage of Mr. Tod's house to rescue the babies from the oven. Soon enough the rabbit family is reunited, Old Mr. Bouncer is given a new pipe and some tobacco, and everyone has dinner together while Peter and Benjamin tell their story. Domestic order is restored in the rabbit burrow.

The moral here, if any of Potter's novels can be said to have morals, seems to be that moderation and vigilance are necessary if one is to have a well-ordered domestic life. Leaving a house to itself is no good: unwelcome visitors may invade and take over. Leaving a house and its inhabitants to a careless caretaker is also no good: again, an invader may come and take what is yours. The invader in both the rabbit home and the fox home is the troublesome working-class Tommy Brock, but in the end Tommy and Mr. Tod fight on into eternity, while the newly cautious and more nearly bourgeois rabbit family have a life of restored order and safety. It is the story of the rabbit home, safe then invaded then safe again, which frames the story of the fox home, deserted, then invaded, then deserted again. Potter is arguing for domestic order and tranquility here, but she is aware that such order is difficult to attain and even more difficult to sustain. There are threats from both without and from within, and even one's closest family members may unwittingly let the enemy through the gates. What wins the day for the rabbits is caution, patience, hard work, and a willingness to risk the dangers inside Mr. Tod's house in order to regain the peace of the rabbit burrow.

The Tale of Pigling Bland[5] is a much sunnier tale, one in which the natural world of pigs left naturally to themselves leads to happiness ever after. The only villains are the unnatural humans, and even they are not entirely without their merits. *Pigling Bland* is also one of the very few texts into which Potter inserts herself, both in text and in illustration. The narrator tells us that "Aunt Pettitoes and *I* dragged" Alexander out of the trough by his hind legs (11), that "*I* went into the garden" to find misbehaving baby pigs and to "[whip] them *myself*" and lead them out by the ears (14; my emphasis). The narrator has a conversation with Aunt Pettitoes concerning the worthiness of the piglets (17) and is pictured giving Alexander his traveling papers. The illustration is clearly a self-portrait of Potter herself, in recognizable tweeds and floppy hat. Potter had a role in earlier books, either as an authorial voice commenting on the action (as in the end of *Mrs. Tiggy-Winkle*) or as a minor figure in the action, the person whose wheelbarrow is stolen at the end of *The Roly-Poly Pudding*. Here, for the first and last time, she is completely integrated with the animal world of the novel, a fully participating figure in it and a collaborator with, if not an equal to, Aunt Pettitoes. It is as if, in this last of the Sawrey books, Potter has truly become one with the landscape and the farmyard, as the animals and their world have become one with her. There is still hierarchy here but it is a hierarchy of human over animal and of legalities over individual desire, not a hierarchy of class or social position. There is still fear of being eaten—there is mention of bacon in this novel—but the threat is not nearly as serious as it is in earlier books and is counterbalanced by the pigs and their peppermints. And although there is one imprisoning house in the novel, in the end Pigling Bland and Pig-wig seem headed off into a sunny domestic future that will, the reader is sure, include a lovely house or stye of their own.

The story begins with a description of Aunt Pettitoes's family of eight baby pigs, nearly all of whom cause exasperation and difficulty by getting stuck in troughs or hiding in laundry baskets. Potter-as-character says to Aunt Pettitoes, "Every one of them has been in mischief except Spot and Pigling Bland" (17). As a result, Aunt Pettitoes resolves to send all the pigs but one away—Spot shall remain to do the housework. The humor here is that in real life pigs being sent to market or to another farmer would be destined to become ham and bacon, but here we are told that Pigling and his brother Alexander are being sent to market to be "hired" by a farmer, and they are warned by their mother to beware of "traps, hen roosts, bacon and eggs; always walk upon your hind legs" (20). Aunt Pettitoes knows the fate of many a pig, and knows her sons—dressed in waistcoats and jackets—will be safer if they seem more human than porcine as they make their way to market, carrying with them licenses for safe passage.

It is Potter herself, as the human proprietor of the farm, who both delivers a stern warning to the traveling pigs and also foreshadows the happy ending for one of them. She says, "impressively," "if you once cross the county boundary you cannot come back" (22), and exhorts them to take care of the licenses permitting the pigs to travel to market in Lancashire, because "I have had no end of trouble in getting these papers from the policeman" (23). As Judy Taylor has pointed out, the characters in this tale begin in a recognizable Sawrey and travel much farther afield than other characters in Potter's novels do. In fact, the characters travel right out of the county and into their own happy future, never once glancing behind. By 1913, when this book was published and Potter had become Mrs. Heelis, she herself must have felt as if she had gotten safely over the bridge and away from interfering policemen and social rules and constrictive parents, and perhaps even away from the difficulties of publishing a book a year for Warne. A major factor in the overall sunniness and joy of *Pigling Bland* is the increasing sunniness and joy in Potter's own life. The darkness of the illustrations to *Mr. Tod* has vanished, and here even the interiors in Mr. Piperson's kitchen have a certain warmth and coziness to them that mitigates any fear we might have of the farmer's intentions toward the pigs.

Pigling and his brother Alexander start off for market together, and the reader is led to believe that this original partnership is the important one in the novel. Pigling is the staid and serious brother, trotting "steadily" for a mile while the more ebullient Alexander "made the road half as long again by skipping from side to side" (27). He also sings—the well-known nursery rhyme of "This pig went to market as he skips." He is improvident in his consumption of peppermints as well. He and Pigling have been given eight "conversation peppermints" by Aunt Pettitoes, peppermints that are wrapped in little screws of paper printed with "appropriate moral sentiments" (25). Those peppermints have a contradictory nature. Even the name of the candy is contradictory, made of the sharp "pepper" and the sweet "mint." These confections are meant to give pleasure and not nourishment, yet they are wrapped in papers with pious moral sentiments printed upon them, suggesting that they in fact do have a serious purpose.

The contradictory nature of the peppermints complements the contradictory natures of the two pig brothers, one so serious and the other so playful. They also function to foreshadow the arrival of another singing pig, Pig-wig, who is as cheerful and playful as Alexander but more careful and cautious than he, if not as cautious as Pigling. Whereas Alexander eats his peppermints all at once, Pig-wig will eat hers little by little; Pig-wig pays attention when Pigling tells her not to do anything to wake up the farmer, and obeys Pigling's instructions once they are on the road together. Pig-wig, for all her high spirits, is more mature and settled than Alexander and an altogether more suitable partner for the maturing Pigling. By the end of the story the peppermints suggest not the contradictory nature of two pigs but the joyous union of two pigs: the peppermints are what send Pigling and Pig-wig on the road to domestic happiness. They provide the link between the lost home of the mother and the new home with the wife.

The peppermints are one of several food references in the story, but the imagery of eater and eaten in this last of the Sawrey novels works differently than it has in the past. Potter mutes the possibility that her protagonists may end up in the skillet or roasting on a spit. Even when Alexander must be returned to the farm after he has lost his license, he is not turned into bacon, or at least if he is Potter gives us no hint of this fate. She merely remarks that "I disposed of Alexander in the neighbourhood; he did fairly well when he had settled down" (32). The verb "disposed" is rather ominous, but then Potter goes on to tell us that Alexander had "settled down," which suggests that he lives on, not that he ends up as someone's breakfast or dinner. It is the good Pigling—so good he tries to catch his brother up when the missing license is discovered but gets lost in the woods instead—who faces the threat of death. When he emerges, wet and cold from the woods, he comes across a hen house in which he can shelter. He knows he has been warned against hen houses, "but what can I do?" he laments (38), even as the chickens in the roost cluck "Bacon and eggs, bacon and eggs" (39). But the picture Potter gives us of the hen roost is not the least bit threatening. We see plump and attractive chickens sheltering a round and curious-looking pig as the entire roost is lit a soft yellow by Mr. Piperson's lantern as he comes to collect chickens to take to market.

Mr. Thomas Piperson—a play on "Tom, Tom, the Piper's son" of the nursery rhyme—is not a pleasant man. He is described as being an "offensively ugly elderly man, grinning from ear to ear" (42), a grin that might remind us uneasily of Tommy Brock's toothy and predatory grin. He is delighted to have discovered a pig on his property, a pig for whom he can discover no proof of ownership. That he does not immediately treat Pigling as a potential meal and that he has hidden Pig-wig away in the cupboard is no comment on Piperson's kindliness toward pigs. It is perfectly clear that Pig-wig (as she herself tells us) is a stolen pig, and that Piperson is concerned that someone may come looking for her and for Pigling. Piperson is constrained by the law, and as we find out later in the story, the newspaper is full of advertisements for lost and stolen pigs, and good citizens are on the lookout to help the constabulary find such pigs. There is, in fact, a great deal of emphasis placed on the law in this story: pigs need licenses to travel; policemen escort unlicensed pigs home; there are county laws forbidding pigs who have left the county to return. The law brings order to the countryside, but it is only by subverting the law that Pigling and Pig-wig can live happily ever after.

Mr. Piperson must feed and fatten up his new-found pig before he can figure out what to do with him, and so fixes three plates of food for himself, Pigling, and for a mysterious someone else who makes smothered noises from a locked cupboard. The reader is well aware that the only reason Piperson is feeding Pigling is in hopes of fattening him up for eventual sale or slaughter, but Pigling himself seems oblivious, despite the fact that Piperson feels his ribs and consults an almanac, only to discover that "it was too late in the season for curing bacon"

(46). Nonetheless, Piperson looks at the "small remains of a flitch" (a side of smoked bacon) and looks again "undecidedly" at Pigling before allowing him to sleep on the rug in front of the fire (46). He is uneasy because the chickens have seen this pig, and the farmer is risking legal trouble if he slaughters a pig who is not his own.

With Piperson, as with the figure of Potter earlier in the story, there is a more complete integration of the fantasy animal world and the human world than there has been in earlier Potter novels. Not only does the same legal authority seem to rule over both pig and man, but pigs and people eat the same food as well. Piperson worries that the chickens are legal witnesses to his thievery and could testify against him. Whereas in *Peter Rabbit, The Tale of Two Bad Mice*, and earlier novels, the humans saw the animals among them simply as animals, in this novel the humans see the animals as having personalities and lives of their own: they come alive for the human *characters* in the novel as well as for the reader. Both animals and humans are constrained by the same social order in this novel: the policeman, that icon of social control, has authority over both the animal and the human world. The humans, or at least Piperson, are as predatory as we think animals often are, and the animals are sweet and human and fall in love just as we do.

The pig who falls in love does so endearingly. Pigling, who is left in the cottage by himself when the farmer heads off to market, first does some exploring and in piglike fashion eats some potato peelings he finds, but then in a human like and tidy fashion washes up the porridge plates from breakfast, all the while singing bits of the nursery rhyme "Tom, the piper's son," a rhyme that tells us that "Even pigs on their hind legs would after him prance."[6] Pigling is also interested in the noises coming from the locked cupboard and as an experiment pushes a peppermint under the sill, where "It was sucked in immediately" (53). Pigling then pushes through the remaining six peppermints during the course of the day, without a word being passed between him and the mysterious someone in the cupboard, beyond the moral sentiments printed on the peppermint wrappers: the pigs are a kind of comic Pyramus and Thisbe. Fortunately, when Piperson returns he is "affable," forgets to lock the meal-chest, and locks the cupboard door but fails to have the door catch properly: the adult reader suspects he has made a stop at the village pub while at market because he goes to bed early and "told Pigling upon no account to disturb him next day before twelve o'clock" (54). Pigling sits by the fire alone until he hears a voice at his elbow demanding he make more porridge.

"A perfectly lovely little black Berkshire pig stood smiling beside him. She had twinkly little screwed up eyes, a double chin, and a short turned up nose" (57). From a pig's point of view she is delightful, although any human female with those characteristics could hardly be cast as a romantic heroine. The illustration accompanying this shows us a startled Pigling, spoon stopped in midair as he turns to stare at this apparition of beauty dressed in a dotted blue-and-white dress. Pigling, both flustered and alarmed by Pig-wig's sudden appearance, "hastily" gives her his porridge plate and "fled" to the meal chest. Pigling, who seemed so self-possessed and mature when we saw him with Alexander or cleaning up around the cottage, becomes suddenly shy and unsure when faced with the cheerful, attractive, self-possessed female pig. She tells Pigling "cheerfully" that she has been stolen for "Bacon, hams," prompting the horrified Pigling to ask "Why on earth don't you run away?" (57). Pigling is no sooner faced with an attractive pig of the opposite sex than he suggests subversion and rebellion to her. (Pigling himself feels protected by his license and seems unaware that his danger is as great as Pig-wig's.)

This brief initial interaction between Pigling and Pig-wig is a telling one. We know that Pig-wig is more socially self-assured than Pigling and also that she is less cautious. She says she will start on her escape "after supper"—like Alexander, her appetites can overrule her common sense. We also see that although Pigling's confidence initially flees when faced with an attractive female pig, his maturity and his masculinity will come back as soon as he sees that Pig-wig does not have the skills to make an escape on her own: he becomes protective of her, finally offering to take her on his way to market: "I might take you to the bridge; if you have no objection" (59). Here Pigling is as polite and formal as any gentleman offering to accompany a single woman on a walk, although he is "much confused" as he asks and then becomes embarrassed at Pig-wig's gratitude.

The interaction between Pigling and Pig-wig is Potter at her best, in the sense that so much is conveyed in so few words and with such understated and ironic humor. Here we have, in miniature porcine form, the flustered suitor who does not even know he has been smitten; the charming maiden who slays her suitor without knowing how she is doing so; the romance happening beneath the surface, with no explicit romantic words being exchanged between the two suitors. This is romance as Potter must have experienced it with Norman Warne, and perhaps again with William Heelis. The romance continues, again with exquisite slowness, as we learn that Pigling is so flustered by Pig-wig that he shuts his eyes and pretends to sleep. He cannot keep up the pretense for long, and when he smells peppermint wakes suddenly to say to Pig-wig, "I thought you had eaten them," to which Pig-wig replies, " 'Only the corners,' studying the sentiments with much interest by the firelight" (60). Pig-wig's control of her appetite suggests her attraction to the provider of the candies—she wants to keep mementos of him—but Pigling is alarmed, fearing that the farmer may smell the peppermints and awaken. He is oblivious, as male suitors often are, to the fact that the object of his affections is being sentimental, saving little keepsakes from Pigling (eating only the corners of the peppermints) and studying the wrappers as if they contain coded love notes from her beloved. And Pig-wig, in a charmingly oblivious way, demands a song from Pigling, an irrational request if he is worried about waking the farmer. Pigling, "much dismayed," begs off, claiming a toothache, so Pig-wig sings instead.

The burgeoning romance between the two pigs in the kitchen is worthy of anything in a Jane Austen novel. The two pigs are clearly meant for each other, are clearly charmed by each other, but neither is a self-conscious flirt or a scheming romancer. They will need to find a way to be together without ever overtly expressing their feelings, not even to themselves. Pigling is attracted to Pig-wig because of her natural charm, her ebullient spirits, her musical skills, and her cheerful nature: qualities any young man of Austen's time or Potter's youth would have found attractive in a young woman. After she serenades Pigling with several verses of song, Pig-wig gradually falls asleep and the considerate—and smitten— Pigling covers her with an antimasscar and stays up all night in fear that Mr. Piperson will wake before the pigs have a chance to escape.

If Pig-wig has charms we might not suspect in a pig, Pigling has unsuspected qualities as well. When we see him in the company of Alexander he appears stodgy and older than his years: the goody-goody brother. Yet it is his maturity and his willingness to think things through that will, in the end, save the day for both him and for Pig-wig. It is he who wakes up Pig-wig in the hours "between dark and daylight" and who cheers her up when she sits and cries in fear of being caught. The two pigs slip away "hand in hand" across a field and to the road, while the sun rises, "a dazzle of light over the tops of the hills. The sunshine crept down the slopes into the peaceful green valleys, where little white cottages nestled in gardens and orchards" (68–69).

This might have been the end of the novel. Here we have a gorgeous sunrise over the bucolic countryside, a counterpart to the rain that plagues Pigling's journey before he finds Piperson's farm; a counterpart to the dark confines of chicken roost, kitchen, and locked cupboard; a counterpart to Piperson's untidy field and unkempt farm; a promise of domestic bliss to come. But the tale is not yet over. The pigs have escaped but their courtship is not complete, and will not be until they brave the dangers of the road and the possibility of an argument before they are ready to begin a life together. Pig-wig looks over the hills to Westmoreland and begins to dance while she sings "Tom, Tom, the piper's son, stole a pig and away he ran! / But all the tune that he could play, / was 'Over the hill and far away!' " (70). The accompanying illustration shows us a misty blue and green view of the enticing hills, while Pig-wig, her back to the viewer, dances as lightly on her feet as any of the dancing mice Potter had earlier drawn. A bemused Pigling looks on, worried that they must get to the bridge before too many interfering and authoritative humans appear on the scene. Pig-wig wants to know why Pigling is so eager to go to market, and Pigling says he isn't: "I want to grow potatoes." Pig-wig, in a non sequitur, asks "Have a peppermint?" Pigling refuses "quite crossly," only grunting when Pig-wig enquires if his tooth still hurts (70). Here, in miniature, the future lives of the two pigs are sketched out for us: the cheerful and solicitous wife who wants to dance and sing, the quiet and occasionally grumpy farmer who appears only to tolerate his wife but secretly adores her and would do anything for her, as we see in the following pages where the escaping pigs are threatened first by the appearance of a ploughman and then by a tradesman's cart upon the road.

Here Pigling has his shining moment, proving himself to be a shrewd and chivalric hero and a worthy companion for Pig-wig. He uses his wits to escape the clutches of the interfering tradesman, who demands to see the pig licenses and is suspicious of a female pig whose name is apparently Alexander. Pigling, quick-witted enough to think ahead, pretends to be both slow-witted (he has missed the market by a day) and lame, hoping the tradesman will be lulled into complacency, as he is. Even though he "knew that pigs are slippery . . . surely, such a *very* lame pig could never run!" (79; Potter's emphasis). Pigling makes Pig-wig wait until the tradesman looks back to make sure they are still in the road, and until he is sure the tradesman's horse still has a stone in his shoe (it is the horse who is lame, not the pig), before saying, "Now, Pig-wig, NOW!" as the pigs "race and squeal" toward the bridge, which they cross hand in hand and, as the novel ends, "then over the hills and far away she danced with Pigling Bland!" (84). The last illustration in the text is a black-and-white sketch that shows both pigs dancing as the sun sets and as they are watched by a trio of rabbit musicians. The pigs dance themselves right into the nursery rhyme, into happy-ever-after, and into immortality.

Potter assured friends that Pigling was not a portrait of William Heelis, who was tall and thin and not piglike at all, and because she wrote herself into the story it is hard to see Pig-wig as Potter's self-portrait (*Letters*, 214). There is not much in the story that is directly autobiographical, beyond the information we get about the lives of pigs and the wonderful drawings of them that clearly show Potter's delight and love for these animals, despite her Christmas gifts of homegrown smoked pork to families and friends. The atmosphere in the novel and the way it ends in what will clearly be a bright future for the pigs surely owes something to Potter's own changing circumstances. She herself had been constrained by many things throughout life, not least of which were her parents and their insistence Potter stay single and care for them in their old age. Potter had assimilated enough of her culture's expectations for daughters to be susceptible to parental pressure, yet she managed to defy her parents not once, but twice, and to make a good marriage and a happy home with William Heelis. She herself must have felt like dancing once she married Heelis, even though he was the country dancer and she more often the observer. She now not only had a home of her own but a husband and the kind of social standing she could never have hoped to attain as a single woman, whether or not she was a best-selling author and champion sheepbreeder and farmer. Potter, like all Victorian young ladies, grew up believing that marriage was a woman's proper state, and she had finally achieved it.

Graham Greene believed that in 1912 with the publication of *Mr. Tod*, Potter's "pessimism reached its climax." Although in her earlier novels she "had gracefully eliminated the emotions of love and death" that so dominate *Mr. Tod*, in *Mr. Tod* "the form of her book, her ironic style, remained unshattered. When she could not keep death out she stretched her technique to include it."[7] What Greene means by "emotions of love and death," I think, is the *expression* of the emotions raised by both love and death. Certainly one of the hallmarks of Potter's artistry is the ironic distance she keeps from such emotion: Mrs. Rabbit merely remarks that her husband had an "accident" and was "baked into a pie," with no more emotion or expression than she would use speaking of the weather—but the context of her remark is what emphasizes its importance and her anxiety. This kind of ironic distance is stretched in both *Mr. Tod* and in *Pigling Bland*. In the former, the anxieties caused by potential rabbit-death are enormous and we see them expressed both in word and action. Benjamin Bunny sounds nearly neurotic as he searches for his missing children, and both he and Peter are frightened out of their wits by the evidence of death around the cottage that holds the kidnapped baby rabbits. But their fear leads them only to self-burial in the tunnel they have dug: their fear will have to be overcome before they can resurrect themselves and then the rabbit children. In the latter novel Potter is more in control of ironic distance as she develops the love affair between the pigs, but ultimately cannot constrain either herself or her characters: the pigs break into song and dance as they escape Lancashire for Westmoreland, and Potter herself seems very nearly to dance and sing in the lyrical and lovely ending to almost the only love story she ever wrote.

The other tale that is very nearly a love story is *The Tale of Two Bad Mice*, where Potter gives us a portrayal of happily married mice who take what they need from the lifeless dolls. She cannot show us courtship in that book, however, only the partnership in love and crime that Tom Thumb and Hunca Munca share so profitably. It is significant, however, that the two novels she wrote that focus on either romance or happy marriage are the two she wrote while she herself was involved in courtship, first with Norman Warne and then with William Heelis. Both novels resonate with an energy and a happiness that outweighs any of the anxieties the characters may have. In both *Two Bad Mice* and *Pigling Bland* the protagonists subvert the rules and run away from home in order to have a home of their own—not unlike what Potter herself had to do. *Mr. Tod* is the dark before the light, the novel in which Potter is at her most pessimistic. True, she does restore the family of Benjamin Bunny and does not show us the deaths of Mr. Tod and Tommy Brock, although their fight is so vicious one fully expects them to die. In a kind of dark mirror image of the other house of destruction in *Two Bad Mice*, Mr. Tod's house is completely destroyed, "smashed to atoms," and the rabbits take nothing useful from it, except perhaps experience. Although Greene thought Potter must have had some dreadful personal crisis the year *Mr. Tod* was written and published, I think it more likely that the novel was simply the pessimistic conclusion of many years of unhappiness for Potter, despite her literary success and her ownership of land and property in Sawrey, amplified perhaps by the tensions caused by her engagement to William Heelis.

Pigling Bland, where the rabbits make their final appearance as musical accompanists to the escaping pigs, is very nearly Potter's farewell from the literary scene altogether—it's as if the rabbits who gave her her first taste of freedom are finally letting her go to cross that bridge into a life of private happiness. After its publication in 1913 and her October marriage to William Heelis, Potter never again writes with the brilliance she showed earlier in her career, and with nothing like the sophistication she shows in the novels published between 1905 and 1913, the novels that are largely based in her new home of Sawrey. Marriage and farming came to preoccupy her; World War I began and provided further worries, preoccupations, and practical difficulties for anyone wishing to write and publish; her eyesight was failing and making it difficult for her to work on small and detailed watercolor illustrations. Even after the war there were difficulties, not least of which being the financial woes of Warne, whose director, Harold, had been arrested for forgery in 1917 and left the company on the brink of financial ruin. Even before the arrest, Potter had been growing exasperated with the company's business practices, although remaining close to Millie Warne and to other members of the family. There were still two books of nursery rhymes to come, as well as *The Story of Johnny Townmouse* and *The Fairy Caravan*, but these were part of the coda of her career, not the culmination, which occurred with the Sawrey books.

Notes

1. Beatrix Potter, *The Tale of Mr. Tod* (London: Warne, 1912; 1987), 11. Unless otherwise noted, all text references are to the 1987 editions.

2. Leslie Linder, *A History of the Writings of Beatrix Potter* (London: Warne, 1971), 212.

3. Judy Taylor, *Beatrix Potter's Letters* (London: Warne, 1988), 198.

4. Celia Anderson, "The Ancient Lineage of Beatrix Potter's Mr. Tod," in *Festschrift: A Ten Year Retrospective of the Children's Literature Association* ed. Perry Nodelman and Jill May (W. Lafayette, Ind.: Children's Literature Association, 1982), 46.

5. Beatrix Potter, *The Tale of Pigling Bland* (London: Warne, 1913; 1987). Unless otherwise noted, all text references are to the 1987 editions.

6. Iona and Peter Opie, eds., *The Oxford Book of Nursery Rhymes* (London: Oxford, 1955), 164.

7. Graham Green, "Beatrix Potter," in *Only Connect: Readings in Children's Literature*, 2nd ed., ed. Sheila Egoff, G. T. Stubbs, L. F. Ashley (New York: Oxford, 1980), 263.

7

Coda and Conclusions

Potter's novels often had long codas to them, pages of exposition giving further details about the lives of the characters whose adventures had just come to an end: the coda in *Two Bad Mice* about the arrival of the policeman and the mouse trap; the coda in *The Roly-Poly Pudding* about the adult lives of the cats; the coda in *Jemima Puddleduck* about Jemima's next adventure in brooding, and so forth. The codas sometimes continued beyond the covers of the books into miniature letters Potter wrote in the voice of her characters and sent to child correspondents.[1] Potter's own career had a kind of coda, marked by the beginning of the First World War and the start of her marriage, years in which she still wrote and published, but without the brilliance of either text or illustration of her earlier work. There were other events that contributed to the waning of Potter's career as well: her farming duties took up more and more of her time and attention; her father's health failed and he died in 1914, leaving Mrs. Potter entirely on her daughter's hands; her eyesight was getting weaker; and her publisher fell into serious financial difficulties, leading her both to attempt to bail them out and to desert them for an American publisher. The best of her books were behind her by 1913; what is successful in the books at the end of her career can be attributed more to earlier, resurrected artwork and ideas, rather than to a continued growth in her artistry.

The beginning of the First World War slowed nonmilitary business nearly to a standstill, including publishing, but even if publishing had been unaffected it is doubtful if Potter would have published much. She was newly married, for one thing. William Heelis' health precluded him from military service, but he had duties as a civilian warden and had been issued a helmet. On the farm there were shortages and worries about horses and property being requisitioned for the war effort. And in London, Warne—who had gotten increasingly haphazard in its financial accountings to Potter—was becoming impossible to deal with. In 1914 Potter wrote to Fruing Warne to say, "I promised not to ask the firm for payments when times were so difficult; but I think you will allow that the failure to send any statements at all is a trial of patience; the overlapping and punctuality had begun *long before the war*" (Potter's emphasis). She goes on to say that if accounts are not gone into satisfactorily within a few months, "I shall have to take some steps about it—not in any unfriendly spirit, but to put the matter on a more businesslike footing."[2] Potter was uneasy enough to alter the wording of her contracts with Warne in 1916 in order to protect her copyrights.

Potter's fears, to her dismay, proved well-founded. In March of 1917 Harold Warne was arrested near Covent Garden and charged with "uttering a bill of exchange for £988.10s.3d. knowing it to be forged."[3] Harold had been dipping into publishing monies and forging bills in order to support a failing family fishing business, apparently without the knowledge of his brothers. He was ultimately convicted of forging nearly £20,000 and sentenced to eighteen months imprisonment with hard labor. The consequences first for the Warne family, to whom Potter had remained close even after Norman's death, were devastating, as were the consequences for the business (now under Fruing's control) and for Potter as its main source of income. Potter wrote sympathetic letters to Millie and others in the family concerning the loss of the family home in Surbiton and promised to look after Winifred's old doll house, the house that had been the model for the one in *Two Bad Mice*, and did her best to help the company survive. It was in her best financial interests to do so as she was their single largest creditor.

Warne asked Potter for a new book in order to help the firm get back on its financial feet as it was being restructured; Potter offered *Appley Dapply's Nursery Rhymes*, writing that "I find I could scrape together sufficient old drawings" (*Letters*, 234). As we have seen throughout this book, Potter had a longtime love of nursery rhymes, stemming at least in part from a childhood love of Randolph Caldecott's work. There are rhymes—some of them very old and not well known and others old favorites—in many of her small novels, ranging from *The Tailor of Gloucester* straight through to *Pigling Bland*. She had been thinking about doing a book of nursery rhymes since at least 1902, and she and Norman had discussed and partly planned out a nursery rhyme book in large format, getting as far as doing a dummy book. Potter's interest in the rhymes was partly historical, based on her interests in the rhythms of older forms of English, partly an interest in the mysterious and often riddling aspects of the rhymes (this was a woman who invented a written code, after all), and partly a desire to follow in the steps of Randolph Caldecott, for whom she had a "jealous appreciation" (441). In 1902, in corresponding with Norman Warne about the publication of *Peter Rabbit*, she says that she has "sometimes thought of trying some of the other nursery rhymes about animals, which [Caldecott] did not do" (64). The original idea in 1902 and

1903 was to illustrate the rhymes and frame them with a decorative border in a large-format book, but other book projects delayed the nursery rhyme book. By the time Fruing Warne asked her for a new book to help the struggling company, she no longer felt up to the task of a large-format book, and instead offered to "scrape together" old drawings to fill a booklet the size of one of the small books in the *Peter Rabbit* series. Judy Taylor points out that some of the pictures in this "compilation" display Potter's "earlier style and show how many of the drawings had been in her portfolio for some time, even if they had been reworked for publication."[4] Potter did rework a number of the illustrations (although not all of them), but *Appley Dapply* is more a miniature portfolio of Potter's earlier, discarded work than it is an integrated, well-designed book.

The charm of *Appley Dapply*[5] lies in the illustrations rather than in the text, which like most nursery rhyme collections is a series of short verses rather than a sustained narrative. Most successful illustrated collections of rhymes give unity through style and design, but *Appley Dapply* lacks this quality. Some of the illustrations date back to 1891 while others are leftovers from the 1913 *Pigling Bland*. Not surprisingly, Potter's work changed stylistically over the years, stylistic changes than are encapsulated in *Appley Dapply*.

The first illustration is of the title character, a small mouse Potter had originally sketched when she was only twenty-five, some years before the illustrated letter to Noël Moore (*Artist and World*, 155). The mouse illustrations, framed in careful rectangles, show a young and very talented artist at work: the fineness of the line, the meticulous graining of the skirting board, the fluidity of the mouse's movements, and the combination of human and mouse characteristics in one figure show us a young artist who has enormous control of technique, as well as originality of vision. By the time we get to a late illustration for the rhyme "Gravy and potatoes in a good brown pot," Potter was recycling more recent work, this time a sketch left over from *Pigling Bland*. While Potter was still in control of her pen and brush, the style of this illustration is quite different from that of the mouse that opens the book. The earlier illustration is done with a much drier brush and is much more concerned with the straightness of lines and the almost photographic realism of the skirting board: one feels that a carpenter's level placed on that board would show it to be absolutely level and square. The later illustration of the pig pays much less attention to the straightness of the lines of the rafter or the table legs; the texture of the pig's skin is suggested rather than meticulously lined out hair by hair, and the entire illustration is looser, more fluid, and less detailed than the illustrations that open the book. Comparing these two illustrations shows us the ways Potter grew in confidence as an artist, as well as the ways failing eyesight changed her style over the years.

Not only are the illustrations from different periods in Potter's career, but they are all framed differently. In 1903, during correspondence about *The Tailor of Gloucester*, Potter became incensed when her framing lines to the illustrations were left off by the printer, and provided her publishers with a lengthy explanation of how and why borders worked and how using them made for a different kind of illustration than vignetting pictures did. Yet in *Appley Dapply* we have squared-off pictures without frames (as in the illustrations of the mice), vignetted pictures (of the mole and his shovel, for example), and squared-off pictures with framing lines (the pig and his potatoes). Potter did little reworking of these illustrations, allowing the original format, vignetted or framed, to stand, thus amplifying the discontinuity of the book rather than ameliorating it. While the original *Appley Dapply* planned for 1905 was apparently a well-integrated and designed work, the published version of 1917 is a hodge-podge, clearly produced under pressure and without much editorial control. It is hard to imagine the Potter of ten years earlier allowing such a poorly designed book to be printed under her name—but by 1917 she had other priorities and interests. She and Warne both knew that her name alone would sell books, regardless of quality, and she was willing to compromise her artistic standards. *Appley Dapply* sold out its first edition of 20,000 copies by the end of 1917 (*Letters*, 247).

Potter wrote one more nursery rhyme book, *Cecily Parsley's Nursery Rhymes* (1922), but between the two rhyme books she wrote one more small novel for Warne, *The Tale of Johnny Town-Mouse* (1918). This is a more successful work than the rhyming books, but even it relies on the reworking of earlier sketches and ideas. The story is a variation on Aesop's tale of the country mouse and the town mouse, and Potter tips her floppy brown hat to Aesop in the dedication to the book. Here, controlled by the original story, Potter does not wander from the narrative track. The story has a pleasing shape to it, as first Timmy Willie mistakenly travels to town, where he is alarmed and made unhappy by the details of town life, and then Johnny Town-Mouse visits Timmy Willie's garden and finds it altogether too damp and dull. Each mouse tries to be a good host, but as Potter comments in the conclusion, "One place suits one person, another place suits another person. For my part I prefer to live in the country, like Timmie Willie."[6] Neither mouse convinces the other to move to new environs. This is Potter's variation on Aesop's original moral to his fable of "The Town Mouse and the Country Mouse": "A simple life with peace and quiet is better than faring luxuriously and being tortured by fear."[7] Potter's country mouse is "tortured with fear" by the housemaids and cat he encounters in town, whereas the town mouse is alarmed by the country sounds of mowing machines and mooing cows. Fear and peace and quiet are in the eye and ear of the beholder.

McDonald shrewdly points out that this little novel emphasizes the "urban" life of the house in Hawkshead in the text but gives pride to country life in the illustrations, further noting that Potter's point of view strays from the mouse's when she illustrates the house, but consistently stays at mouse-eye view when illustrating Timmy Willie's country life.[8] This is true so far as it goes, but it is worth noting that Potter does stray from mouse-eye view when Timmy Willie begins his journey in the country: we see him from a higher, human point of view in our first picture of him, when he is standing on two legs and looking curiously at the hamper that will mistakenly bear him to Hawkshead. When we see him from a mouse-level point of view he is either enjoying the luxuries of food in the garden or telling Johnny of these pleasures. But a number of the illustrations set in the house are from a human point of view. The human point of view emphasizes the greater human qualities of the town mice (who are always clothed, whereas Timmy Willie remains unclothed) and the dependency of the town mice on humans. Ironically, the town mice depend on the crumbs and leavings of the same humans who expend much energy trying to eradicate them. Timmy Willie, on the other hand, relies on nothing but the bounty of the garden. The garden may be planted and tended by humans, but because he does not invade or threaten human habitation, Timmy Willie is left to himself. Unlike Peter Rabbit, he does not raze gardens or do noticeable damage, so he is ignored by the human gardeners. When he does invade human space by climbing into the garden hamper, he is on the road to trouble. Even if humans are not actively pursuing the mouse, the proximity of mouse to human habitation leads to anxiety and danger for Timmy.

Again we have the theme of the eater and the eaten and of anxiety about domesticity. But here, later in Potter's career and after she has largely quieted her own domestic anxieties, Potter puts literal distance between the anxiety-ridden house in town and Timmy Willie's "peaceful nest in a sunny bank" (*Town-Mouse*, 33). Timmy's house barely deserves the title "house": it is open on one side and garden plants creep in from outside. The illustrations of his house show quite literally that one can make a house in the country and in fact totally integrate domestic life into natural country life, thus visually supporting the "moral" of the tale. The integration of text and illustration supports the theme of the story, as was the case with all of Potter's best books.

Potter also returns to social satire in this little book. Timmy Willie literally crashes a formal dinner party, falling down a hole and straight into the middle of Johnny's dinner table, smashing glasses and cutlery along the way. The town mice, dressed in white tail, never lose a beat. Johnny, "after the first exclamation of surprise" "instantly recovered his manners" (21). Timmy Willie is properly introduced and invited to join the dinner party, where as honored guest he sits at the head of the table despite the fact that, unlike the town mice, he is not dressed nor does he have a suitably long tail. However, the mice "were too well bred to make personal remarks" (22) and resort to polite conversation, which does little to calm the nervous Timmy Willie, on edge because of noises of cats and servants and other mysterious things coming from upstairs. Johnny, like the good well-bred gentleman mouse he is, does his best to make Timmy Willie comfortable, offering him delicacies from the table and the best bed in the house—although the food gives Timmy indigestion and the bed smells of cat, so Timmy opts for sleeping beneath the fender instead. Johnny finally, politely, says "It may be that your teeth and digestion are unaccustomed to our food; perhaps it might be wiser for you to return in the hamper" (38), thus gently suggesting that Timmy leave if he is uncomfortable and barely concealing his annoyance when he realizes that Timmy did not understand that the hamper he arrived in is returned to his own garden once a week. It is the exasperation of someone so used to his own world and his own point of view that he cannot understand that of an outsider, but the exasperation is cloaked in good manners and polite speech. Johnny is to some extent hypocritical, but his hypocrisy is of the common social sort that exists in order to oil the wheels of human interaction. His hypocrisy is not for personal gain nor is it a result of pretension: it is a result of his social standing. Potter is both amused by and scornful of the ever-so-polite town mice, as she always was of characters (and people) who were impressed more by appearances than by reality, and who lived on the labor or leavings of others rather than on their own labor.

Timmy has been a good guest, however, and offers hospitality in return. He has painted a lovely picture of life in the garden, a life we get to see glimpses of when he returns in the hamper. His garden is filled with "roses and pinks and pansies—no noise except the birds and bees, and the lambs in the meadows" (34). He is visited in the spring by Johnny Town-Mouse, who comments that "it is a little damp" and who holds his elegant tail out of the mud. Johnny remains dressed in his town best, totally unsuitable garb for the countryside. Johnny finds country life too quiet (although he is as alarmed by the cows and by lawnmowers as Timmy was by the cat and the human racket in the house) and gratefully returns home.

The illustrations for this tale are vignetted as they were in the earlier books and have some lovely garden views. The mice in the country are often framed by beautifully drawn foliage, yet Potter's waning eyesight had taken a toll. The drawings are not nearly as detailed as they had been earlier in her career, and not all of their muddy quality can be attributed to the deterioration of the plates: the work is not up to her earlier standards, although the elegant mice at the dinner table very nearly are. The entire book shows Potter near the top, but not at the top of her game. She is still critical of the merely decorative and largely useless, she still provides ironic commentary on social life, but her commentary is not as sharp or ironic as it has been in the past. Some of this is no doubt due to the neutral tone of the original Aesop tale, but some is also due to her growing lack of interest in writing small books. What we see in *Johnny Town-Mouse* is the last glimpse of Potter at her best, although her best is fast fading.

The writing of *Johnny Town-Mouse* coincided not only with the war, but also with the unexpected death of Beatrix's brother Bertram and the permanent move of Mrs. Potter to the Lake District. Bertram remains a shadowy figure in the documented version of Potter's life. The published letters contain no correspondence between the two of them, nor is he mentioned in Potter's letters to friends,[9] but

Bertram and Potter had been close in childhood. It was Bertram who was her coconspirator in her first attempts to publish her work, Bertram who accompanied her on tramps in the countryside to study wildlife and wildflowers, Bertram who had the microscope Potter used in her studies of insects and fungi. Closeness apparently persisted, because when Bertram was appealed to in 1913 to help his parents stop Potter's marriage to William Heelis, he announced that he himself had been married since 1902 and had simply kept this information from the family. Bertram was as good at keeping secrets and leading a private life as was his sister, and his reluctance to share his marriage (to someone his parents would have found socially unsuitable) suggests that the elder Potters wanted to exert unusual control not only over their daughter but also over their son. They failed with both, but Bertram did not have as happy or as long a life as his sister. He had had problems with alcohol since he was a young man—Potter referred to this as the "family weakness"—and his sudden death by cerebral hemorrhage in June 1918, at the age of forty-six, was probably hastened by long-term abuse of alcohol. Taylor tells us that Potter had seen little of Bertram since her marriage, but his death was a shock and she felt his loss keenly.

It was not much consolation to have her mother nearby. Mrs. Potter had a fairly lonely life after the death of her husband in 1914, and Potter herself was unwilling to travel much to London to be with her. When Lindeth How, a Lake District home the Potters had rented and summered in came on the market, Potter bought it for her mother and Mrs. Potter moved with "four maids, two gardeners and the coachman-turned-chauffeur" (*Artist and Countrywoman*, 144) on the other side of Lake Windermere from Potter. Although we have no letters or journal entries to tell us Potter's feelings about this move, at the least she must have been exasperated by the number of support staff her mother seemed to need. Potter and Heelis needed far fewer, for far more extensive property, and Potter was never in favor of excess of any sort. She must have been especially annoyed because her mother would often refuse to send the car to pick her daughter up at the ferry, leaving the arthritic Potter to walk between the ferry landing and Lindeth How. A further irritation was Mrs. Potter's reluctance to use any of her money to help her daughter buy up threatened farmland in the district, even though such use of her money would have been a wise financial investment for her.

In this war period Potter was also concerned with supporting local charities and local social events. She kept Willie company when he joined the local folk dancers, negotiated with villagers about the leasing or borrowing of one of her fields for celebrations of one sort or another, and helped set up a local nursing association in 1919. She had also not lost her taste for national politics, and we know that in 1919 or 1920 she gave £3 to the Southern Irish Loyalists, thus supporting her staunch opposition to Irish Home Rule, opposition she had held since Gladstone's time in the 1880s (*Artist and Countrywoman*, 149). She was also still learning to be a farmer, still buying up property in the Lakes, and was becoming a partner with Willie. Even at the end of her writing career Potter's energy seems prodigious, in keeping with her beginnings as an industrious Victorian.

So it is no surprise that Potter was increasingly reluctant to spend time writing small stories for children: her work on the books must, at this point in her life, have seemed trivial compared to the day-to-day realities of life as a farmwoman and wife during a time of war. Warne kept pressing her, after *The Tale of Johnny Town-Mouse*, for another new book. She did promise one called *The Tale of Jenny Crow* but did not make much progress on it, noting to Fruing that "You do not realize that I have become more—rather than less—obstinate as I grow older. . . . I never have cared tuppence either for popularity or for the modern child; they are pampered and spoilt with too many toys and books" (quoted in *Artist and Countrywoman*, 149). She also noted that "It is absolutely hopeless and impossible to finish books in summer," the busiest season for a farmer (150), and finally writes that "you don't suppose I shall be able to continue these d . . . d little books when I am dead and buried!! I am utterly tired of doing them" (150). The strength of the language here is quite unusual for Potter, and suggests that indeed her exasperation and indifference to the books was genuine, at least on the day she wrote the letter.

Potter might have stopped writing for publication altogether if not for a visit by Anne Carroll Moore, children's librarian with the New York Public Library, who began a correspondence with Potter that grew into a visit, a friendship, and a strong American connection. It was Moore who encouraged Potter to work on a second nursery rhyme book, which ultimately became *Cecily Parsley's Nursery Rhymes* (1922),[10] the last of the little books to be printed by Warne.

Cecily Parsley is a more integrated and successful nursery rhyme book than is *Appley Dapply*. There are fewer rhymes in *Cecily Parsley*, they are more familiar rhymes (with the exception of the rhyme about the guinea pigs and their garden, which is apparently original to Potter), and there is almost a feeling of separate chapters in the very short, thirty-three-page book. Most of the rhymes are split over several pages and have several illustrations to them, giving the reader a chance to both savor a rhyme and a chance to move on to something new fairly quickly: a good strategy for a nursery rhyme book intended for small children. As in *Appley Dapply* the illustrations are for the most part salvaged and reworked illustrations from Potter's portfolio, but here Potter seems to have put more effort into the reworking and has been more careful about matching illustration to rhyme. For example, the opening rhyme about Cecily Parsley living in a "pen" while she brews ale for gentlemen is accompanied by a drawing of rabbits outside her pub, which is in a tree and is appropriately called "The Pen Inn," with a signboard featuring a large quill pen on it. Potter has not merely recycled an old drawing of rabbits, but has reworked the drawing so that it is more closely integrated with its associated rhyme. Some of the illustrations of the cat and dog having tea are reworkings of drawings for *The Pie and the Patty-Pan*, and the mice by the candle in the last illustration are reminiscent of the mice around the bunsen burner in Potter's illustration of "A Dream of Toasted Cheese," first done as a commemoration of the publication of one of Potter's uncle Sir Henry Roscoe's publications of a chemistry book, and later recycled as the cover for *The Tailor of Gloucester* (*Artist and Her World*, 85–86).

Cecily Parsley is the last of what most would consider the "canon" of Potter's work. It is the last to be published solely by Warne and the last of the short narratives: late in her career Potter was more interested in writing longer prose narratives than in writing shorter illustrated texts. Potter became increasingly divorced not only from her interests in drawing for children but also from dealings with Warne and Company. The company was always urging her, their best-selling author, to write a novel a year, pressure Potter found increasingly irritating. On the other hand Potter had made two important American friends in Bertha Mahony (editor of *Horn Book Magazine*) and Anne Carroll Moore, the New York City librarian. These women admired Potter's prose as much as her art and did not pressure her to write for the profit of their own enterprises. Moore was a librarian and out of the private financial sector altogether, and Mahony's primary purpose was to promote excellence in children's books, not to turn a profit in publishing (although she did own a children's bookstore and had some financial interest in the selling of children's books). Furthermore, Mahony gave as much as she took from Potter. The *Horn Book* was the first publisher of *Wag-by-Wall*, thus assuring the magazine healthy sales for that issue, but Mahony also facilitated the sale of fifty signed *Peter Rabbit* drawings for the benefit of the National Trust, with whom Potter was working to save land in the Lake District (*Artist and Her World*, 194).

Potter made a third important American friend, Philadelphia publisher David McKay, who in 1927 made an "alarming visitation . . . in search of a book that doesn't exist," as Potter wrote (*Letters*, 309). Hobbs and Taylor note that Potter felt McKay "understood an aspect of her writings not appreciated" in England (*Artist and Storyteller*, 161) and was flattered by his admiration of her prose, which he thought as highly of as did Moore and Mahony. She agreed to rework some earlier stories and print them with McKay rather than with Warne, despite the unpleasantness this was bound to cause. Some of the stories were reworkings of early attempts at fairy tales and others were original stories about animals, longer than but not dissimilar to the stories she had told in the series of little books for Warne. Many of them were tales she had shared with a child friend, Henry P. Coolidge, who shows up as a character in the stories and to whom *The Fairy Caravan* is dedicated. She wrote to him in 1928 both to praise the boy's written account of his visit to Sawrey and to explain that farm chores had interfered with completion of the tales that were to become *The Fairy Caravan*. Potter wrote to McKay: "I don't want all this stuff published in England"

(*Letters*, 313), feeling the material was too personal. Some of the material certainly spoke more realistically of her life than the little books had, but the novels published with Warne are far more revealing of Potter's personality than are the tales in *Caravan*. Nonetheless Potter made certain to secure a British as well as an American copyright for the book. She was very pleased with McKay's work and wrote to him that she hoped the book would give satisfaction "to my most exacting critics—my own shepherds and blacksmith. I do not care tuppence about anybody else's opinion" (316). This echoes her earlier pleasure at a good review of *The Tailor of Gloucester* in a tailoring journal, and indicates Potter's respect for the working people with whom she had contact during her lifetime.

The Fairy Caravan[11] shows Potter interested in longer narratives less reliant upon illustration but it also shows a Potter who, without strong editorial control, tended to ramble on and lose the thread of her narrative. Warne & Co. had been aware of this weakness and had, in her early books, consistently encouraged her to shorten and tighten her narratives. *Peter Rabbit* was accepted only in shortened form, for example, and *The Tailor of Gloucester* lost many of its rhymes in the transformation from manuscript to printed book. Potter was aware of this weakness in *The Fairy Caravan*, writing to Henry P. Coolidge that "the wanderings of the circus company go on and on without end" (*Letters*, 311) and to McKay, "I am afraid I am long winded about my sheep. . . . I am conceited enough to say I am the only person who could have written about the sheep; because I know them and the fell like a Shepherd; but the Herdwick men are not articulate" (313). *The Fairy Caravan* today is almost unreadable, although one can see the misty outlines of not one, but several promising stories in it. The book begins with the story of Tuppenny, a short-haired guinea pig who lives in the town of Marmalade, a town where the snobbish long-haired guinea pigs look down upon their short-haired cousins. Tuppenny becomes the unfortunate "guinea pig" (and one is certain Potter had the pun in mind) who tries out the hair tonic promised to grow hair by Messrs. Ratton and Scratch, two rats with a traveling snake oil show—only the snake oil works, and Tuppenny begins to grow so much hair neither he nor his wife can control it. In these early pages one can see Potter the social satirist at work. The long-haired guinea pigs are "affronted" by the hundreds of placards put up by Ratton and Scratch (a word Potter used earlier to describe Tabitha Twitchit's feelings about her unruly children), but the short-haired guinea pigs "twitter" both hopefully and nervously, unwilling to spend money on an untried tonic unless someone else tries it first: hence Tuppenny is persuaded to be an experimental subject.

The beginning of the story is promising. Potter quickly sketches the social life of the town of Marmalade and pokes fun at both sorts of guinea pigs. She presents us with an unlikely protagonist, a guinea-pig who "suffered from toothache and chilblains; and he had never had much hair, not even of the shortest" (13) and who is "too depressed" (13) to argue with the guinea pigs who want him to try the elixir. He is further plagued by a short-tempered wife. When his hair grows and grows, completely out of control, he becomes a laughingstock, flees the town, and "wandered into the world alone" (20). But this is only the first chapter of a very long prose narrative that is interspersed with quick and lively pen-and-ink illustrations, some of them quite amusing (Tuppenny fleeing Marmalade, looking like a dustmop come to life).[12] Whereas Tuppenny is presented as the protagonist in the opening chapter, as he wanders off into the narrative he becomes only one of many animal characters who meander, as does the "fairy caravan" they travel the countryside with, and he ultimately trails out of the narrative much as the caravan itself does.

The Fairy Caravan is a loose set of stories centered on a traveling animal circus that is invisible to humans but highly popular with the animal populace of the countryside. The story of such a caravan might have been the basis for a good short illustrated tale, but here becomes simply a vehicle for Potter to string together a number of stories she found amusing or illustrative of life in the Lakes, as well as to write herself and one or two of her friends in as characters. Potter is at her most indulgent in the chapters where some Herdwick sheep tell stories. The sheep tales are filled with esoteric information about sheep (we hear of various breeds of sheep, of sheep getting crag fast (trapped on narrow mountain ledges), of sheep being buried in winter snow drifts and with dialect from the Lake District. One of the Herdwick sheep says "it takes strong hemp to langle us" (87); another says "I doubt you *were* a twinter, or a two-shear at most!" (90; Potter's emphasis). The sheep who survive being buried in a snowdrift emerge "quite lish and cheerful" (91). Potter had once commented that children appreciate a "fine word" every now and then, but the fine words here do little beyond show that Potter is conversant with the Lancashire dialect and the habits of sheep. Furthermore, although the adventures of being crag fast or buried in snow are potentially exciting, they are told by the sheep as they placidly crop grass long after the adventures are over and done with. There is no suspense to the stories they tell and a bewildering amount of information about sheep—who are owned by "Mistress Heelis." The sheep stories are better suited for a farming journal than for a children's book.

Potter had, in fact, been trying to get short pieces about country life published in magazines and journals devoted to farm life. As early as 1913, just after her marriage, Potter tried to place in *Country Life* stories she had written in 1911. Of the four pieces she submitted, "The Fairy Clogs" was accepted, but " 'Pace Eggers' is not topical. 'The Mole Catcher's Burying' is for a children's paper, and 'Carrier Bob' I do not think quite happy."[13] The editors' comments here suggest that Potter was having difficulty moving from the children's book market into the adult. "The Mole Catcher's Burying" personifies a group of moles who are so happy the mole catcher is dead that they dig the grave gratis. Its theme is rather grim, but one can well imagine the sort of illustrations Potter might have done for a small children's version of the story, and in fact one of the illustrations in *Appley-Dapply* would have been suitable for such a story. "Pace Eggers" is about an old folk custom and is dependent upon rhyme and song, a longtime interest of Potter's. "Carrier Bob" is the most realistic of the tales, even if the story of a long faithful but now deceased dog was "not quite happy," according to the editors. In all these stories we can see Potter struggling, unsuccessfully, to move from fantasy writing to more realistic writing. She had become a countrywoman and was attempting to marry her new state in life to her writing, but with little success.

Potter's final illustrated narrative is a book based on a story she had been thinking of since at least 1883 (*Artist and Her World*, 165), *The Tale of Little Pig Robinson* (1930).[14] While Taylor and Hobbs think the novel shows Potter's talent at sustained narrative, and while it is more assured than *The Fairy Caravan*, it lacks narrative drive and forward motion. Potter was certainly capable of complex narratives that moved forward with alacrity—both *The Pie and the Patty-Pan* and *The Roly-Poly Pudding* prove this—but late in her career she became much more discursive and was unhappy when editors tried to keep her from being so: Warne cut a number of illustrations from its edition of *Pig Robinson*, but Potter convinced David McKay in Philadelphia to include them in the American edition.

The entire first chapter of the book—and it is a book with chapters, which is unusual for Potter—is not about Pig Robinson, but about a cat named Susan and her human masters who live in a seaport and eat herring for dinner. Susan is told by her mistress to go meet the ship and collect that night's supper. While on the docks she is puzzled by the sight of a pig on the deck of a ship called *The Pound of Candles*. There is a suggestion that as Susan drifts off to sleep at the end of the first chapter, she merely dreams the story of the pig, and the first chapter is meant as the frame for Pig Robinson's story. However, if that was Potter's intention she seems to have forgotten it because at the end of the story we hear no more of Susan, who is not one of Pig Robinson's final visitors to the island. There is no dream-frame of falling asleep and then awakening as there is in *Alice in Wonderland*, for example. Susan merely disappears from the tale.

A second framing device of the story is the tale of Robinson Crusoe, but the references to that tale are slight. Pig Robinson shares a name with Crusoe and lives on a deserted island, but despite having no Man Friday, he is not as isolated as was Crusoe: by the end of the tale he has several visitors to his island. The threat to his life comes not from cannibals but from hungry sailors on the ship from which he escapes. A third framing device is Edward Lear's poem "The Owl and the Pussycat," a poem Potter quotes at the beginning of the second chapter just before Pig Robinson is introduced. Pig Robinson is the pig "with a ring at the end of his nose" living happily beneath the Bong-tree. Potter supplies what might today be called the "back story" to Lear's poem and thereby enriches both Pig Robinson's story and Lear's. Potter answers the question of how the pig got to the island in Lear's poem, and Lear's poem gives Potter atmospheric details for her island. Despite all this, the multiple framing of the story is not entirely successful. Potter seems unable to interweave narrative threads as skillfully as she did earlier in her career. Pig Robinson's story of nearly becoming a birthday dinner for the ship's captain is framed by Lear's poem, by Crusoe's story, and by the story of the cat Susan and her mistress, but these narrative frames never merge into a single integrated frame as they do in *The Tailor of Gloucester* or *Mr. Tod.* As is common in much of Potter's later work, the lack of editorial control allows her to indulge her weaknesses as a writer.

Despite the narrative weakness of the tale, it does show that later in Potter's career she was still interested in the themes of the eater and the eaten and the difficulties of domesticity. Here, however, our pig hero does not so much escape the confines of domesticity as he does the confines of a ship crewed entirely by men. Pig Robinson, unlike Pigling Bland, does not trot off into the sunset with a lady love but lives out an isolated bachelor existence on an island, leaving marital bliss to the owl and the pussycat. There are echoes here of Potter's great themes, but they are echoes only: her heart seems to have gone out of them as her life as farmer supercedes her life as writer.

The illustrations for this novel are more interesting than the story itself. The pen-and-ink sketches are lively and detailed: Potter makes up for the lack of many color plates by giving the reader interesting and detailed scenes of countryside, port town, and ship in pen-and-ink. There is a liveliness to the port community that the quickness of her sketches perfectly suits. Whereas in her earlier books the sketches were generally small, here many of the sketches take up an entire page, giving Potter ample room to sketch in the details of ship rigging or people jostling on the streets. These full-page sketches, in fact, largely take the place of the full-page color illustrations in the earlier books in terms of their importance to the narrative pace and to our understanding of the characters. There are only seven color plates (including the cover and the frontispiece) in 123 pages of text, while there are twenty-two full-page, black-and-white illustrations as well as several smaller ones interspersed throughout the text.

The illustrations of Pig Robinson as he sets out to market provide a clear example of how at this point in her career Potter could accomplish more in black-and-white sketches than she could in color. The first illustration of him is a full-color representation of the pig heading off to market with his basket, down a path cutting through a sheep field, with a background of hills and a glimpse of the sea behind. It is a lovely illustration, one that captures the quality of light near the seashore, but the portrait of Pig Robinson himself is curiously flat, lacking much facial expression. In fact, the background is given more attention than Pig Robinson himself and was probably a reworked illustration from earlier in her career, with the pig pasted in for this novel. The next two sketches of Pig Robinson are full-page, black-and-white illustrations, and they provide much more detail than the color illustration does. In fact, in the entire book the color illustrations are "sketchier" than the sketches are. The first black-and-white illustration we see of Pig Robinson shows him crossing a small bridge; his personality is much clearer here, accomplished in a few pen strokes. His floppy ears are better defined, his facial expression is clearer, and he is livelier than he is in the color illustration. The next illustration shows him carefully climbing down a narrow stile, and here his caution and his concentration are clear through both his posture and the intensity of his gaze on his next footstep.

As Potter's eyesight became weaker, doing the fine and meticulous brush work and color work of the earlier color illustrations became more difficult. The bold contrast of black ink against a white page, however, gave her enough contrast to see and work by and allowed her to do busier sketches than she had been able to do in the earlier watercolors. For example, some of the street scenes include twenty or more people, a half-dozen or more animals, carts, shop fronts, and cobblestone paving. None of Potter's earlier watercolor illustrations contain nearly as many figures. Potter can include so many figures because she does so sketchily, giving the impression of figures, barely sketching their outlines rather than working them up in any detail. The one full-color street scene she includes, when examined carefully, turns out to be another pen-and-ink sketch with a thin watercolor wash over most of it to suggest the color of clothing, storefront, and street. The only figure who merits a full watercolor treatment is Pig Robinson himself.

Potter published several more books, only one of them during her lifetime and none of them illustrated by her. *Sister Anne*,[15] a gothic retelling of the Bluebeard story, was published in 1932 by McKay, with illustrations by Katherine Sturges. *Wag-By-Wall*[16] was published in 1944 by both Warne and the *Horn Book*, with proceeds from the American publication going to both the magazine and the National Trust. *The Tale of the Faithful Dove*, long desired by Warne but dismissed by Potter because of a lack of variety in the proposed illustrations, was published first in 1955 and again, with illustrations by Marie Angel, in 1971.[17] These last stories reflect Potter's lifelong love of fairy tales (both *Sister Anne* and *Wag-By-Wall* have their origins in older fairy tales); of country life (*Wag-By-Wall*); and of the difficulties of domestic life (*The Faithful Dove*). It is this last story, whose origins lie earlier in Potter's career, that is the most interesting and has the closest ties to the body of work that secured her reputation.

Potter first wrote to Warne about *The Faithful Dove* in 1908 from Bolton Gardens, during the fruitful period of the Sawrey books. She wrote to Harold Warne that the story "is about a chimney and laying eggs. It was made before Roly Poly and Jemima. . . . The story has been lying about a long time, and so have several others. . . . I should like to get rid of some of them."[18] But Warne did not pursue publication until 1918, at which point Potter could not be convinced to do the illustrations. She suggested another artist who might do the illustrations but Warne turned down her suggestion.

The story shares not only chimneys and eggs with *Roly-Poly Pudding* and *Jemima Puddleduck*, but once again the familiar themes of claustrophobia and the dangers and delights of domesticity. A pigeon couple fleeing a predatory hawk is separated, with the female pigeon flying down a chimney she then cannot escape. She has had to desert one egg in fleeing the hawk but lays another in the chimney. She is aided by a very polite and formal mouse who says, "I fear I have no refreshment to offer to you, Madam. . . . We removed to our present abode on account of the owls. I am a mouse of genteel descent" (quoted in Linder, 343). The mouse helps send word to the cock pigeon, who is then able to feed his poor trapped wife until eventually she and her newly hatched chick are released by a roofer's apprentice.

The story has clear thematic links to the works Potter wrote at her peak. There are natural threats to the pigeons even in domesticated Rye (the setting of the story). The pigeons are still wild but also domestic enough to live in close proximity to dangerous humans who like to eat pigeon pie. A traditional symbol of domesticity (the chimney) both saves and entraps the female pigeon and also serves as a safe nursery for her chick. What sets *The Faithful Dove* apart from the other Sawrey books is that we begin, for the only time in Potter's career, with a happily married couple who are reunited at the end and manage to raise a child of their own, even if their first egg must be abandoned when the female pigeon flies into the chimney.

Potter's career is one long exercise in both writing and living in code. As a Victorian woman hemmed in by conventions of class and gender she needed to find a way to break free while still appearing conventional. Ironically, her way out seemed to constrict her further, while in fact giving her an opportunity to critique restrictions. She appeared to constrict herself by limiting her artistic output to a marginalized and feminized genre: children's books. She further appeared to constrict herself by focusing her talents on a traditionally feminine medium: miniature watercolors. But being a children's writer was not Potter's first choice: scientific illustration and inquiry was. When the doors of Kew and the scientific societies closed to her due to her gender, she had to find another path.

The small books she created for children proved, in the end, to be far more lucrative than science could ever have been and provided Potter with financial independence. The books appeared to be a genteel occupation for a single woman living at home—although her parents were never happy at the daughter's involvement in trade—but in fact allowed Potter to explore her own anxieties about domesticity, power, hierarchy, and class. Although the books are not consciously coded, as was her journal, they are coded nonetheless. What we see, when the code is deciphered, is an Edwardian woman writer with deep anxieties about both gender and class, a writer with rebellious if not subversive tendencies, and above all a writer with a strong individual voice and vision.

Potter's tales led her to both entrepreneurial and political activities—unusual for a woman of her class and time. Today many of us bemoan the commercialization of children's texts—the endless *Harry Potter* tie-ins, the stuffed Sendakian Wild Things, the *American Girl* phenomenon—but commercialization is not new and in fact was largely invented by Potter. She was an astute businesswoman, both in publishing and in farming. She was intensely private, but willing to become publicly active when roused by a cause she cared about.

This is not to say that Potter was entirely unconventional. She wanted marriage and the respectability the married state would bring her. When she married William Heelis she all but gave up her literary career, yet she never became a passive wife or mere helpmate to her husband. Interestingly, both Norman Warne and William Heelis were business as well as romantic partners. She married late, when she was her own woman and was past childbearing age. She may have given up her literary career, but she substituted farming for it, beginning the substitution long before she married Heelis. She accumulated thousands of acres of land in the Lakes to leave to the National Trust, not to her husband. Her letters and her editorial writing remained sharp and even acerbic to the end, and she never lost her interest in politics. In 1936 she wrote in a letter to an American friend that King Edward "by his obstinate wrong-headedness proved himself utterly unsuited to reign as a constitutional monarch."[19] When the Second World War broke out, Potter wrote that if "Mr. Chamberlain believes in [Hitler's] passions he must be an incurable . . . I haven't much faith in Mr. Chamberlain."[20] True to form, Potter was not uncritically patriotic during the war years, but was an astute reader of the press and commentator on British politics.

Potter was not cut off from the world and was not a woman who lived in any sort of fantasy world. She used her animal fantasies as a way to break free of restrictions of gender, family, and class, and from a very young age was an active observer and commentator on the social and political world in which she lived. The genius of her work is that she managed to be topical and timeless at the same time. Those who know enough to recognize the references to Free Trade and class issues gain a further insight into the Edwardian period; those who do not, still enjoy the face-offs between the more and the less powerful characters in the books. Those who know something of Potter's biography may see the ways in which the stories parallel some of the major events in her life; those who do not can still enjoy the tales of miniature houses and trickster animals and daring adventures into forbidden worlds. There is always in Potter more beneath the surface than one might expect in such small books.

In fact, in many ways Potter—who wrote so often of tricksters—may be seen as a trickster herself. She plays on the reader the trick of hiding serious issues between small covers and within pastel drawings. She tricks us into thinking surface is all—when the fox in *Jemima*, Tommy Brock, and the heroines of *The Pie and the Patty-Pan* should clue us in that seeing surface qualities only puts us in danger of not seeing what is truly important.

Potter's final trick may be that she has masqueraded as a children's writer when in fact a number of her books can be seen as miniature novels. Many of her books provide in miniature what all novels provide: complex interwoven plots, major and minor characters who develop over time, symbolic and metaphoric use of language and object, and moral ambiguity and complexity. Potter's novels may be written for a younger audience and they may be illustrated, but this does not mean they are not novels. After all, we refer to books for young adults (many of which are illustrated) as novels and there is the relatively new genre of the "graphic novel," meant for adults but illustrated in a comic-book style that for many critics is more closely associated with childhood than with adulthood. Critics had no difficulty in reviewing Art Spiegleman's *Maus* (the story of the Holocaust with a cast of mice and cats) as a novel. Potter's books may be miniature in size and they may have pastel illustrations, but they are as serious of purpose as any novel meant for adults and often as complex. But whether she be novelist or not, like all tricksters she leaves us in admiration of her linguistic and artistic talents. When we learn to read what is hidden beneath these short narratives, when we break the "code" beneath them, we realize that Potter left us an even richer body of work than we imagined, one that will continue to provide us pleasure and food for thought for at least another one hundred years.

Notes

1. See Judy Taylor, ed., *Letters to Children from Beatrix Potter* (London: Warne, 1992) for a number of these letters, written in the voices of more than a dozen of her characters. These letters often suggest that the animal characters exist in a unified fantasy animal world. For example, Squirrel Nutkin writes to Dr. Maggotty, "I am sending back the box of blue beans, I think they have a very funny smell & so does my brother Twinkleberry," thus combining characters from three separate novels (90).
2. Judy Taylor, ed., *Beatrix Potter's Letters* (London: Warne, 1986), 222.
3. Judy Taylor, *Beatrix Potter: Artist, Storyteller and Countrywoman* (London: Warne, 1986), 138.
4. Judy Taylor, Joyce Irene Whalley, Anne Stevenson Hobbs, and Elizabeth M. Battrick, *Beatrix Potter 1866–1943: The Artist and Her World* (London: Warne, 1987), 155.
5. Beatrix Potter, *Appley Dapply's Nursery Rhymes* (London: Warne, 1917; 1987).
6. Beatrix Potter, *The Tale of Johnny Town-Mouse* (London: Warne, 1918; 1995). 59. Unless otherwise noted, all text references are to the 1995 edition.
7. Aesop, *The Fables of Aesop*, tr. S. A. Handford (New York.: Penguin, 1954), 43.
8. Ruth K. McDonald, *Beatrix Potter* (Boston: Twayne, 1989), 78–81.
9. I have not had the opportunity to study any of the unpublished letters, which may contain information that tells us more about the relationship between brother and sister.
10. Beatrix Potter, *Cecily Parsley's Nursery Rhymes* (London: Warne, 1922; 1987).
11. Beatrix Potter, *The Fairy Caravan* (Philadelphia: McKay, 1929).

12. There are also a half-dozen full-color and full-page illustrations tipped into the printed volume. Most of these are reworked illustrations from earlier years, and they function as "set pieces" rather than as integral parts of the text. They function the way illustrations do in nonpicture books.

13. Quoted in Leslie Linder, *A History of the Writings of Beatrix Potter* (London: Warne, 1971), 376.

14. Beatrix Potter, *The Tale of Little Pig Robinson* (London: Warne, 1930; 1987).

15. Beatrix Potter, *Sister Anne* (Philadelphia: David McKay, 1932).

16. Beatrix Potter, *Wag-By-Wall* (London: Warne, 1944).

17. Beatrix Potter, *The Tale of the Faithful Dove* (London: Warne, 1955; 1971).

18. Quoted in Linder, *History of Writings*, 338.

19. Unpublished letter to Mrs. Perry, 16 December 1936. Philadelphia Free Public Library RBD PB ALS P429S.

20. Unpublished letter to Mrs. Perry, 4 October 1938, Philadelphia Free Public Library RBD BP ALS P429V.

Bibliography

WORKS BY BEATRIX POTTER

The Tale of Peter Rabbit. London: Warne, 1902; 1987.

The Tailor of Gloucester. London: Warne, 1903; 1987.

The Tale of Squirrel Nutkin. London: Warne, 1903; 1987.

The Tale of Benjamin Bunny. London: Warne, 1904; 1987.

The Tale of Two Bad Mice. London: Warne, 1904; 1987.

The Tale of Mrs. Tiggy-Winkle. London: Warne, 1905; 1987.

The Tale of the Pie and the Patty-Pan. London: Warne, 1905; 1987.

The Tale of Jeremy Fisher. London: Warne, 1906; 1987.

The Tale of a Fierce Bad Rabbit. London: Warne, 1906; 1987.

The Tale of Miss Moppet. London: Warne, 1906; 1987.

The Tale of Tom Kitten. London: Warne, 1906; 1987.

The Tale of Jemima Puddleduck. London: Warne, 1908; 1987.

The Tale of Samuel Whiskers; or, the Roly-Poly Pudding. London: Warne, 1908; 1987.

The Tale of the Flopsy Bunnies. London: Warne, 1909; 1987.

The Tale of Ginger and Pickles. London: Warne, 1909; 1987.

The Tale of Mrs. Tittlemouse. London: Warne, 1910; 1987.

The Tale of Timmy Tiptoes. London: Warne, 1911; 1987.

The Tale of Mr. Tod. London: Warne, 1912; 1987.

The Tale of Pigling Bland. London: Warne, 1912; 1987.

Appley-Dapply's Nursery Rhymes. London: Warne, 1917; 1987.

The Tale of Johnny Town-Mouse. London: Warne, 1918; 1987.

Cecily Parsley's Nursery Rhymes. London: Warne, 1922; 1987.

The Fairy Caravan. London: Warne, 1929; 1987.

The Tale of Pig Robinson. London: Warne, 1930; 1987.

Sister Anne. Philadelphia: Alexander McKay, 1932.

"Wag-by-Wall." *Horn Book* 3 (1944): 199–202.

The Faithful Dove. London: Warne, 1956; 1970. Illus. M. Angel.

LETTERS AND JOURNALS

Linder, Leslie, ed. *The Journal of Beatrix Potter 1881–1897*. London: Warne, 1966.
Morse, Jane C., ed. *Beatrix Potter's Americans: Selected Letters*. Boston: Horn Book, 1982.
Taylor, Judy, ed. *Beatrix Potter's Letters*. London: Warne, 1989.
————. *Letters to Children from Beatrix Potter*. London: Warne, 1992.

WORKS ABOUT BEATRIX POTTER

Anderson, Celia. "The Ancient Lineage of Beatrix Potter's Mr. Tod." In *Festchrift: A Ten Year Retrospective of the Children's Literature Association*, edited by Perry Nodelman and Jill May. W. Lafayette, Ind.: Children's Literature Association, 1982, 44–47.
Avery, Gillian. "Beatrix Potter and Social Comedy." *Bulletin of the John Rylands University Library of Manchester* 76, no. 3 (1994): 185.
Battrick, Elizabeth. *The Real World of Beatrix Potter*. London: The National Trust, 1986.
Carpenter, Humphrey. "Excessively Impertinent Bunnies: The Subversive Element in Beatrix Potter." In *Children and Their Books: A Celebration of the Work of Peter and Iona Opie*, edited by Julia Briggs and Gillian Avery. Oxford: Clarendon, 1984, 271–98.
Crouch, Marcus. *Beatrix Potter*. London: Bodley Head, 1960.
Eastman, Jackie F. "Beatrix Potter's Tale of Peter Rabbit." In *Touchstones: Volume Three*, edited by Perry Nodelman. W. LaFayette, Ind.: Children's Literature Association, 1985, 100–7.
Fletcher, John. "On Some Complexities of Beatrix Potter." *International Fiction Review* 4 (1977): 71–72.
Frey, Charles. "Victors and Victims in the Tales of 'Peter Rabbit' and 'Squirrel Nutkin.' " *Children's Literature in Education* 18, no. 2 (1987): 105–11.
Godden, Rumer. *The Tale of the Tales*. London: Warne, 1971.
Golden, Catherine. "Retrieving Beatrix Potter's Revision Process." In *Victorian Authors and Their Works*, edited by Judith Kennedy. Athens: University of Georgia, 1991, 29–40.

———. "Beatrix Potter: Naturalist Artist." In *A History of Book Illustration: Twenty-Nine Points of View*, edited by Bill Katz. Metuchen, N.J.: Scarecrow, 1994, 626–41.

Greene, Graham. "Beatrix Potter." In *Only Connect: Readings in Children's Literature*, 2nd ed, edited by Sheila Egoff et al. New York: Oxford, 1980, 258–65.

Grinstein, Alexander. *The Remarkable Beatrix Potter*. Madison, Conn. International Universities Press, 1995.

Harris, W.C. "Undifferentiated Bunnies: Setting Psychic Boundaries in the Animal Stories of Potter, London, and Seton." *Victorian Review* 23, no. 1 (1997): 62–113.

Heelis, John. *The Tale of Mrs. William Heelis*. Hawes: Leading Edge, 1993.

Hobbs, Anne S., ed. *Beatrix Potter's Art*. Rev. ed. New York: Warne, 1990.

Hobbs, Anne S., and Joyce I. Whalley, eds. *Beatrix Potter: The V&A Collection*. London: Warne, 1985.

Hollindale, Peter. "Aesop in the Shadows." *Signal* 89 (May 1989): 115–32.

Hutchings, Margaret. *Toys from the Tales of Beatrix Potter*. New York: Warne, 1973.

Jay, Eileen. *A Victorian Naturalist: Beatrix Potter's Drawings from the Armitt Collection*. London: Warne, 1992.

Kutzer, M. Daphne. "A Wildness Inside: Domestic Space in the Work of Beatrix Potter." *Lion and Unicorn* 21, no. 2 (1997): 204–14.

Lane, Margaret. *The Tale of Beatrix Potter: A Biography*. Rev. ed. London: Warne, 1968.

———. *The Magic Years of Beatrix Potter*. London: Warne, 1978.

Lightner, Karen J., *Beatrix Potter: A Guide to the Collection of the Rare Book Department, the Free Library of Philadelphia*. Philadelphia: The Free Library, 1992.

Linder, Leslie. *The Art of Beatrix Potter*. Rev. ed. London: Warne, 1972.

———. *A History of the Writings of Beatrix Potter*. London: Warne, 1987.

Luce-Kapler, R. "The Seeing Eye of Beatrix Potter." *Children's Literature in Education* 25, no. 3 (1994): 139.

Mackey, Margaret. *The Case of Peter Rabbit: Changing Conditions of Literature for Children*. New York: Garland, 1998.

———. *Beatrix Potter's Peter Rabbit: A Children's Classic at 100*. Latham, N.J., and London: Scarecrow, 2002.

McDonald, Ruth. *Beatrix Potter*. Boston: Twayne, 1986.

———. "Why This is Still 1893: *The Tale of Peter Rabbit* and Beatrix Potter's Manipulation of Time into Timelessness." *Children's Literature Association Quarterly* 10, no. 4 (1986): 185–7.

———. "Narrative Voice and Narrative View in Beatrix Potter's Books." In *The Voice of the Narrator in Children's Literature: Insights from Writers and Critics*, edited by Gary D. Schmidt and Charlotte F. Otten. New York: Greenwood, 1989, 54–60.

McEwen, J. "Tales from the Dark Side: Beatrix Potter, Artist and Storyteller." *Art in America* 76, no. 6 (1988): 4.

Nikola-Lisa, W. "The Cult of Peter Rabbit: A Barthesian Analysis." *Lion and Unicorn* 15, no. 2 (1991): 61–66.

Parker, Audrey. *Cottage and Farmhouse Detail in Beatrix Potter's Lake District*. London: Beatrix Potter Society, 1993.

Pennington, John. "From Peter Rabbit to Watership Down: There and Back Again to the Arcadian Ideal." *Journal of the Fantastic in the Arts* 10, no. 2 (1991): 66–80.

Rahn, Suzanne. "Tailpiece: The Tale of Two Bad Mice." *Children's Literature* 12 (1984): 232–39.

Redfield, James M. "An Aristotelian Analysis of Miss Moppet." *Chicago Review* 34, no. 4 (1985): 32–41.

Robison, Roselee. "The Journal of Beatrix Potter." *Prose Studies* 7, no. 3 (1984): 232–39.

Scott, Carole. "Between Me and the World: Clothes as Mediator between Self and Society in the Works of Beatrix Potter." *Lion and Unicorn* 16, no. 2 (1992): 192–98.

———. "Clothed in Nature or Nature Clothed: Dress as Metaphor in the Illustrations of Beatrix Potter and C. M. Barker." *Children's Literature* 22 (1994): 70–89.

Sendak, Maurice. *Caldecott & Co.: Notes on Books and Pictures*. New York: Noonday, 1988.

Sircoff, Seth. "Prickles under the Frock." In *Children's Literature: The Great Excluded*, edited by Francelia Butler. Storrs, Conn.: Children's Literature Association, 1973, 105–9.

Tabbert, Reinbert. "National Myths in Three Classical Picture Books.' In *Aspects and Issues in the History of Children's Literature*, edited by Maria Nikolajeva. Westport, Conn.: Greenwood, 1995, 151–63.

Taylor, Judy. *Beatrix Potter: Artist, Storyteller and Countrywoman*. London: Warne, 1986.

———. *That Naughty Rabbit: Beatrix Potter and Peter Rabbit*. London: Warne, 1987.

———. *Beatrix Potter and Hill Top, Cumbria*. London: National Trust, 1989.

Taylor, Judy, Joyce Irene Whalley, Anne Stevenson Hobbs, and Elizabeth Battrick, eds. *Beatrix Potter 1866–1943: The Artist and Her World*. London: Warne, 1987.

Whalley, Joyce Irene, and Wynne K. Bartlett. *The Derwentwater Sketchbook*. London: Warne, 1984.

OTHER WORKS CONSULTED

Alderson, Brian. *Sing a Song for Sixpence: The English Picture Book Tradition and Randolph Caldecott*. Cambridge: Cambridge University Press, 1986.

Bailey, Peter. " 'A Mingled Mass of Perfectly Legitimate Pleasures': The Victorian Middle Class and the Problem of Leisure." *Victorian Studies* 2, no. 1 (1977): 7–28.

Blewett, Neal. *The Peers, The Parties and the People: The British General Election of 1910*. Toronto: University of Toronto, 1972.

Bulmer-Thomas, Ivor. *The Growth of the British Party System: 1640–1923*. New York: Humanities Press, 1966.

Brown, Penny. *The Captured World: The Child and Childhood in Nineteenth-Century Women's Writing in England*. New York: St. Martin's, 1993.

Cole, G. D. H. *A Short History of the British Working Class Movement, 1789–1947*. London: Allen and Unwin, 1948.

Gilbert, Sandra, and Susan Gubar. *The Madwoman in the Attic: The Woman Writer and the Nineteenth-Century Literary Imagination*. New Haven: Yale University Press, 1979.

Harris, Joel Chandler. *Complete Tales of Uncle Remus*, edited by Richard Chase. Boston: Houghton Mifflin, 1955.

Hawkins, Angus. *British Party Politics, 1852–1886*. London: Macmillan, 1998.

Hunt, Peter, ed. *Children's Literature: An Illustrated History*. Oxford: Oxford University Press, 1995.

Inglis, Fred. *The Promise of Happiness*: *Value and Meaning in Children's Fiction*. Cambridge: Cambridge University Press, 1981.

Kirk, Neville. *Change, Continuity and Class*: *Labour in British Society 1850–1920*. Manchester: Manchester University Press, 1998.

Marsh, Peter T. *Bargaining on Europe*: *Britain and the First Common Market, 1880–92*. New Haven: Yale University Press, 1999.

McCord, Norman. *Free Trade*: *Theory and Practice from Adam Smith to Keynes*. New York: Barnes and Noble, 1970.

McGavran, James Holt, Jr., ed. *Romanticism and Children's Literature in Nineteenth-Century England*. Athens: University of Georgia, 1991.

McLean, Ruari. *Victorian Book Design and Colour Printing*. Berkeley: University of California Press, 1972.

Nelson, Claudia. *Boys Will Be Girls*: *The Feminine Ethic and British Children's Fiction, 1857–1917*. New Brunswick, N.J.: Rutgers University Press, 1991.

Nodelman, Perry. *Words about Pictures*: *The Narrative Art of Children's Books*. Athens: University of Georgia, 1988.

Opie, Iona, and Peter Opie, eds. *The Oxford Book of Nursery Rhymes*. London: Oxford, 1955.

Read, Donald. *England 1880–1914*: *The Age of Urban Democracy*. London: Longman, 1994.

Watt, Ruth. *Gender, Power and the Unitarians in England, 1761–1860*. New York: Longman, 1998.

Wilbur, Earl Morse. *A History of Unitarianism in Transylvania, England, and America*. Cambridge: Harvard University Press, 1952.

Index of Subjects

Aesop, 24, 139, 156, 158, 159
Alice in Wonderland (Lewis Carroll), 38, 164
American Girl series, 168
Anderson, Celia, 139
Angel, Marie, 166
Austen, Jane, 2, 7, 12, 15, 140, 149

Bailey, Peter, 28
Biddle, John, 16, 18
Blake, William, 52
Brefeld, Oscar, 36
Bright, John, 127
Brontë, Charlotte, 12,140
Brooke, Leslie, 66

Caldecott, Randolph, 1, 24, 154
Carpenter, Humphrey, 2, 11, 19, 23–24
Carroll, Lewis (Charles Dodgson), 1, 115
  and *Alice in Wonderland*, 38, 164
Chamberlain, Joseph, 6
Chamberlain, Neville, 168
Chambers, Robert, 24
Class, social, 4, 5, 7, 12, 14, 15, 22, 27, 28,
  61–62, 74, 75, 78, 79, 126, 168
  and leisure, 28, 29
  in *The Tailor of Gloucester*, 15, 19–20, 22

in *The Tale of Jeremy Fisher*, 119, 121
in *The Tale of Johnny Town-Mouse*,
  157–158
in *The Tale of Mrs. Tiggy-Winkle*, 79
in *The Tale of Mr. Tod*, 136, 138,
  141–142
in *The Tale of the Pie and the Patty-Pan*,
  83–88
in *The Tale of Squirrel Nutkin*, 25, 27,
  28, 29, 30
in *The Tale of Two Bad Mice*, 67,
  74–76
Cole, G. D. H., 27
Coolidge, Henry P., 161, 162
Country Life magazine, 128, 163
Crompton, Jessy (grandmother), 6, 12, 13,
  17, 18, 35, 37, 42, 140
Cromwell, Oliver, 16

Darwin, Charles, 6, 17
Dickens, Charles, 6
Dodgson, Charles. *See* Lewis Carroll
domesticity
  and Potter's life, 8, 47–48, 50, 62, 66, 67,
  71–72, 74, 76, 78, 81, 91, 101, 116,
  122, 134–135. *See also* gender;
  Beatrix Potter and parents

Index of Titles